AF227611

Blessed Beyond Belief
The Life, Loves, & Labours of Stu Silvester

© 2020 by Stu Silvester

Published by: H&E Publishing, Peterbourough, Ontario
www.hesedandemet.com

Paperback ISBN: 978-1-989174-66-1
Ebook ISBN: 978-1-989174-67-8

Cover painting:
"Peaceful Pastures" by Lloyd Silvester.
"My father Lloyd Silvester painted it in 1983. My dad painted and sold numerous pictures until age 95, and I'm blessed to have several of his original prints. He died in his 99th year after a fruitful and faithful life." – Stu Silvester

Blessed Beyond Belief

The Life, Loves, & Labours of
Stu Silvester

Contents

Prologue
Dedication to Bev

It is with a grieving heart but also a very grateful heart that I write these thoughts in an effort to thank the Lord for bringing Beverly MacLean into my life sixty years ago. Her love for the Lord and for me, combined with a Christ-like spirit and God-given wisdom, produced a perfect partner for me. It was her prayers, sacrifice, and encouragement that allowed me to go to seminary at twenty-eight years of age with two little daughters. Bev taught school in Toronto for five years enabling me to earn two degrees at Central Baptist Seminary, preparing me for ministry.

For the next fifty years, Bev supported me as my wonderful wife, loving mother of three lovely daughters, and one who many called a "perfect" pastor's wife, and an efficient school librarian; as well as a grandmother of ten and great grandmother of nine. She also impacted hundreds of lives with her gifts of mercy and hospitality.

Bev used to say that everyone has a life-story. She encouraged my dad to write his autobiography years ago. It was at her insistence that I started to write this book and often on our drive home from Florida she would say, "It's time to start dictating your book again." Now that she has gone home to her Lord and reward in heaven, I am freshly motivated to complete "our story of God's faithfulness and blessings". I encouraged her to record some of her memories of our life and labours together. The largest section was from her diary on our six-week trip to Zambia and it reveals her fears and faith as we faced dangers and difficulties.

It is my prayer that the story of God's faithfulness in our lives will encourage you to be "Steadfast, unmoveable, always abounding in the work of the Lord, forasmuch as you know your labour is not in vain in the Lord." (1 Corinthians 15:58.)

1

Stu's Story
1935–1941

It was in the summer of 1935 that Lloyd and Kathleen Silvester were expecting their third child. They already had two boys, Roger and Grant, and were probably hoping for a girl but it was not to be. On a hot summer day in southern Saskatchewan, in a prairie town called Chaplin, halfway between Moose Jaw and Swift Current, I was born in a small house with the help of a midwife, Mrs. Hieie. It was July 9 that I first saw the light of day, and according to what my father told me years later, my mother had a very difficult time with my delivery. Apparently, from that time until my mom died at age fifty-two, she suffered from migraine headaches almost every month. I remember she would have to go to bed for a couple of days each month and her lovely dark hair turned prematurely white in the area where the pain was the most severe. She was a wonderful mother, and I always felt badly that I had caused her so much pain. She never complained and was a wonderful example of Christian patience and love.

My mother" Kathleen Hamilton" and my Father "Lloyd Silvester" were both born in Ontario. My mom was born near Laurel, south-west of Shelburne on Sept. 23, 1908. My dad was born near Burk's Falls on April 25, 1905. Both of their parents migrated to Saskatchewan to farm the prairies which had been opened up to settlers. My mother went to school in Toronto to train to be a teacher and she graduated at the top of her class! She taught one year in Laurel

Ontario, and two years in Saskatchewan at Sunflower and Rosneath schools. My dad was destined to be a farmer and worked hard to provide for his family of five sons. They had married in 1930 following a long distant courtship by phone and letters. They were married in Bingham Baptist Church in Saskatchewan and were the finest Christian parents who made many sacrifices for their five boys.

The drought on the prairies started awhile before I was born, and lasted for seven years, until 1942. This difficult time was called the "Dirty Thirties" and, to make things worse, the "Great Depression" with the stock market crash of 1929 was creating a double whammy. These years were very difficult for my parents because for seven years there were no crops to harvest. My dad raised pigs, chickens, and a few cattle in order to provide us with food and some money; however, because of lack of rain the grass burned up and my dad had to cut Russian thistles to feed the cattle. Dirt storms were another result of the drought and the sun would be blackened out; the dirt would blow in under the windows and form drifts on the windowsills. The drought also made water scarce, and one year my dad had to dig three wells (I remember helping pull up pails of dirt with a rope as he filled them). It seemed that when any grain did grow the grasshoppers would come by the thousands and eat it before it could be harvested. Also, hailstorms would come and beat down the grain crops. How we ever survived without discouragement is a miracle. These difficult years sounded a lot like the ten plagues of Egypt recorded in the Old Testament.

When my parents couldn't afford gas for our car, we would go to church on the "stone boat" pulled by our horses. Another thing they did was take the motor out of their car and put a wagon tongue in the front so it could be pulled by the horses. These became known as "Bennett Buggies" because the Premier of Saskatchewan was Mr. Bennett. The winters on the prairies were very cold and windy. One time the temperature never got above forty degrees below zero for a whole week and the water froze in the house even though we had three stoves going. Part of the problem was the houses had no insulation other than some newspaper pasted on the boards. My Dad had to haul coal ten miles from Chaplin by horse and sleigh, and often had to run or walk behind the sleigh to keep from freezing in subzero weather.

When I was born, we lived at the Hamilton place which had been the house/homestead of my mother's parents. Then we moved to the Silvester homestead, and the house my grandfather had built in 1917. These places were only a couple of miles apart and about ten miles south of Chaplin where I was born. The community where we lived was called Droxford and the little white church and cemetery was about a mile north of our home. It was called Bingham Baptist Church, after Pastor Bingham who had been the pastor at Burks Falls Baptist

Church. This church had started in my great-grandfather's home years earlier and eventually the congregation could afford to build a brick church on the main street of Burks Falls. The church was a member of the Convention Baptist Church of Ontario and Quebec. When the Silvester's left Burks Falls in 1909 for the prairies, Pastor Bingham was persuaded to go west, so they named the church after him. I well remember our whole family sitting in a pew near the front and singing, etc. One hymn stands out in my mind which is, "Verily, verily, I say unto you" and I thought they were saying "Beverly, Beverly, I say unto you". I guess I was planning ahead to when I would meet Beverly MacLean.

The following are some of the events I remember when we were still living in Saskatchewan; getting lost in a field of wheat or rye; shoveling snow using a license plate; Christmas and seeing Santa at the church; thousands of grasshoppers; terrible dirt storms; and sizzling hot weather. The most frightening memory is my getting stuck in a slough with sinking sand; the more I struggled the deeper I sank. I yelled for help and our hired man Arthur Morden came to my rescue; but I lost my rubber boots. It could have been a lot worse. I still recall the day they moved Grandma Silvester's house with two tractors so it would be closer to where we lived. For a number of years, we had no electricity. But my dad was very creative and built a wind charger with a three-bladed propeller he had made. It was hooked to a car generator and battery so that we were one of the first to have electric lights in our home.

After seven years of drought and the depression, my parents were forced to make a major decision regarding the future and their family. My dad walked the fields praying for the Lord's leading regarding whether to stay or move. The grasshoppers had eaten the crops in 1940 and my Dad lost his John Deere tractor to the bank; so, it would be impossible to carry on farming. On September 21, 1940, my brother, Alan was born. The family was getting bigger and there was less money to make ends meet. That winter was very cold and it was difficult to heat the house.

A decision was made in 1941, in the midst of the continuing drought and crop failure, to leave the west for the east. Good-bye Saskatchewan … Hello Ontario.

My Dad had a 1929 Nash he bought in Moose Jaw for two hundred and fifty dollars. He sold some of his Holstein cattle to start building a trailer to move our family's earthly possessions to Ontario. He paid ten dollars for a model T rear end and built an enclosed trailer. Uncle Gene and Aunt Marjory Lanning (my dad's sister and husband) were persuaded to move too. They had a similar car and also built a trailer. I still remember watching them build them; Uncle Gene's was more streamlined and Dad's was more square with rounded corners with one window - I believe — and a door. This was the upgraded model of early pioneers when they headed west by covered wagon or by settler cars as dad's family did in 1909.

In the summer of 1941 with temperatures reaching a hundred degrees Fahrenheit and another crop failure, the time had come to pack up and leave Saskatchewan — the "Land of the Big Sky" and head east. Dad had sold the cattle and anything he could to make some money and, after putting four new tires on the 1929 Nash, he only had eighty dollars left, with a two-thousand-mile trip ahead. This took a lot of faith and fortitude. Sounds a lot like Abraham when he left the Ur of the Chaldees, not knowing where he was going but endeavoring to follow the Lord's leading.

In August 1941, after saying goodbye to friends and some family members; the two 1929 Nash cars pulling homemade trailers headed east toward Moosejaw. In the Lanning's car was Uncle Gene, Aunt Marjorie and their two daughters, Gloria and Marietta, ages seven and five. In our car was Dad and Mom, Roger, Grant, Alan, and myself. This trip was a great adventure for young kids but more trying for the parents. One day I remember traveling in the Lanning's car and, while sitting on the floor in the back seat, Gloria taught me at age six how to tie my shoes. I was probably a slow learner compared to today's standards. As I recall we camped in parks on the fourteen-day trip. I remember when we crossed from Canada into the US, the border official made my Mom and Dad throw out a geranium plant that my Mom wanted to keep. My Dad was

2 Nash Cars & Trailers leaving for Ontario

not a happy camper. My Mother kept a diary of our trip to Ontario and I will try to share some of that with you.

SILVESTER – LANNING 1941 TRIP

Moving from Droxford Saskatchewan to Ontario
From the diary of Kathleen Silvester

Date	Activity
Tues. Aug 19	• We did the final packing, had dinner at Aunt Lucy's then went to Margories"s
Wed. Aug 20	• Packed and entertained, Gene sold cows – had supper at Nelson's
Thurs. Aug 21	• Pancake breakfast at Nelson's – Left Gene's about 9am – called at "Home" cemetery = Vin's, Hughes & Chaplin (took snaps) – reached Leslies's 2:45pm – shopped, saw Grandma – went to Tourist camp
Fri. Aug 22	• Went back to Leslie's and said good-bye to all. Reached Daisy's at 2 pm D.S.T. Regina – camped at Weyburn late PM
Sat. Aug 23	• Fixed Gene's radiator and left late, crossed at Portal, USA late in the afternoon, intending camping at Kenmore but drove on to "Devils Mountain" and stopped in Donnybrook ravine
Sun. Aug 24	• Sunday – made late start, started to rain in afternoon. Parked at Devil's Lake
Mon. Aug 25	• Our shift lever broke off so made for a late start – stayed at Cookston, Minnesota camp
Tues. Aug 26	• Stopped at Solway, Minn. Later trailer wheel gave trouble, spent night at Floodwood garage
Wed. Aug 27	• Passed through Duluth and Superior. Spent night in Wakefield park
Thurs. Aug 28	• Lovely scenery in Michigan, started to rain at Escanoba - camped at Thompson, Michigan
Fri. Aug 29	• Crossed at the SOO on the ferry 4pm – it started to rain and soaked our things in trailer – spent night in cabin at Green Bay near Bruce Mines, Ontario
Sat. Aug 30	• Made poor time on account of Gene's radiator, spent night at Webbwood Ont. – rained during night and morning
Sun. Aug 31	• We drove partly through rain on to North Bay and spent night in tourist camp

Mon. Sept 1	• Got to Burks's Falls and visited old places etc. – went on and spent the night at Huntsville
Tues. Sept 2	• Went on to Barrie, had flat tires on trailer and bearing wear out – continued to Rich Hill with Bob "Home at last"
Thurs. Sept 4	• Left for Toronto and spent night at New Toronto 3rd St. – went to see Belfrys
Fri. Sept 5	• Moved out to Port Credit
Sat. Sept 6	• "big wind" and Genes left for St. Thomas
Sun. Sept 7	• The gang came along and we went up to Laurel
Mon. Sept 8	• Had dinner at Jessie's and then went back to Port Credit
Tues. Sept 9	• Washed, went to Marge and Charlies – kids came back
Wed. Sept 10	• Blackout
Thurs. Sept 11	• Left for Union on in day – arrived after dark
Fri. Sept 12	• Gene started to work – we moved into Blacks late at night
Sat. Sept 13	• Lloyd got his job
Sun. Sept 14	• We rested
Mon. Sept 15	• Lloyd and Gene started on night shift – went in at 6pm
Tues. Sept 16	• Marge & I drove into St. Thomas

ST. THOMAS 1941–1946

After coming east, Dad immediately looked for a job in Mimico (Toronto) at the Goodyear plant, but there was nothing available. Uncle Gene went to St. Thomas because his folks lived there. He knew the Weatherhead Co. was hiring, so Dad applied there and was hired in the fall of 1941. He got thirty-five cents an hour and so we left Port Credit, where we had been camping, and headed south to St. Thomas.

He found a house owned by Mr. and Mrs. Black. They lived in a newer part of the house, but a portion of the house was empty. It was in Union between St. Thomas and Port Stanley. We had no furniture. We slept on the floor in blankets. I remember the mice running over us in the night. Dad went to the dump and found an old hot plate which he rewired so meals could be cooked. I remember Mrs. Black, our neighbour bringing us cookies and squares on a paper plate, and it seemed like manna from heaven. I'm sure she felt sorry for us as kids and a family and wouldn't know how we'd even survive the coming winter. Dad made a couple of chairs and a table out of orange crates. We lived there about six

Black's Old House in St. Thomas

months then moved to the River's place in St. Thomas, near to where the Timkin Roller Bearing plant was located. The school was across the street. I couldn't go until I was seven because I had trouble talking properly. My mom taught me to speak and once I got started, there was no stopping me. From there we moved to a home near Waterworks Park; 115 Alma St., called the Jansky Place. Dad rented it with the option to buy but we were unable to take that option, as the price was fifteen hundred dollars. We lived there for two years. I went to Loches, a school a half mile from the house. At this school I had my mouth taped shut and Roger, Grant, and I got the strap for making fun of a smelly family. We chanted:

> Father Moses shot a skunk
> Mother Moses cooked a chunk
> Baby Moses ate a hunk
> Holy Moses how they stunk.

Dad's mother (Louise Silvester) was living out west and wanted to be with us. Dad agreed to her coming but in later years regretted it because we had so very little and it put so much more responsibility on Mom who already had four boys and few resources. Our house wasn't well equipped either. All four of us children got measles and mumps and had to be quarantined with a sign on our house.

The doctor said we might have to return to Saskatchewan where it was drier and less humid, but we stayed and survived the challenges.

Because it was war years, there was rationing of gas and on many occasions we walked. Hiawatha Street Baptist was one and a half miles away. It was a good church. Soldiers were part of the congregation because they trained nearby. The pastor was Mr. Wheaton. He was a good preacher, as well he painted as he spoke to convey his message.

My Dad bought a house on 113 Balaclava St. It was a double lot with a house for two thousand dollars. The Weatherhead Company was just around the corner from our house where my Father worked during the Second World War. We went to Manitoba St. School about three blocks away. Dad was foreman of thirty-five women on the assembly line making aircraft brass shells. The factory had previously made brass brake fittings for cars. We went to clubs at the church and a missionary, Elma Birch, taught me in Sunday School. Dad was the superintendent. We'd go to a bakery and get stale bread goods for free. Roger and Grant had paper routes and I'd help them. A quart of milk was ten cents and Jersey milk was thirteen cents delivered to the door. The iceman would bring a 50-pound block of ice for the icebox. Jumbo, the famous elephant from P.T Barnum's circus, had been killed on the train track, just one block from our house. In 1946, when the war ended, I remember the soldiers returning at the train station downtown. Dad's job was cut back. so, he had to do something else to support the family. I learned to ride a bike while at this house. Because of my delayed speech, I started school a year late, but caught up by doing grades two and three together. I finished grade four when I was ten years old, before we left St. Thomas in April 1946, to move to a farm near Shelburne Ontario.

2

The Old Rich Hill Farm
1946–1957

On April 2, 1946, we arrived at Rich Hill farm, after leaving St. Thomas where we had lived for five years during the second world war. The name "Rich Hill" came from a town in Ireland. My mother's great grandparents, David and Jane Spence were born in Ireland and emigrated to Canada in 1844. They were teachers and had a house built in Churchville just south of Brampton in 1845 and it is still there. In 1851 they moved to Amaranth township and homesteaded Rich Hill Farm, named after Rich Hill in Ireland. They started a Methodist Church in their home, which later became Whittington United Church. This farm was in our family until we sold it in 1956 and moved to St. Thomas.

It was a wood frame house that was now covered with red bricks; a two-story home with four bedrooms, a kitchen, living room, and parlour but no bathroom. When we arrived, it had no electricity and we had to use coal oil lamps and lanterns for the next two years (1946-1948). We had left St. Thomas being used to hydro so it was like going back to the dark ages. We had one big lamp that pulled down over the dining room table and Uncle John, from whom we had bought the farm, used to pull it down and read there while the rest of us sat in the dark. My Grandmother Hamilton and her brother Uncle John lived

Rich Hill Farn House (Brick)

with us for a number of years as part of the arrangement when my Dad bought the farm. So, nine of us had to live in cramped space, with limited resources. My mother's mother was a lovely Christian lady who was a poetess and, being separated from Grandpa for many years, needed a place to live. Uncle John, however, was a bachelor who should have been a professor rather than a farmer as he was not overly ambitious. He mainly read and slept. About the only time he would be seen working was when someone came to visit. Then he would leave his bedroom and head out to the pump to get water and take the swill pail out so he would be seen as helpful otherwise he did very little; however, he loved his meals. One of the memories was when my mother put out a big dish of jam to be used by the whole family. Uncle John took five or six slices of toast and all of the jam for himself. Finally, my Mother made individual dishes of jam for each of us; which meant a lot more work for her.

In order to have some spending money (since we didn't receive an allowance), I did caretaking at Rich Hill School, located on the northwest corner of our farm. I started when I was in grade eight and continued for five to six years. This involved sweeping the floors, dusting the desks, and emptying pencil sharpeners and garbage cans. In the winter I lit the fire in the pot-bellied stove. My pay was fifteen dollars a month. It was good discipline for a teenager. When the school was torn down, buses then took the children to a centrally located school. This school has since been torn down and modern two-story home stands in its place. All five of us boys attended the school and the teacher taught grades one to grade nine. We had double desks, so someone sat beside us and we used ink wells, pens and pencils. Ball point pens became available when I was in grade seven or eight. We couldn't afford them. One of my friends, Wilmer Little, got one and when it ran out of ink, I bought it from him for ten cents. I put regular ink in it thinking it would work but, to my chagrin, the ink leaked out and I got covered — along with my notes — with ink. Bad idea.

The two hundred and twelve-acre farm had become run down because hundreds of loads of manure had never been put on the land but was in a huge pile behind the barn. It would take several years to build up the land again and lots of hard work. In order to try to survive, my father decided to do a couple of things; the first was to buy a thousand little chicks to help produce meat and eggs. We had them all in one brooder house and we had to build another one because there was not enough room. By the time we got it built, half of the chicks had died because of disease caused by overcrowding. My job was to carry all the chicken feed and water in big pails making sure the chicks always got fed. As a result, I became interested in raising chickens and later had between five hundred and six hundred laying hens when I started working for Skyline Farms in Aurora. I sold several thousand chickens, covering Dufferin County in my '39 Mercury Coupe, for a couple of years. I took a course at the Ontario Agricultural College in Guelph and learned how to treat disease in chickens in order to service my customers.

The second way my father tried to feed the family was through building a sawmill. He purchased a portable Bell Saw from the US and, since our farm had close to one hundred acres of mixed bush, which included hemlock, tamarack, spruce, birch, maple, cedar, etc. All of the trees had to be cut by hand using a crosscut saw, so he hired a nearby neighbor, Gordon Wright, because we boys were too young to do that heavy work. At the Shelburne Fair in 1946 he saw a Hornet two-man chain saw weighing sixty-five pounds and purchased it, as he knew it was the way of the future. He took on a contract for one hundred and twenty-five cords of hardwood to supply the schools in Amaranth Township — another source of income to help us survive. When neighbouring farmers learned that we had a sawmill, they started to bring logs from their bush lots to have them cut into lumber to use on their farms. Some Saturdays there would be up to six different farmers coming in with their tractors and wagons with loads of logs from their farms. My Dad charged four dollars per hour for cutting their lumber and I rolled the logs with cant hooks up to the sawmill carriage and shoveled sawdust. I also helped flipping the logs on the carriage. Roger and Grant worked at moving the lumber — tail-sawing before we would run it through the edger to take off any bark and, if the customer wanted, we ran it through the planer. We worked at this for ten years to make additional money. We would cut up the slab wood from the logs and on Saturdays we would do three truck loads, delivering it to farmers or town's people. It was fifteen dollars for five cords delivered to their home. In order to get rid of the sawdust, we would store it in the basement of our house and Uncle Gene, my father's brother-in-law, designed a sawdust burner that we used to heat our house. Once a day a hopper would be filled and it would gravity feed. All that was left of the sawdust at the end of the winter was one big tub of ashes, like cement, so it was very efficient. I also used sawdust as bedding for some of our dairy cows that were in stanchions; I made up a machine that spread sawdust from a turntable from an old phonograph player. The rest of the sawdust was spread on the fields as fertilizer.

The Dairy Farm
When we first went to the farm in 1946, it was called "mixed farming" with Black Angus beef cattle, pigs and chickens. My Dad was looking for more means

Family Picture at Rich Hill Farm, 1950

Barn & Milking Parlour on the farm

of supporting the family and a neighbouring successful dairy farmer, Bill Clark, encouraged Dad to go into Holsteins and they would buy the milk for their dairy in Orangeville. Soon Dad bought ten registered young cows from Cardinal, ON, near Ottawa. We sold all our Angus cattle to purchase the Holsteins. We sold thirty to buy ten. Unfortunately, when we sold them the price was low for the Angus and within a year the price almost tripled to about five hundred dollars each. If we had known, we could have made a lot of money with less work and less outlay of money because at that time farmers were selling four to five beef cattle for enough money to buy a brand-new car. As our dairy herd increased in size and production, partially through artificial breeding, the work of milking up to thirty cows every morning and night kept us busy. In 1953 we were able to change to the newest method of milking and built a milking parlour. The cows came through in an assembly line and I did all the milking for four to five years. The assembly line made it faster as it was the first Surge milking parlour in Ontario. It was clean and efficient and many people came to watch how it worked. I only missed two milking days in four years and that was to attend Roger's wedding in Sarnia.

I am constantly amazed how God guides in His sovereignty and how one decision can impact our lives for years to come. This was especially true in what led to us leaving our farm near Shelburne and moving to Sarnia.

It started in the fall of 1953 when my oldest brother, Roger, was asked to be a messenger and driver, along with Pastor and Mrs. Harold Charlton of Orangeville Baptist Church and go to the first Fellowship Convention at Temple Baptist Church, in Sarnia. I remember telling my dad that we needed Roger to help us finish building our new milking parlour. It was late October and winter was around the corner but dad responded by saying Roger had been working hard and a few days away would be a good experience for him. Yes, father knows best. It was at the convention he met Gwen Smith, pianist for the convention, who would become his wife. A couple of years later in March, the family drove to Sarnia to see them. It was a warm spring-like day in Sarnia as we headed north; I remember my mother remarking that it was probably the same at home. She didn't want to leave Rich Hill Farm since her forefathers had purchased and developed it. When we got close to home there were great snow drifts and we couldn't get to our farm by the road, so that we had to walk the last quarter mile across a field. The house and barn were plastered with snow from a fierce storm. Now my mom saw what had taken place and was willing to consider moving.

Although our local doctor had treated my mother for eczema, it soon became apparent that she had contracted breast cancer. My dad was very upset since the doctor drank a lot and Dad remarked that a veterinarian looked after our Holsteins better than our physician looked after my mother. Dad spent a lot of money to take mom to the Mayo Clinic in the U.S. for a mastectomy, but later the return of mom's cancer led to the decision to sell our farm and sawmill business and move to Sarnia. A family from Sarnia (Hosies) purchased our farm in September of 1956. Dad then procured a lovely home and five acres near Mooretown south of Sarnia. It was decided I should move to our place near Sarnia so the heat could be left on and the place maintained. I departed the day after Christmas in my '39 Mercury Coupe and left my six hundred laying hens and milking parlour responsibilities for my dad to manage.

I returned to the farm from Sarnia in January 1957 in my 1939 Mercury coupe. I had to drive at night through an ice storm and the defroster wasn't working. Thankfully I arrived safely to assist at the auction sale of our herd of Holsteins, my 600 laying hens, as well as all our farm machinery. The day of the auctions was sunny and cold, with hundreds attending. By the end of the day everything was sold and we were grateful to God for a wonderful outcome.

Years later, after we had moved to Huntsville, we saw a store called "Rich Hill Candles" in Bracebridge. We were curious about the name since our farm was called "Rich Hill". We learned later that the Hosies who had purchased our farm in 1957, when we moved to Sarnia, had sold the farm again. Three university students (hippies) rented the old farmhouse and started their candle company. They named it "Rich Hill Candles" after the farm. The candle company grew and they moved to Orangeville and then to Bracebridge where they employ a large number of people and ship candles around the world. I took Dad to meet the owners and he gave them the book he had written — much to the excitement and pleasure of the owners.

3

Arriving in Sarnia
1956

Roger knew a fellow who headed the Fuller Brush franchise and he got me a job. On December 28th I started selling with him on St. Claire Avenue in Point Edward, where Bev's family moved to in 1958. The only thing that I sold that morning was a package of toothbrushes for one dollar and ninety-five cents, and I made forty percent profit. Now I thought I was going to starve to death if I didn't become a better salesperson. Of course, the worst time of the year to sell anything was between Christmas and New Year's when everyone was broke, busy, or probably both. In the new year I went to a sales training meeting in Windsor and learned to never try and sell one thing but to do it in pairs or three's, then you could negotiate and ladies felt they were winning. The approach I used was simple — when I rang the doorbell or knocked on doors to introduce myself, I would tell them I had a free gift for them, pick up my black sales case, start taking off my black rubbers, and take a step forward. Usually they would let me in where it was warm. My sales grew to one hundred dollars a day and I became the top salesperson in the area. The downside was that I sold for five days and, after getting all my Fuller Brush inventory which ran from brushes, mops, cleaners, women's cosmetics, I had to take most of Saturday to deliver all of the merchandise to the scores of homes. Often about half the people were away and I had to return later that day or the following week to deliver the goods and collect my money. By June I was ready for a change and had serviced all of northern Sarnia and Point Edward two times. Going door to door was great training when I went into the ministry. I did some visitation in Toronto but mainly in Bramalea where I canvassed thousands of homes and seeing many come to Christ and to our church.

One of the deacons at Temple Baptist Church was Laird Nixon and he was in charge of hiring at the Polymer synthetic rubber plant, which was government-owned. Roger worked there (and later Ernie) and Laird interviewed me. I got a job for about one dollar and sixty cents an hour, wherein I started at the bottom of the labour gang. It was hot, dirty work, which included cleaning big tanks and high columns filled with hot, sticky rubber. We had to wear rubber suits, boots, and hats. Sometimes in styrene tanks we wore masks and had air pumped into us like astronauts, so we wouldn't be gassed. After one worker died, they paid us additional danger pay of twenty cents an hour. I was able to get a couple of promotions during the next six years; however, I was used to working hard and my boss told me to "cool it" because I was making the other workers look bad. I knew I didn't want to spend the rest of my life working there but I got a lot of overtime and did okay. One year our Atomic and Chemical Workers Union said that we needed to go on strike, so we'd get higher wages. As a result, we were on strike in 1959 for ninety-six days and we had to picket regularly. Our weekly pay was only fifteen dollars and free haircuts. I had completed a 1931 Ford hot rod and I'd drive it in to picket. I was hurting financially and I had gotten a job with a friend, Florent Vogels, who worked with me and also owned a forty-acre farm north of Sarnia. He grew sugar beets and I got a job for a month 'blocking' or thinning them out. My pay was three dollars an hour; not very much for the back-breaking work in the hot sun. Work there ended a fellow worker from Polymer, Bob McGregor, and I decided to drive to B.C. and back. His dad owned a used car lot in Petrolia and we took a 1957 M.G. roadster— white with a black top. We packed a tent, clothes, stove and some food, plus Bob's golf clubs. He was club champion in Petrolia and played several others in Windsor and B.C. Our first day started great as we headed north in Michigan. We got a speeding ticket (Bob driving) and then our battery died. We continued to travel for a total of three weeks. In Saskatchewan we found Chaplin where I was born. We started looking for an old farm we had left in 1941— eighteen years earlier. We headed down a dirt road and stopped and to ask a farmer if he knew where Oscar Silvester lived. He said, "Go south a mile to the main drag and go east a mile and turn north a little where there is a Lloyd Silvester living across from Oscars". I informed him that Lloyd was my dad and we had moved away in 1941. It was unbelievable he lived four miles away and hadn't known that.

M. G. Roadster going west

We reached beautiful B.C. and had fun when we met two young gals who were driving a white 1957 M.G. as well. We asked them out for brunch and the gal with long dark hair with whom I was sitting with turned out to be married, so we had to scuttle any further 'fellowship'. Bob wanted to play golf at the lovely and expensive and private Capilano Golf Club; so, we got there in the evening and drove up the side of the mountain/course, moved one of their fancy benches and parked our car, put up our tent, and slept there. Early the next morning, we headed to the clubhouse and walked in. Bob McGregor was 6'2" tall and possessed a lot of nerve; when the man in charge asked, "Who invited you here to play golf?" Bob said, "I've driven all the way from Ontario where I am a club champion and I have my caddie with me". The man said, "Fine, we're happy to have you as our guests", and we played one of the most beautiful golf courses in the world. Subsequently, we went to another course where the Canadian Champion was a member and played there too. To conclude our western visit, we went up Grouse Mountain on a chairlift, sleeping that night in the car. I was driving so I had to sleep behind the steering wheel. The next morning, we headed back east.

We covered Alberta and into Saskatchewan, and by about 5:00 p.m. arrived

Bob & Stu at Grouse Mt. B.C.

in Moose Jaw. Phyllis Silvester, my second cousin, who later married my dad, lived with her parents and we found their home just in time for supper. We were hoping they would invite us to sleep overnight, even on the floor in our sleeping bags. When they asked us where we were going and we said we were heading home, they merely wished us a safe trip. So much for western hospitality. We headed toward Manitoba and drove through the night until we ran out of gas around 5:00 a.m. Guess who had to find a service station and wake up the owner — yours truly. Driving for about thirty-six hours straight we arrived home, in the rain late that evening; tired but glad to be alive and home safely. Friends said the strike was nearly over and the American-based union officials said they were heading to the US. The only raise we received was two cents an hour. We had lost about fifteen hundred dollars, but I had an exciting and eventful trip that summer.

One icy morning, on my way to sell Fuller Brushes, I was in a three-car accident and was crushed in the middle in my '39 Mercury, which was totalled. I then purchased a 1951 black and yellow Meteor hardtop, using the parts from my Mercury-transmission, rear end, dash, etc. to build a hot rod. I installed an Oldsmobile V8 "88" motor and did the welding and painting myself. It was less than perfect. I painted it tropical rose, a '55 Ford colour. It cost me a total of one thousand dollars and one year's work, but it was featured in the January 1960 Hot Rod Magazine, as it would accelerate 0–60mph in six seconds. I drag raced other cars and motorcycles and no one ever beat me. I joined the "Rod Benders" car club and had tons of fun. My brother Ernie later purchased it after I had taken the Olds motor out and put it in my 1940 black Ford Coupe. I had this car until I sold it in 1963 when I went to seminary. Cars were one of my loves/idols/ gods to which I had to say good-bye in order to, as St. Paul said in Philippians, "Forgetting those things which are behind and looking unto Jesus the author and finisher of my faith." (Philippians 3:13)

As a twenty-one-year-old, I was profoundly impacted spiritually in terms of my life and future ministry by two ministries: Temple Baptist Church and Youth for Christ. As I sat under the faithful ministry of Dr. Hal MacBain, my faith was strengthened and my life challenged. Sunday after Sunday people responded to the invitation to accept Jesus as Savior and Lord; the church grew as the Sunday school increased and youth ministry grew. I became involved in teaching junior-aged boys and we had Sunday school contests in which I tried to bribe them to come by giving them chocolate bars. It worked for a while but after they melted in my pocket, I found a better way was to invite them to our home and take them on hikes, thereby investing time and effort in their lives. I was asked by Dr. MacBain to give leadership to the high school-aged young people and teach some. Youth for Christ (YFC) was a great ministry that had been started in the 1950's by Billy Graham. I had attended their rallies in Orangeville and Shelburne and my mom and dad used to sing at many rallies. Men like Charles Templeton and his wife Constance would speak and sing while I attended YFC bible studies as well.

Bob Simpson, a young man from Toronto who had gone to Bible school in the US, became the director for Sarnia, London, and Windsor YFC. He was a gifted speaker and leader and asked me to assist him. For two years I was the announcer for the half-hour radio broadcast on Saturday mornings on CHOK. Occasionally I spoke when he was sick and this was great training for ministry in the future. The first formal sermons I ever preached were from the back of a pop truck owned by Les Morris of Temple, in a park on the St. Claire River, and another time in Sears Mall Plaza.

I helped lead our jail ministry in the Port Huron jail across the river in Michigan. A team of guys and gals would go and sing, give testimonies and visit with the prisoners. On one occasion they let me go into solitary confinement with a young man guilty of murder and lesser crimes. I remember receiving many letters of appreciation from young men to whom I had ministered and/or led to Christ.

It was in September of 1959 that I first met Bev MacLean, who would become my wife. Prior to meeting her, I had dated several girls from Sarnia and surrounding area, as well as one in St. Thomas, for about a year. The saying back then was "playing the field" and I was guilty of playing the whole farm. Then it was group or casual dating without getting too serious. One day, my younger brother, Alan, brought home the high school yearbook from Central High, when he was in grade thirteen. I was looking at pictures and saw a gal who he said was a Christian and had recently come from Montreal. Her name was Beverly MacLean and she caught my attention. Possibly the thought that she was French piqued my interest. Anyway, it was our first fall YFC rally and I offered to take them home in my 1954 Studebaker Commander Coupe any girls who needed a ride. My youngest brother, Ernie, was with me and I packed four or five girls into my car. Bev was one of them and I took her to her house in Point Edward as my last delivery. I decided to phone her from a pay phone. I don't know how I had gotten her number, but when I called fifteen minutes after I had left her at home her mother answered. She said Bev wasn't home to which I responded, "Are you sure?" She said her daughter had gone bowling with a girlfriend at Marcin's Bowling Alley in Point Edward. Apparently, this was the night the clocks were to be turned back so she decided it was too early to stay home. I persisted and later called her to invite her to go to a football game at the stadium near her home the next Saturday night where the Sarnia Imperials were playing an American team. I don't recall who won but I know I certainly did as we walked, talked, and held hands. She would not let me kiss her until the fourth date, playing "hard to get" because she knew I had dated others and her plan ultimately worked. The second date was the following Sunday, to a soul-winning class sponsored by YFC. She was only seventeen and I was twenty-four, but she seemed a lot more mature than gals I had dated who were older. However, Bob Simpson wanted me to meet a gal in Windsor so one Saturday off I went in my Studebaker. I got to Chatham and headed west toward Dresden before I realized I was already an hour behind schedule so for ten miles drove between eighty and ninety miles per hour. I kept an eye on my rear-view mirror as I passed cars finally reaching a stop light and then taking off with tires spinning. As I looked in my rear-view mirror, there was a police car with lights flashing as I pulled over. I said, "I guess I took off too fast from the light". He asked what kind of motor I had under the hood then said "I've been trying to catch up to you for ten miles and couldn't. What is the hurry?" I told him I had an appointment in Windsor and was late so he suggested to take a different highway south to Windsor since there were no police and I could make better time. Wow. No ticket and some help to keep speeding. I met this lovely Christian gal who worked in Detroit

Girl Friend Bev & 1954 Studebaker

from a wealthy family and we went to an opera in Windsor, fur coat and all. On the way home on Sunday evening I almost had a serious accident on a road that had a 'Bailey Bridge' which narrowed down to one lane. My mother asked me next day why I was still 'in the hunt' as she felt Bev was the right girl for me. I finally listened to my mom and that was the counsel God used to help confirm my need to be serious with Bev. We exchanged Christmas presents and went on a youth retreat in Alton, at Friendly Acres. By February I was convinced Bev was the right gal for me. She had prayed for a Christian fellow to be her husband as her home wasn't a Christian home and her father had a drinking problem.

In February on Valentine's Day I purchased a nice engagement ring, placed it in my jacket pocket and her brother Keith took my jacket to hang it up and the bag with the ring it fell on the floor right in front of her. Thankfully the ring didn't fall out and later that evening I proposed in the car as that seemed to be the only private place I could find; not very romantic but Bev said "yes" and we began our plans to be married on August 13th, 1960.

Bev had been attending teachers' college for a year (1959–1960) and during that time we wrote numerous letters and she graduated in June. During the summer she got a job in a local restaurant as a waitress to make some money. I would drop in to see her, but the owner didn't like me hanging around unless I was buying something. Her dad made a generous offer to me when he found out we were planning to get married. If we were willing to wait a year, he would give us the lot next to their home which he owned. I said, "Thanks, but no thanks," since I would rather have his daughter than the property and I was not sure how it would work out living next door to my in-laws. The other problem was the cost to build a new home. In order to buy furniture for an apartment and get a newer car for our honeymoon, I decided to sell my 1932 V/12 Cadillac Brougham Coupe. I had purchased it years earlier, when living on the farm, for seventy-five dollars. It was a rare car from Guelph, which had been chauffeur-driven and owned by a businessman in Orangeville. It had power brakes, adjustable ride control, dual exhaust, and all the toys. I sold it to a Cadillac dealer for five hundred dollars and they restored it to the point at which it was worth about seventy-five thousand dollars. I purchased a beautiful 1955 Pontiac hardtop — beige and brown with a big V8 and stick shift.

Our wedding at Temple Baptist Church in Sarnia was on August 13th, 1960. Dr. MacBain married us and we held the reception in the auditorium under the sanctuary. My brothers Roger, Grant, and Alan were in the wedding party. Bev had three of her close girlfriends stand up with her. My mother and father were both at our wedding. My mother died the following spring from cancer at the age of 52. It was a beautiful day with many family members and friends in attendance.

As we took off on our honeymoon with the car covered with syrup, confetti and cans tied on, I was able to outrun all of the cars that chased us as we headed for Niagara Falls. I had to push it to one hundred and twenty miles per hour to finally beat the last Plymouth and Pontiac. It was like a snowstorm inside the car with the windows open and confetti flying around. Oh, to be young again — or maybe not. This was the beginning of a great two-week honeymoon in New York City, the New England States, and Quebec to visit Bev's relatives and then home for the start of an adventurous life together.

RAISING CHINCHILLAS 1955-1958

After I moved to Sarnia/Moosetown in 1955/1956 I purchased several chinchillas from my friend Eldred Turner. He had headed up Youth for Christ (YFC) in the Orangeville/Shelburne area as well as running a farm near ours. I paid one thousand dollars for several male and female chinchillas and their cages, which was a lot of money back then. Chinchillas had a beautiful blueish and silver coloured fur and brought a high price for making fur coats.

Unfortunately, in my busyness with my work, cars, sports, dating girls, and church work, I didn't look after them very well. I raised some and sold them but, in the end, I really didn't make much money, so I sold them a while before I got married in 1960.

Stu & Bev's Wedding in Sarnia Aug 13/60

4

Our First Home
1960–1963
from Bev

In August 1960, after our honeymoon, we moved into the Kember apartment we rented, at the corner of London Road and East Street in Sarnia. I could walk to the school I taught at — Hanna Memorial on Maria Street. Ours was a one-bedroom apartment on the first floor. There were four three-story buildings built in a square with a swimming pool in the center. I don't even remember using the pool.

Our first company was a group of young people from the church who poured in unexpectantly. I was somewhat embarrassed since we were not very settled. Stu had enough money from the sale of a 1932 Cadillac to buy the furniture we needed. I have never heard the end of this sacrifice. We had a green chesterfield and chair, a kitchen suite with metal legs, and a book headboard bedroom suite, they were our base furniture until after we had three children and had lived for quite a while in Bramalea.

When we found out at Christmas that I was pregnant, we knew we would have to find a larger place and, because I would have to leave teaching, a place that was cheaper. I had to leave my job since it was not proper to be teaching when you showed too much in those days. I continued until May. In the summer of 1961, we moved to an apartment a little way out of town where Stu could have a second job extracting honey from the bee-hives and cutting grass for the owner. The building had been a big chicken house that was made into six nice apartments. Stu felt more at home living in the country setting. He did some work on cars in the back of the apartment building, moving a motor from one car to another. It was at this time that Stu's Mom died after fighting cancer for several years. We were so glad she was able to be at our wedding and that she knew I was pregnant with Lois. From her hospital bed she gave us an envelope with five dollars in it for a gift for the grandchild she would never see. Lois was born two months after she died in 1961.

We had only one car, a 1955 Pontiac which we got for our honeymoon. Later Stu eyed a 1955 Thunderbird which was lots of fun but a little crowded when we had Dale. We had it until August 1963 when we went to Toronto. Stu worked for Polymer Corporation - a government-owned company and he belonged to the Atomic and Chemical Employees Union.

This apartment on Confederation Street was Lois's first home. She came home in our little 1955 Thunderbird in style. We were getting her ready for her life with Bruce. I remember holding her in the front seat when we had a little

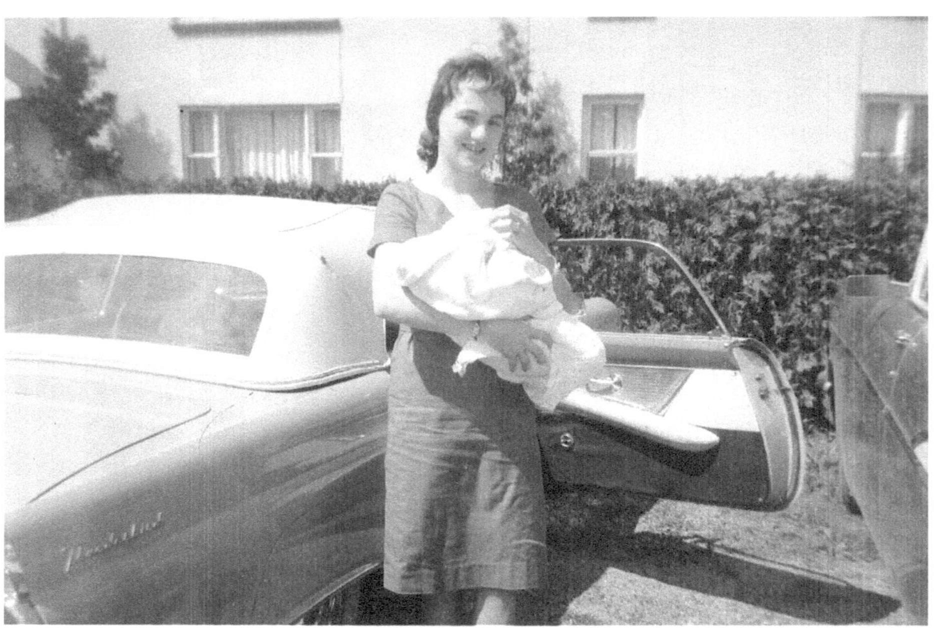

Bringing Lois home in T-Bird - Aug 13/61

accident one day and, realizing years later, how unsafe it was in those days with no seat belts. This new place was really good to be with a little one. There was lawn to sit on and lots of safe places to walk with the stroller. Our friends, Carol and Bob Eley, lived in the same building so it was nice to have that company. I stayed home with Lois until Christmas then Aunt Donna said she would babysit as she was at home with our nephew David who was just a little older than Lois. It was hard to let someone else look after Lois.

During this time Stu taught Sunday school and I worked in Pioneer girls. I went back to work Jan. 3, 1962 until the end of June. I had to have two years of teaching under my belt to get my permanent certificate; however, just before I started back, I discovered I was pregnant again. Dale was on the way, but I was allowed to teach until the end of the teaching year this time. Stu's Mom had died just before Lois was born so we had Stu's Dad and Ernie at our place quite often because they were alone. I especially remember Christmas morning with them.

We washed a lot of diapers in those days and often hung them out to dry. I was given two weeks of diaper service but went back to the routine. Disposable diapers had not been invented then. We had wood floors that had to be waxed quite often. One day I happened to leave the wax out and Lois thought she'd take a turn at doing it. She reached from her playpen another day, got a box of Kleen-ex, and pulled every one of them out of the box before I noticed. Lois and Dale shared a room for the next year. Then we were off on a new adventure as Stu was quitting his job and going to seminary in September 1963.

OUR FIRST HOUSE: AN OLD FARMHOUSE
IN BURK'S FALLS. 1966-1978

In early 1966 Stu's Dad heard that the old house that his grandfather had built near Burk's Falls in 1896 was for sale. It was originally a farmhouse on a hundred and fifty acres but the farmhouse with five acres was severed and was for sale for twenty-five hundred dollars; the one hundred and forty-five acres were sold to a local farmer, Ed Miller, a fine Christian dairy farmer. Years later when Ed died, I was asked to take his funeral at Burk's Falls Baptist Church. My Dad thought it would be good if the five boys could each put in five hundred dollars and buy the house to get it back into the family again; however, none of my brothers were interested since the old place had been vacant for three years except for the mice that had taken up residency. I was the only one who was foolish enough or adventurous enough to consider buying it. A man by the name of George Still owned it and I went to see if I could negotiate a better price since I didn't have near enough money. After a time of bartering I got him down to a price of one thousand eight hundred dollars. We had a reserve of a one thousand dollars

Burk's Falls House built by my Great Grandfather Silvester in 1896

saved up before going to seminary in case Bev got pregnant. I'm not sure how I scraped together the other eight hundred dollars, but the deal was finalized in the summer of 1966 and we were the proud owners of the seventy-year-old house my great grandfather had built...and our first real estate acquisition. The taxes where only thirteen dollars a year.

And so, began a twelve-year adventure and a source of many new memories, especially for our children. The house had no running water or indoor facilities. We had to construct a new outhouse behind the garage. One day Lois asked, "Where do you flush it?" It was handy that it was a two-seater.

There was a lovely spring at the back of the property which flowed continuously. A pressure pump had been installed between the spring and the house. There was a tap with one pipe into the house and my brother Ernie brought up a used sink he had and we installed that in the kitchen area so we had spring water (when it worked). We had to prime the pump often to keep it going, so made lots of trips carrying water. The house was surrounded by overgrown cedar hedges and I tried to get them under control or at least down to seven feet in height. The house had some lawn out front plus a two-acre field in the front of that. I decided to cut the field to make the place look better and I remember purchasing a power lawnmower for forty dollars in Toronto in order to try to get the field under control. Before we finished our two weeks of vacation that first year, we had made the house and the yard fairly presentable including the old pantry which we papered with some wallpaper that someone gave us. The boards had been covered with old newspaper and it was so interesting reading the old news. There was some old furniture left in the house and we kept it.

A family in Forward Baptist Church in Toronto, where I was ministering, had an antique dining room and bedroom suite. They gave this furniture to us and we had to move it by car and trailer to Burk's Falls. The furniture made the old house more livable, and twelve years later in 1978 we sold the house and Ed Ross, the realtor, purchased the furniture. Years later, in 2012, when I was a chaplain in Muskoka Landing, I visited him just before he died.

In 1967 we decided to have the annual Silvester/Lanning reunion at our place because it was centennial year. The old house hadn't been painted for many years. We decided it needed to be covered with oil first, so we tried to spray it, but the oil disappeared. We used brushes and many gallons were applied. We chose white paint with green trim, for the house. Bev's dad helped us paint and he said it was like painting the bark on a tree. I think we used twenty-five gallons of oil and paint using four-inch brushes. We were pretty proud of the finished product. Between twenty and thirty came for the reunion and we filled all five bedrooms, plus tents. It was a memorable event as we celebrated the Centennial of Canada as a country in this seventy-one-year-old house. We made many memories at that great old house: one was tearing down the old back shed and burning the old wood and tar paper. We found hundreds of bottles and cans smashing and shooting a lot of them. Probably in retrospect we should have kept some of these antiques. While cleaning out the basement, which had a dirt floor, I found a special round shaped stone. My dad later identified it as an Indian hammer head which I still have. It would have had a leather strap around it with a wood handle.

Another funny incident and memory occured in 1976 when Bev and I were tearing down the brick chimney that had been pulling down the roof because it was sinking in the basement dirt floor. We had taken off the top of the chimney and we threw big bricks out the upstairs windows as we dismantled it. We were both dirty, with black soot on us, when up our driveway came a big beautiful Mercury car. Out stepped a businessman in a three-piece suit. This man, whose name I can't recall, owned a crane company in Winnipeg, Manitoba. I had preached at the Baptist church he attended a few months earlier and actually had stayed at his home. Their former pastor, Lester Laird, had resigned and now they were in need of a new pastor. So, without any notice, this man jumped on a plane and flew to Toronto then rented this Mercury and drove to Bramalea

Baptist. He was looking for me and Jessie Wright, my secretary, said I was on holidays at our Northern Retreat. Nothing could stop him from pursuing me and we had no phone so he headed north to the old house. When I recognized who he was I was really embarrassed as I'm not sure if he recognized me or not. He said he was there to extend a call to me to become their new pastor and to make matters worse, he insisted on taking a picture of Bev and me. I admired his persistence but said I wasn't ready to leave Bramalea Baptist church.

OUR FIRST PERMANENT HOME — BRAMALEA

In March 1969 I was asked to speak for a call at the little Bramalea Baptist Church. They had a part-time pastor but had grown to sixty members and felt they could afford a full-time pastor for a salary of seven thousand five hundred dollars per year. I spoke Sunday morning and evening, and also led the Wednesday night prayer meeting. They asked if I could play the piano on Wednesday and I could since I achieved grade six in music. I said, "If you're calling me on my playing, I'll probably never make it." I received a call by ninety-three percent of the people. I accepted the call and began my first Sunday of formal ministry in June of 1969.

Our First home - 15 Banbury Ct. Bramalea

After being in five apartments (two in Sarnia and three in Toronto), we wanted to buy a home in Bramalea. All the homes were quite new and, after looking at several we found a three-year-old split-level at 15 Banbury Court. It had sold for sixteen thousand nine hundred dollars in 1966 and now in 1969 we had to pay thirty-one thousand dollars in a private deal. We only had one thousand dollars for a down payment. The former owner took back a second mortgage for ten thousand dollars at eight percent interest for five years. Fortunately, I had left five dollars in the Polymer Credit Union in Sarnia where I worked and they loaned me another five thousand dollars for three years. So, with three mortgages totalling six hundred and fifty dollars a month in payments and my salary being six hundred and twenty-five dollars a month, it meant that Bev had to start teaching full-time as a librarian, so we had money for food, clothes, etc. Within four and a half years we had paid off the fifteen thousand dollars using our savings, not buying dining room furniture, and trusting God to meet our needs.

We really loved our home, which had three bedrooms and three baths, but the basement was unfinished. I decided to try to finish the lower level, which included building a stone fireplace. We hauled granite stones from up north and I split them, doing most of the stonework from 11:00 pm to 2:00 am following

Fireplace & Rec Room Stu built

a full day of ministry. It was a great challenge and diversion from my ministry responsibilities. For months my fingers were bleeding from the mortar work but by Christmas the fireplace and all the walls were finished, covered with walnut panelling and the floor with yellow shag carpet. We had a great Christmas with Dad, Phyllis, and Bev's Mom and Dad.

A couple of years later, Bruce Fitter Jr. had started to date Lois and following his schooling, he started to build decks and recreation rooms. We asked if he could construct a deck off our kitchen. He agreed, and when he came Bev asked, "Where are the drawings?" to which he responded, "In my head." So by faith we believed this young budding builder. We had a 'Hollywood' style kitchen and had to open up a wall below one window. I offered to assist but, after an hour or so, Bruce suggested I go back to my church work and he would do the construction. By the end of the day a sliding door was in and a deck almost completed with built-in seating, and we could hardly believe it. Bruce was on his way to becoming a very successful designer and builder of many magnificent houses as well as restaurants.

Another event including Bruce was in 1982 when we were getting ready to move to Cheltenham. He had a new pickup truck and he loaned it to me to move some firewood to our new place. I was being overly cautious, not wanting to scratch it. I was loading it beside our house and a young fellow was standing in the back holding up the limbs of the red maple. I was looking out the back window, making sure he lifted the limbs up so they wouldn't scratch the truck which seemed to be stuck so I stepped on the gas and suddenly I heard a terrible sound. I had the driver's door open and it had caught on the trunk of the tree and bent the door back so far that now it was even impossible to close. I had to confess my sin to Bruce whereupon he forgave his father-in-law, refusing to let me pay for the damage.

5

Seminary Days:
A Big Change
A Difficult Decision

When I was eighteen, I was involved in the young people's group at Orangeville Baptist Church and in YFC in Orangeville. I wrestled with the possibility of going to Bible school or seminary, but it went no further than getting some literature. I was the main worker on the farm with my Dad, and was needed to work the farm and sawmill, so it would be hard to leave. Then my mother became ill with cancer. She had prayed that one of her boys would go to seminary and felt I would be the one. As a result of her illness we ended up selling the farm and moved to Sarnia; that move gave me further exposure to Christian ministry at Temple Baptist Church as well as in YFC. In the interim, my brothers Alan and Roger went to seminary, so I felt that I was off the hook.

Bev and I talked and prayed about the possibility of going into Christian ministry before we got married, but it was not until after my mom died in 1961 that I began to ponder it more seriously. I went to Dr. MacBain to see what he thought, hoping he would discourage me from going, as I did not like public speaking. His response however, was positive and he said he was waiting for me to come to tell him that. He suggested that both he and I pray about it for a week and then meet again, so we did, and he encouraged me to go to seminary.

He said he didn't encourage everyone who came to him regarding serving to go and several had gone against his counsel and it hadn't worked out for them in the ministry. I valued his wisdom, love, and prayers then and throughout my ministry. I decided to pursue God's call, but we knew we had many hurdles to overcome before it could happen.

We decided to put out a fleece, like Gideon, to see step by step if the obstacles could be overcome. First, I had not finished high school so wasn't sure that I would be accepted. Without my income, Bev would have to find a teaching job in Toronto. We had two little girls, Lois (almost two) and Dale (almost one) and they would need a baby sitter. Finally, we needed an affordable place to live. We left for Toronto one day after I had applied, and grandma watched the girls. I had an interview at Central Baptist Seminary and was accepted on the condition that I take a couple of extra courses in English for my enrolment in the three-year Licentiate in Theology degree with a minor in Christian Education. Bev had an interview with the school board and was assigned a school in North York (Gulfstream - just off Weston Road north of the 401). We looked for a place to live near the school so Bev could walk, as we would only have one car and I would need it. We found a low rental on the ground level only a couple of blocks from the school; there were three bedrooms, so I had one for studying. We met someone in the building who knew a lady wanting a job as a babysitter just to get out of the house and she enjoyed the children. We couldn't believe that she would come by bus, stay all day and charge so little. She must have been an angel. Bev was making only three thousand one hundred dollars a year, so we had to be very careful with our money.

We drove back to Sarnia knowing that it was God's will that I pursue a ministry career. We thought the Lord would send us to the mission field or to a small country church where we would fit in. This was going to be a big leap for us. Bev's dad thought we were crazy. We were just saving up money to buy a house; however, we knew that it would be best to follow the Lord's leading and so pursued that. One of the first things we had to do was to trade in our 1955 T-Bird for a 1960 Ford Falcon. It was an even trade and it had more room and better economy, but Bev had to learn to drive a gearshift over a weekend. We left early in September 1963, with our friend Don McLean pulling a U-Haul trailer.

Getting settled with both of us beginning new ventures, as well as the kids' adjusting to a new babysitter, made it a stressful time. I found the assignments, the reading, the driving in Toronto all stressful and I had headaches for the first time in my life. I got into the seminary quartet singing bass which required practices and traveling most weekends to churches in order to promote the seminary, which cut in on my study time. As I was the oldest, I often spoke or gave a testimony at those churches. One time, when speaking in Montreal, an English professor was in the congregation; he congratulated me on a good message and my enthusiasm but criticized my dangling participles and split infinitives (I didn't even know what he was talking about). I struggled to get rid of my grammatical errors and Bev was my critic and mentor. It took some time, but I conquered most of the bad habits I had and I thank the many people who endured my practicing time.

I remember one incident with the CBS quartet. We sang at the morning service in a small-town church in Minden. In the afternoon we went back to the church to practice for the evening service. We got talking about what we had eaten at the homes we went to for dinner. At the home where my friend and I went to eat the lady said, "I hope you had a good breakfast because we only have a light lunch at noon." I hadn't even eaten any breakfast. The other two fellows were bragging about the good meals they had enjoyed. The second home I went to for supper before the evening service seemed okay but the lady said, "I hope you had a good noon meal because we only have a small meal before church." I remember kicking the other guy under the table and hoping we'd have enough energy to sing and speak as well as to drive back to Toronto.

In the summer of 1965 our quartet and lady's trio, with Dr. Irene Robertson, and George Barton travelled in a big Dodge Station wagon to British Columbia and back. We went to many churches, starting with North Bay, holding special meetings with Dr. Denzil Raymer and preaching to promote Central Baptist Seminary. It was a tiring few weeks, but I believe it bore some fruit in new students and financial support for our school. I remember I had to do some of the driving to spell off Mr. Barton. I recall him getting upset when we started repeating one of his sermons which we had heard numerous times. The last time I saw the Bartons was in 1996 in Virginia while we were on our way to Arizona the year we first retired. He had been my Greek professor and a great encouragement in pursuing ministry.

SEMINARY DAYS IN TORONTO CBS — 1963–1968

Once I was enrolled in the three-year Licentiate Course, I found the expectation of studying and reading for hours each day a challenging experience. I hadn't been in school for over ten years and at age twenty-eight with a young wife and one and two-year-old daughters the experience was daunting. The first week was the hardest with every professor assigning books to read and assignments to complete. My head was aching from pressure for the first time I could remember. I recalled thinking maybe I had made a mistake in leaving my job in Sarnia and enrolling at CBS. However, with prayer, determination, and Bev's support

I kept going. I studied long and hard in my office/study bedroom and found I could keep up with the younger students. My experience of being in the workplace and being ten years older than most of the students, gave me a different perspective on life and ministry. I saw young students walking out of a test/exam after they thought they had done enough to pass the sixty-five percent threshold. I stayed to the last minute to try and do my very best. I knew the Bible said, "Whatever your hand does, do with all your might." At the end of each semester and year I found God enabled me to pass all the exams. In my third year I had eleven courses and I was able to average over eighty percent. My favourite subject was Homiletics (the art of preaching) and each year I was at the top of the class (P.T.L.). On the other hand, my Greek wasn't anything to write home about.

I enjoyed the practical work they encouraged at seminary like street preaching in downtown Toronto at noon hour and going to the Yonge Street Mission. The sign above us said "Stand Up, Speak Up, and then Shut Up". I was better at the first two than the third. These people had to listen or endure our speaking before the mission would feed them. I travelled for three years with the seminary quartet; this required practice time and being away most weekends. Bev had to stay home with Lois and Dale and try to get to church on Sundays. She demonstrated amazing patience, wisdom, and endurance for a young mother as well as teaching school full-time. She deserves a special medal for faithfulness. She is a Proverbs 31 wife.

CBS Seminary Quartet - 1964

SUMMER 1964 — SIMCOE

The seminary wanted the male students to use the summer months serving as summer interns in our Fellowship Baptist Churches. I was asked by Rev. Norman Pipe, the chairman of Home Mission, to come to his church, Bethel Baptist in Simcoe, Ontario. It meant Bev and the girls had to stay at our apartment in Toronto while I was gone six days a week, with Mondays off. Bev went to her parents' home for a month while she took a summer school course. She asked me if I had enough sermons prepared and I said I had sixteen; however, on one Sunday I spoke six times. I started at 8:30 a.m. with a half hour radio broadcast then taught a young people's Sunday school class, preached, and led the 11:00 a.m. worship service with four hundred attending. In the afternoon, I spoke at a senior's residence, then spoke at the 7:00 pm evening service, wrapping up with a youth meeting afterwards.

After leading and speaking at these six services, I went home and to bed and didn't wake up until 11:00 am the next day. Now I had only ten messages left, and this was only the beginning. It was a 'baptism by fire' and good training for future ministry in years to come. To make things worse, the church was in the middle of a split because about half the congregation felt Pastor Pipe should resign following thirty-five years of ministry. I was caught in the middle as a young fellow in the church split. My buddies back at the seminary blamed me, but I said I was the only fellow who had planted a 'new church'. In August when Pastor Norman Pipe went to his cottage on the Ottawa River, Bev was asked to prepare meals for Pipe's two grown children who worked at a local canning factory. She was only twenty-two years old and found these responsibilities very demanding. Bev tells the story that I had only one white shirt and she had left a burn mark on the back. She warned me not to take my suit jacket off when I was out, but I forgot and took it off because it was hot. The other embarrassing story Bev recalled was her making cherry pies from the locally grown cherries; however, because of other domestic demands, she didn't take the pits out of the cherries. When we had company join us, it was a bit embarrassing and hard on people's teeth.

These months of ministry stretched me almost to the breaking point but helped prepare me for future challenges in the ministry. I did a lot of visitation to the sick and shut ins. One ninety-year-old lady told me her parents had attended Spurgeons' Tabernacle in London, England. She said she had often sat on Spurgeon's knee, as following his preaching he would take little ones on his knee, just as Jesus did. At the end of the summer, the Pipes invited us to their cottage for a time of rest and renewal.

WESTON — 1963–1965 (per Bev)

When Stu got accepted at Central Baptist Seminary in 1963 and I got a job teaching for North York, we moved onto Weston Road. It was a low rental (ninety-three dollars per month) apartment just two blocks away from the school I was assigned to. We were in a three-bedroom flat with hardwood floors throughout. The girls had bunk beds and Lois fell out of the top bunk one day. (I often wonder if that was the cause of her scoliosis.) Stu used the third bedroom for his office and it also had a single guest bed. Lois had just turned two and Dale was just one when we moved in. By going to Humberlea Baptist Church we met a family who lived in the same apartment. Mrs. Hollywood looked after the kids for a while and then we got a lady who came to the house each day. She traveled by bus and we only paid her fifteen dollars a week; she was wonderful with the girls and seemed to enjoy her days with them.

Stu had a long drive to Seminary each day. He picked up Roger the first year so they drove together. It was very difficult for Stu to get into reading and studying. Having a wife and family to care for didn't help. He managed to have fun with the single guys playing ping pong and doing pranks. He enjoyed the quartet and, in the spring of 1965, traveled on tour with them out west and on most weekends.

I taught grade three and four at Gulfstream Public School for two years. I was teaching when we got the news that President John Kennedy had been assassinated in November 1963. It happened on Friday and we were able to watch the stunning events unfold on television. It was a tragic event and had a great impact on world affairs.

The first summer Stu went to Simcoe to work in Bethel Baptist Church. He would come home late Sunday night and be home Monday; I was working so didn't see him much. I came home for lunch those days and his brother Roger usually was there to visit. I went with the girls to Sarnia and stayed at my parents' when the school year ended and he'd come for Mondays. At the end of August when Pastor Pipe and family were on holidays, only the girls and I went and stayed at their house. It was hard with two little ones, one being toilet trained. The Pipe's two working adult children came home for their main meal at noon and they had to put up with my cooking. I was twenty-two and still had a lot to learn. Migrant workers would come to the door asking for food. The abundance of fruit in that area amazed us so we canned cherries, which we enjoyed throughout the year (even with the pits in.) At the end of the summer, the Pipes had us up to their cottage in Pembroke. I had my very first motorboat ride on the Ottawa River. The trip up in the car was difficult — no 401 in those days and the girls had car sickness on the way.

The second summer Stu almost returned to Simcoe, but Dr. MacBain made it possible for Stu to work with him at Forward Baptist in Toronto. We moved to Roywood Drive in North York, just off York Mills at the Don Valley Parkway, so we'd be closer to the church. I asked for a transfer in teaching.

6

My Ordination Service at Forward Baptist Church

This service was special to me because it was held on my mother's birthday, September 23rd, 1967. She had prayed that I go into the ministry and now, six years after her death from cancer at age fifty-two, I was to be ordained into "The Baptist Ministry". My dad and stepmother attended, coming from Temple Baptist in Sarnia. There were fifty-three messengers present from twenty-two Fellowship Baptist Churches.

I first gave an account of my conversion to Christ which took place on a snowy Sunday at our farm located between Shelburne and Orangeville. We had been attending Whittington United Church where my ancestors had gone. It was two miles south of our farm, but the roads were blocked to the extent that neither cars or horses and sleighs could get through. I remember listening to the "Old Fashioned Revival Hour" from Long Beach California on our radio and the preacher was Dr. Charles E. Fuller. Following his challenging sermon, I knelt beside the coffee table and gave my life to Christ. I was all alone and age thirteen.

We started attending Orangeville Baptist Church, ten miles south of us because the United Church had become liberal in its beliefs and teaching. I was baptised at Orangeville Baptist at age fifteen and became active in young people's work there until I was twenty-one, when we sold our farm and moved to Sarnia.

My call to the ministry was the second part of being ordained. At age eighteen while still at Rich Hill Farm, I sensed God calling me to train for His service and I sent for some material from Ontario Bible College in Toronto. I had been attending Youth for Christ rallies and Bible Studies and was growing in my faith. It was while living in Sarnia, attending Temple Baptist Church, and working with YFC I finally surrendered to God's call and God's will. When I was married and aged twenty-eight with a wife and two small daughters, I applied to Central Baptist Seminary and was accepted; Bev taught school in Toronto for five years so I could earn my Licentiate degree in theology (L.Th.) and Bachelor of Religious Education.

The third part of ordination was my Doctrinal Statement and Beliefs; I covered about fifteen main doctrines, having it printed out. I won't go over it, in fact I can't because I loaned it out several times and the last person never returned it. One funny thing happened when I loaned it to Don Whiteside to use: there were several pages and when he came to read about his/my belief about "End Times or Eschatology" the last page was missing. His quick response was "I guess it was raptured." (Don had been sent to Kingston Penitentiary for attempted murder and had received a Queens' Pardon.)

I feared the question period following my three-fold presentation, especially when I saw Dean Gordon Brown in attendance. The first question I was asked was, "If you were some place where there was no water and someone asked to be baptized, what would you do?" I thought for a moment and turned to Acts 8 - the story of Philip and the Ethiopian eunuch asking to be baptized out in the desert. My answer was, "If the Lord could provide water for Philip in the desert, He would be able to do the same for Stu Silvester." When they laughed and liked my answer; it relaxed me and I was able to answer other questions to the satisfaction of my questioners. I was so happy when Dean Brown arose to his feet and said, "I think it is time to cease our questioning and proceed with the ordination." I was greatly relieved because I feared he might question me on some Greek Grammar or "Life of Christ," which he taught.

John Bonham was the moderator, Pastor Lyons gave the charge to me, Vince Trimmer gave a charge to the church, Dr. MacBain led the ordination prayer, and my brother Alan gave the ordination sermon. This was followed by a lovely meal and great fellowship. I was thankful I had survived. Now I could perform weddings and carry out my God given call and responsibility of preaching the Word of God for the next fifty years or so. My framed Ordination Certificate hangs on my study wall as a reminder of that day, as well as God's call and faithfulness over the years of ministry.

SERVING AT FORWARD BAPTIST —1965–1969

One of the things I missed the most when I left Temple Baptist Church in Sarnia was the preaching of Dr. MacBain. However, in the sovereignty of God, Dr. MacBain left Temple in Sarnia following twenty-seven years of faithful and fruitful ministry to become the pastor of Forward Baptist following Dr. Jack Scott, who had gone to Ebenezer Baptist in Detroit.

Following my second year at CBS, I was asked by Pastor Norm Pipe to be his summer assistant for a second summer. I was hoping and praying for something in the metro area would open up for me so I wouldn't have to leave Bev and our two girls in Toronto. I finally told Pastor Pipe I'd return to Bethel Baptist in Simcoe. The very next day Dr. MacBain phoned to ask if I would come to Forward Baptist from May to September. I reminded him that if he had called a day earlier, I would have been thrilled to go. He said to leave it with him and he would take Norm Pipe out for lunch and see what could be arranged. I don't know what he did or said, but Norm released me to go to Forward. I think I said, "Hallelujah and Praise the Lord." Not only had Dr. MacBain married Bev and me, but he'd encouraged me to go to seminary.

Beginning in May 1965 I served in areas of youth ministry, Christian education, visitation, teaching, and some preaching. When I returned to seminary in September, Forward Baptist kept me on part-time and this arrangement continued until I graduated in May 1966, with my L. Th. In May 1966, I began full-time as Assistant Pastor to Dr. MacBain. What a blessing and privilege to be mentored by such a gifted and godly servant of God. What a thrill to sit under his powerful preaching again and learn the importance of pastoral visiting as well as deacons' meetings and how he ran them. Some members started to leave Forward because they felt Dr. MacBain's preaching didn't measure up to Jack Scott's. I asked, "How are you handling this?" He replied, "It's not my church, it is the Lord's and I'll continue to feed and lead". Dr. MacBain may not have been the orator that Dr. J. Scott was, but he was a great pastor and shepherd of the flock. Both of these men were gifted and great servants of God.

In the summer of 1965, I was heading up Daily Vacation Bible School. I took a lot of the older kids outside to kick a soccer ball up and down the street beside the church. A car pulled up and headed toward me and I thought the person wanted to park so I walked toward it. Suddenly, I heard, "Hold up, bank robbery hold up", and the driver of the car threw the passenger door open and down the street came a short man running hard with a pouch around his waist. Suddenly I realized he was the robber and I ran toward the car to head him off. He jumped in and sped off, but I was able to get the licence plate number. A teller had chased him from the Bank of Nova Scotia at the corner of Gerrard Street and Danforth

Forward Baptist Church - Toronto

Avenue. Actually, the robber had brandished a gun under his sweater the teller fainted; he got away with over two thousand six hundred dollars.

I ran to the bank with the bank employee and fortunately there was an off-duty policeman cashing his cheque. I gave him the licence plate number and he called to alert the motorcycle police what had happened. The bank manager called me into his office and thanked me, saying "You could have been shot (because he believed the robber had a gun). Why did you risk your life?" I said, "This morning Dr. MacBain called me into his office to inform me that a loan for four hundred thousand dollars had been approved from this bank for our building project." I said, "I wanted to make sure the money was here when we needed it." He said, "You will get a reward from the bank", and the Canadian Bankers Association later awarded me two hundred dollars. The week before at a deacons meeting, when Dr. MacBain was challenging the twelve deacons to be willing to pledge up front money. Many of them made one thousand dollar promises and I made one for five hundred dollars. At the time I didn't have five dollars extra, but God supernaturally provided much of it for fifteen minutes' worth of work. Later the City of Toronto awarded me a lovely Citation for Bravery which I have hanging in my office. At the time of the robbery the T.V. cameras arrived and I was interviewed by a reporter. The caption in the Toronto Star was "Local Priest

Helped Apprehend Bank Robber". Some of my seminary friends heard it and said, "It sounds like something Stu Silvester would do. Were the bank robbers apprehended?" Yes, a cop on a motorcycle received the licence plate number and chased the car, which had been stolen. The car pulled over and the men went in two directions. He chased and caught one in a back yard. The other man jumped over the fence into the same yard and he captured him too. Within fifteen minutes both men were arrested and later sentenced to two years in jail. One lived near the church and in early 1969 they were being released, so I thought it might be a good time to "get out of Dodge" and I left for Bramalea Baptist Church. The new auditorium seating one thousand was completed in 1967.

The other story regarding money and God's providence began while visiting an elderly member of the church at her home. I read and prayed with her and shook her hand as I left. She slipped some money into my hand. I said I'd take it and make sure it got in the offering. She said, "I've already looked after my offering. God told me you had a personal need and the money is for you." When I got to my car, I counted it and it was eight dollars. Our little girl Faye was sick and we had a prescription but no money to get the needed medicine. I went to the drug store and got the medicine and it was seven dollars and ninety-five cents. When I returned home, Bev asked, "How did you buy the medicine since we had no credit card?" I said, "The Lord provided through a godly widow."

While I continued ministering at Forward from 1966 to 1969, I did a lot of youth work which also included speaking at youth retreats for FBYPA and other churches. The church allowed me to continue my studies at CBS on my Bachelor of Religious Education (BRE degree), studying two half days a week and in May 1968 I graduated.

I thank the Lord for my wonderful wife Bev who not only raised three lovely daughters but taught school full-time and part-time, as well as supply taught when we needed to balance our budget. In early 1969 I was contemplating leaving Forward and going out on my own. Dr. MacBain said he could help me get into a good church. I said I would prefer a younger, smaller congregation into which I could grow. I'd observed that an older established congregation was not always flexible and open to new ideas. A friend of mine at CBS, Doug Gale, was going to the new Bramalea Baptist Church in "Canada's First Subdivision City" and he said he'd submit my name if I was interested. I agreed and the rest is history.

7
Twenty Years of Ministry and Memories 1969–1989

I began my ministry the first Sunday in June 1969 at Bramalea Baptist Church, having received a call in March with a ninety-three percent vote. We were excited about going to Canada's first suburban city where the name "Bramalea" came from the name "Brampton", "Malton", and "lea" since it was located between these two cities. Bev and I had three daughters, Lois aged seven, Dale aged six, and Faye two years old. We had lived in five different apartments — two in Sarnia and three in Toronto and we had the challenge of buying our first home. We scraped together one thousand dollars for the down payment (money from insurance when I was rear-ended in Toronto in my 1963 Ford, which I never fixed). The house was a three-year-old side split and cost thirty-one thousand dollars. The owners sold it privately and he took back a ten thousand-dollar second mortgage for five years. I had belonged to a Credit Union in Sarnia and providentially, I had left five dollars in my account. I phoned them and they loaned me the five thousand dollars for three years that I needed to complete the purchase. The three payments totalled six hundred and fifty dollars each month, which was my monthly income as pastor so my faithful wife Bev had to return as a fulltime teacher/librarian so we could live and feed our family. In four-and-

Bramalea Baptist Church 1969

a-half years we had paid off both loans by living carefully and not purchasing dining room furniture.

When I began my ministry at Bramalea I was also working one day a week for the Fellowship Baptist Young People's Association (FBYPA), which involved some travelling, speaking, and publishing of a monthly paper. There were sixty members in a building that held one hundred and fifty people that had been built on one-plus acres in 1967. I remember driving from Toronto for the cornerstone-laying and opening of the church because Bill Hiltz, a professor at CBS and part-time pastor, had he invited students to come. I remember our Fellowship Convention at People's Church in 1965 and my giving a couple of dollars towards buying a portable building to be used at Bramalea, not knowing in 1969 I would become their full-time pastor. The people welcomed us warmly and initially I was responsible for everything, including secretarial and some janitorial work. In the first week I had the joy of leading three to Christ. One was Mac Campbell, a teacher/principal who later became board chairman for over ten years. The second week of my ministry I flew to New York (my first plane ride) with my brother Alan to attend the Billy Graham School of Evangelism. I questioned if I should go, having just commenced my ministry. While in New York I learned the importance of training others; being taught by James Kennedy of Evangelism Explosion, from Coral Ridge Church in Florida.

In studying Scriptures, I realized the Great Commission wasn't "Come and Hear" but "Go and Tell". I trained both men and women on personal evangelism, as well as teams to go door to door considering four areas: Motivation; Methods; Materials; and Message. We used "FORM" as an acrostic meaning Family, Occupation, Religion, and Message regarding church and God. After our first blitz, in which we went out in pairs, four new families began attending the next Sunday. Personally, I visited almost five days a week from two to five hours daily from September to December 1969. We used World Home Bible League material and tried to enlist people in a Bible study.

Let me share three stories growing out of this outreach ministry. The first involved a lady who came to her door after I knocked. I said, "I'm from Forward Baptist Church in Toronto." She looked at me strangely and after I realized what I'd said and corrected myself, she said, "Thanks for calling but I won't be coming because I'm the wife of the Presbyterian pastor in Bramalea." I'm sure she wondered what kind of a guy this is who doesn't even know where he is."

In the second, I met Mrs. Kristel Koehler, (a Lutheran), and talked to her about the Lord and His work. Unknown to me, her mother had recently died, and she was wondering about life after death. She began attending and then the whole family came. All five became Christians and her two sons served as missionaries in Turkey and Mexico.

The third is about thirty ladies enrolled in the Bible study. Some were struggling to complete them. One lady suggested that if she could meet with other ladies it might help her. Out of this need, Ladies Coffee Hour began in February of 1970. They met in a room in our church at 10:00 a.m. with coffee, cookies and a nursery for children. This ministry grew to where we saw hundreds attend and eventually most came to church. Then with follow-up, scores of families were reached. I also held seminars regarding Ladies Coffee Hour Ministry. Many similar ministries began in our Fellowship Baptist Churches across Canada. By the end of 1969, we welcomed forty-one new members; many the result of door-to-door visitation. I recorded the names of every family in a little three ring binder, including the names and ages of all the children as well as a brief history of their beliefs and any church affiliation. Each time I visited them I'd record the pertinent information, thus having a permanent record. I still use the information from four binders with hundreds of families for prayer and had it when called on thirty years later to take one of their funerals. The old adage is "People don't care how much we know, until they know how much we care." This method helped me to memorize and remember over one thousand people's names. (No computer database back then.)

By the spring of 1971 our church attendance had reached two hundred, and we ran out of room. On Easter Sunday we moved the morning service to Bramalea Secondary School a block away. By visitation, advertising and providing space, attendance kept growing. I used to say Spirit, Staff, and Space were basis for growth. Eileen Morley was brought on staff as Christian Educator and Music Director and did a great job, remaining with us for twenty years. We expected to move back to our little church building during the summer months, but we couldn't because we soon reached an attendance of three hundred. We held evening services at our own building for a while, but soon all programs except our nurseries were moved to the school.

At this point after prayer and planning, the membership voted overwhelmingly to sell our property and purchase a larger one, as we were advised by the city planners that we'd have inadequate parking if we built on our existing property. However, a seven percent minority of the congregation worked with the neighbours and got sixty-six signatures opposing the sale of our property as a medical centre and we lost an offer for one hundred and fifty thousand dollars as a result since our property needed rezoning. Then we got an offer for one hundred and seventy-five thousand dollars from the same developer to use our church building as a Montessori School and to build ten houses on the other property. The membership approved acceptance of this offer. Then I received a call from the developer saying he had bad news. He was lowering his offer by ten thousand dollars because in 1967, four feet at the far end of the property had been sold for a carport and he could build only nine houses. I had to go back to the membership with a lower offer and the minority were now more like twenty-seven percent in their increased vocal opposition. I prayed for God's wisdom and help then I took out the survey of our property and noticed one of the ten building lots looked wider than the other ones. I phoned the planning department and told them our dilemma. They said all the lots should be the same size, but they would investigate anyway.

Upon checking the survey, they found the surveyor had made a mistake and the lot was five feet wider than it should have been. They assured me that the property line could be moved through a "Committee of Adjustment", without going to the neighbours. We ended up with an extra foot. We received one hundred and seventy-five thousand dollars in spite of the initial opposition. Because the providence of God had allowed a surveyor to make a 'mistake' and a young pastor untrained in surveying to find it, God's will would be accomplished.

In looking for a larger building site, we found that the ones allocated for churches were only one to two acres. Since our church was growing quickly, we felt we needed at least five acres for building and parking. I decided to go directly to the City's Chief Engineer and tell him our needs; Mr. Smith got out of his chair and said, "It is interesting you are here today, for last night council discussed the use of the five acres at the corner of Dixie Road and Highway #7. Would you be interested?" It didn't take long for me to say "YES." to which he responded with, "Give me a five-hundred-dollar deposit and three weeks." It was doubtful the deal would go through but, with the encouragement of Bill Wright, a deacon, we called a special prayer meeting for Sunday afternoon and one hundred and fifty people met for an hour and walked around the property, praying for God's will to be accomplished. The next day I received a call from the city saying the red tape was gone and the five-acre property was ours for one hundred and twenty-five thousand dollars at the best corner of the city, right across from Bramalea City Centre with two hundred stores. I was so excited I got a four by eight sheet of plywood and made a sign saying, "FUTURE SITE OF BRAMALEA BAPTIST CHURCH". I took it up in the trunk of my 1969 Ford and put it in place at the corner of Dixie Road and Highway #7. When I drove on the property it was frozen hard but when the sun came out the ground had thawed and when I went to move my car, it had sunk to the axles. I thought of Dave Mullen, a new convert who owned a garage and tow truck, and he came to my rescue.

Later that year (1973) we put two portables on the property for office space and nurseries before our new facilities were completed. I remember frozen water pipes and putting down cardboard so people could walk over the mud. Better days were ahead.

Now we could build a twenty thousand square foot facility with an auditorium seating seven hundred and Christian Education rooms for five hundred.

We began a bus ministry which grew to seven buses which were used for Sunday School, Wednesday family nights, camping ministry in Algonquin Park, and choir tours across Ontario.

The seven percent who had opposed the move had grown to more than twenty percent, but they hadn't been able to stop God's will and work from being accomplished. They were telling people that Bramalea Baptist Church was being misled by the pastor and board, and the church would go bankrupt. I remember in the middle of this difficult time getting alone in our recreation room and crying out to God for wisdom and direction. Should I leave or should I stay? The Lord gave me peace to persevere. The people opposing us numbering seventy and led by two former members tried to start a new church but within six months it collapsed because of division. Most of the people returned to us with humble hearts. In September of 1974 our new facilities were dedicated costing seven hundred thousand dollars, excluding the property.

A special treat for Bev and myself after this challenging time, was the gift of a two-week trip to Hawaii which we thoroughly enjoyed and fondly remember.

New people and families came every Sunday, and one hundred and twenty-one new members were received in 1975. Our giving's went up by seventy percent while our attendance grew to six hundred and our staff to six. As a staff and board, we did long range planning and set goals. We introduced a "Family Night" which included a full course meal cooked on site by our own people, to which two hundred and fifty came for the meal. We moved eighteen ministries to Wednesday night and attendance grew to over five hundred. The ministries included Christian Service Brigade, Pioneer Girls; five choir practices, prayer meeting, teacher training, four or five electives, plus family devotions for everyone. It ran from 5:00 p.m. to 8:30 p.m. and there was something for every age including nursery and youth. This enabled families to be together other nights of the week and to accommodate everyone we used several school gyms. I was asked to do seminars promoting Family Night and many of our Baptist Churches commenced holding Family Nights in their churches.

In 1976 we were able to buy another acre from the Department of Highways for six thousand dollars. They wanted fifty thousand dollars, but Bruce Freeman, who had just joined our church and was an engineer working on the expansion with Bramalea, listed eight reasons why the one acre was worth only six thousand dollars. After the presentation to city council we were awarded it. We now owned six acres across from Bramalea City Centre and it was now valued in the millions. We also started Precious Jewels Day Care Centre, with a staff of ten and it became a great ministry for children and families alike.

The Sutera Twins, from the United States, held forty meetings over three weeks. God did a tremendous work of renewal with hundreds of lives being changed. As our speakers noted, "When revival becomes the experience of the church, evangelism will become the expressions of the church." As a church we also formulated a Mission Statement which was "To Exalt Christ, Edify Christians and Evangelize the Community." When our vertical relationship was right with the Lord and our horizontal relationship was right with fellow believers, then evangelism was a natural bi-product. We used the Share Course for discipleship and at one time we had twenty-seven new Christians in it, with me trying to do it all myself. I had to delegate this ministry and approximately one thousand people were discipled over twenty years, using the Share material from our Fellowship. As a diversion from ministry demands, I restored a 1933 Ford Coupe between 1972 and 1976, at my brother Ernie's body shop near Sarnia.

In 1976, I was elected president of our Fellowship. This was a challenging experience with numerous speaking engagements and many meetings. Our Sunday School continued to grow under Eileen Morley's leadership. That year we won our seventh Cross Canada Sunday School Contest in the "A" Division growing from an average of five hundred and twenty-five people in 1977 to seven hundred and thirty-six in 1978 — a forty percent increase. Also, in 1978 we entered the city's large parade called Nitty-Gritty-Brama-Ching-Wing-Ding." and we won four major awards: Grand Marshall Award; Theme Award "Happiness Is"; Most Colourful Float Award; and Church Group Award. It included a large truck float, Sunday School bus, and my 1933 Ford Coupe. We had music and gave out hundreds of leaflets promoting our church.

After ten years of ministry at Bramalea, we were surprised by a lovely evening entitled, "This is Your Life". It was a wonderful celebration of years of blessings with family and friends. Bev and I were given Seiko Quartz watches and our three girls received sets of silverware.

In August of 1979 I broke my leg and it took some months to recover — a time to reflect and re-evaluate my priorities. My first sermon following this was entitled, "A Lesson from a Leg — He stopped me, He settled me, and He strengthened me." To rebuild my leg, I began running and this led to my training and entering five marathons between 1993 and 1997.

By 1980 we had to go to two services and our staff had grown to ten, requiring weekly staff meetings. Our Sunday School had reached one thousand and one hundred and twenty-seven new members were received into membership. I travelled to Columbia, with Dr. MacBain, to speak concerning renewal and interpersonal relationships. This trip helped me to understand more clearly the problems and pressures missionaries face. As a result, our church became more supportive of missions in prayer and finances. We began in 1969 with a mission's budget of six hundred dollars and by 1989 it grew to two hundred and fifty thousand dollars annually. We saw many young men and women train for the pastorate and missions including Steve Jones, who is now president of our Fellowship of the Evangelical Baptist Churches in Canada.

Between 1981 and 1984 we experienced great blessings and growth. Our number of deacons had grown from five to forty with fifteen elected on the administrative board — each with a portfolio and job description. Another twenty-five were caring deacons who were selected and responsible for ministering to fifteen to twenty families each through visits and phone calls.

A building committee was formed for a new facility. God had allowed us to pay off the facility we opened in 1974 in six years and by 1982 we had four hundred and fifty thousand dollars in a building fund. Our total giving's had reached seven hundred and ninety-five thousand dollars, which was a thirty percent increase over 1981. Our business administrator, his wife, and Bev and I travelled to large churches in the USA (including Swindoll's and MacArthur's) to look at buildings and ministries; helping to expand our horizons and plan for a new facility.

A sixty thousand square foot building was designed by Ray Mercer of Chapelstone Contractors and John Siderius, a member, volunteered to be project manager for two years. Initially, not one of the sixteen financial institutions would back us, so we prayed for direction. "With encouragement of Phil Phillips, our deacon of Prayer", God led us to start building by faith. The week after we made that decision, with unanimous vote of support from our membership, a cheque for one hundred and sixteen thousand dollars was received from the former Pine Grove Baptist Church in Woodbridge. This was the first time we had ever received money from any outside source and it was a seal that God would provide. In 1983-84 our staff, board and church members pledged several thousand dollars toward the four million building project. Bev and I made a three year pledge too and promised that all extra money we received would go toward our pledge. She had an old car and we said we wouldn't replace it until our goal was met. Bev's mom needed a new car and I test drove one at Mac Lang Chrysler in Sundridge and I filled out a ballot for a draw for a new car. Out of

Bramalea Baptist New Building 1984-1985

Interior of new Bramalea Baptist Church March 1985

30,000 ballots, mine was drawn and we won a Plymouth Sundance that I gave to Bev to replace the old car. It was another example of God's provision when we are willing to trust Him. We grew in faith and the building grew in size as people gave vehicles, jewelry, bonds and cash resulting in hundreds of thousands of dollars being given toward our building project. Later a trust company approached us, and we received a mortgage for a portion of the costs.

In the spring of 1985, we opened a beautiful new building with an auditorium seating two thousand and twenty-five thousand square feet of new Christian Education space, with a large office complex. This enlarged facility enabled us to continue to grow but was also available for large gatherings like our Fellowship Convention in 1986, when Dr. John MacArthur spoke. There were two thousand three hundred people in the auditorium and four hundred watching by closed circuit television.

Christmas and Easter Cantata were highlights, which attracted thousands of people from the Bramalea community, Toronto and beyond. These cantatas involved up to three hundred people in acting, orchestra, and choirs. Allan Soll, a Jewish man, and one of several people who came to Christ through this special ministry, was baptized, became a member and later worked for the mission organization — Missionary Aviation Fellowship.

From 1986 to 1988 our ministries expanded in all areas, with my brother Alan coming on staff as associate pastor. I also travelled to the Maritimes and B.C. to speak at their regional Fellowship Conventions. The Lord was providing me with increasing opportunities to speak regarding church growth and evangelism. Dr. Roy Lawson, General Secretary for our Fellowship, challenged me to consider coming on staff with the Fellowship as a Church Growth Consultant in the fall of 1988. After six months of wrestling with God to know His will, I left home in Cheltenham after praying with Bev regarding the decision to resign from Bramalea Church. I was to meet Roy Lawson with my decision and I was hoping for a sign from God to confirm my desire. As I drove the ten miles to my office, I listened to WDCX from Buffalo, and heard Chuck Swindoll, who had spoken at our church a few years earlier. He said, "I'm beginning a new series on "Knowing God's Will". I was all ears and he went on to say, "I don't know who all I'm speaking to but there is at least one person who needs to leave where he is and like Abraham obey God, and if he doesn't, he will not accomplish what God desires. I said, "Thank you Lord" and I met with Roy and said I finally had peace resigning in March of 1989 after being pastor of Bramalea Baptist Church for twenty years. I accepted the challenge to work with our Baptist churches across Canada, but it was hard to leave such great people and church after seeing hundreds come to Christ, eight hundred and forty baptized and one thousand six hundred and sixty new members received. Giving's increased one hundred-fold from fourteen thousand dollars in 1969 to 1.4 million in 1989, but I had to realize that it was God's work and not mine.

Our wonderful congregation graciously accepted my resignation in 1989 and honoured us with a week-long celebration entitled "20 years of Ministries and Memories" with all our extended family invited. As well as a generous gift of money, we were given a beautiful book of remembrances, with several hundred personal notes of thanks and appreciation. During those twenty years my slogan was "Minimize the Machinery and Maximize the Ministry". I had said to Bev after leaving Bramalea that I felt like we had accomplished forty years of ministry in twenty years. It was a wonderful conclusion of the privilege of being labourers together with God at Bramalea.

PASTORAL DUTIES AND DANGERS

I vividly recall the day when Roy and Vera Horne who were members of our church, Bramalea Baptist Church (BBC) phoned me with a serious problem. They had two teenage children and had offered to try and help a young fellow who had drug problems. They let him live with them in an effort to minister to him. When they phoned me, they said he had threatened them and there were

Staff at Bramalea Baptist Church 1986

afraid to return home for fear of their lives. I phoned the police for advice and help. They asked me if I knew him and I said I had met him once or twice and his last name was Brown. They felt I would be the best person to try and reason with him and get him to surrender to the police. Their plan was that I would go to the Horne's home in Brampton and knock on the front door. They would back me up with their guns drawn in case something went wrong. Several policemen hid behind trees and I approached the front door after praying. I had never done anything like this before and with a mixture of fear and faith I knocked and waited for a response. In a few minutes I heard the young fellow coming and he opened the front door. He asked what I wanted and I asked if I could come in and talk with him. He let me in, and I followed him to the family room and didn't see any sign of a gun and I told him I wanted to help him. The police entered the home and reasoned with him as well. This episode ended well with the young man getting counselling and I believe later came to Christ. Just another day in the life of a young pastor.

TRIP TO PRAYER BREAKFAST IN OTTAWA – 1985

John McDermott, our M.P. in Brampton who had attended sod turning for our new building in 1985 invited me to be his guest in Ottawa for three days. Mrs.

Final Sunday for me at Bramalea Baptist Church - Mar. 1989

Martin Luther King Jr. was to be the speaker and since she and I were Baptists he wanted me to hear her. It was a special time of meeting her and having my picture taken with her. I met Prime Minister Brian Mulroney as well as several senators including, Robert Stanfield. I sat in the house during a session with Mrs. John Reimer. Her husband was the Conservative M.P. from Kitchener/Waterloo. He has taken a stand against homosexuality and same sex marriage. As a result, she said he had death threats and they had to have security twenty-four hours a day. I saw the scripture verse from Psalm 22:8, "And He shall have dominion from sea to sea and from the river to the end of the earth." This is where the word "Dominion" of Canada was taken from. It was chiseled in stone above the arch going into the parliament building and I also saw another verse but forgot what it was. I returned home with a new appreciation for our heritage and the work that our politicians do on behalf of our country. It reminds me of Apostle Paul's admonitions in Timothy 2:1-2, "I urge then, first prayers, intercession, and thanksgiving be made for everyone, for kings and all those in authority, that we may live peaceful and quiet lives in all godliness and holiness." Too often we have been guilty of complaining rather than praying for our politicians and leaders.

8

Trip to Ten Fastest Growing Churches in the United States

In the spring of 1972, I was taken on a two-week trip to the U.S. by a wealthy businessman who shall go unnamed. He was a recent member of our church and had read the book by Elmer Towns on the "Ten Fastest Growing Churches in the U.S.". Since we were growing quickly and planning for expansion and relocation of our facilities, he felt it would be helpful to learn from successful pastors and churches. He arranged an hour meeting with all ten pastors, and we took off in his Mercedes; our first stop was Temple Baptist in Detroit which Dr. Beauchamp Vick was pastor. My Dad had attended this church back in the 1920's when he was working in Detroit; Bev and I had attended with another young couple one Sunday before we were married. I remember a funny incident when Bev was in College and Career class in which one of the girls asked the teacher, "Where is Detroit on a map of Palestine?" The teacher went over to the map and said, "It must be on here somewhere." Bev and her friends who were in teachers' college weren't impressed by her (the American's) geographic skills.

Our interview there was great and we toured their auditorium (which held three thousand) plus large gyms and Christian education facilities. We went to several churches in Ohio and Pennsylvania before we ended at Lynchburg, Virginia at the Thomas Road Baptist pastored by Dr. Jerry Fallwell. We spent three memorable days with Jerry and his staff. Jerry gave me a lovely New Testament signed with Philippians 1:6 which is my life verse. "Being confident of this very thing that He who has begun a good work in you will continue it until the day of Jesus Christ." I have used this New Testament to this day for hospital visitation, soul winning and other occasions. They had just started what would become Liberty University and were negotiating for several thousand acres up on the mountains. We went out on Sunday School bus visitations as they had one hundred buses. I also saw busloads of young people heading out on singing tours to other churches. The preaching and music on Sunday were very inspiring and helped stretch my vision and faith for what God could do back at Bramalea.

A couple of memories I learned from my trip with my friend were as follows: (a) when we would stop at night at a motel, he always complained about them and we'd go to several before he was satisfied; (b) during our trip he was always talking about his investments and concerned about losing his money. (I said to Bev on return, I hope I never become wealthy like that and I never did. However, I think she would have preferred that I picked out better motels rather than the cheapest one.); (c) shortly after we returned, he moved away and never followed through on his promises to help us with finances for our new facilities. It made me look less to man and more to the Lord for His guidance and provision. (Philippians 4:19 "My God shall supply all your needs according to His richest in Christ Jesus.")

Also, a while after returning, we expanded our bus ministry from one to seven buses. We also had three children and youth choirs and they did tours across Ontario. Lessons I learned from this trip motivated me to expand my vision and ministry outreach.

9
Three Trips
to Israel

MARCH 16–30, 1978

Richard Mitchell, a seminary professor and I were asked to chaperon fifteen graduate students from Central Baptist Seminary on a trip to Israel. We were to spend two weeks at the Institute of Holy Land Studies in Jerusalem, led by Dr. Young, then President of the Institute of Holy Land Studies. We would study for two days and then engage in archeological digging, recovering, and labelling of ancient pottery. We went to all the major biblical sites including the Qumran Caves, where the Dead Sea Scrolls were found by a Bedouin shepherd boy in 1947. We also went to Masada, where the Jews held off the Romans for almost two years, and where Eliezer made an incredible speech, refusing to be taken alive. Some of the young seminary students were Bob Flemming and John Mahaffey who later became fruitful pastors and leaders in our Fellowship Baptist Churches. I was able to counsel some of the students regarding personal problems and issues and regarding God's work. I remember the fun we had with the word "WADI" which refers to a ravine or gully. We competed to see how many "W's" we could use then called ourselves "the weary, worn out wadi walkers who walked warily, wisely and well while walking and wondering in the wild wilderness". We had a lot of fun and returned with many memories and a deeper appreciation for God's Word and His World.

Camel & Stu's first trip to Israel

1984 — PASTORS OF LARGE TORONTO AREA CHURCHES

Ten pastors from the largest evangelical churches were invited to go to Israel to promote tourism in Israel. We left Toronto by bus for Mirabel Airport in Montreal and as we checked our passports before flying to Tel Aviv, I found that my passport had expired. Ironically, I had just signed papers at church so some church members could get new passports. I spoke to the authorities in Tel Aviv by phone and I said I was a minister. The authority said, "I don't care if you're the Prime Minister, we can't let you fly." I was left behind at the airport while the other pastors flew to Tel Aviv. I contacted Rev. Bill Phillips, a pastor friend to rescue me and help me to get a new passport. The next morning, I received one and had to book a new flight to New York. I flew to Kennedy Airport, and had to flag a taxi to go to LaGuardia Airport to get my flight to Amsterdam and then to Israel. The plane was filled with conservative Jews, who were doing their Phylacteries in the aisle of the plane. I believe I was the only Gentile. I had a great conversation with a Jewish teen, but his mother stopped our conversation as soon as I spoke of Jesus Christ. Then the pilot took pity on me and invited me to sit with them in the cockpit as we flew over Greenland and Iceland. This would never be allowed now, since 9-11 in New York. I commented to the two pilots regarding how fast the fuel gauges were spinning and they said it takes three quarters of the fuel for the first quarter of the trip because of the initial inertia with a full load of people and fuel, and the last quarter of the trip they coast to their destination. I arrived in Israel a day late and caught up with the other pastors. We had Moshe Dayan's right-hand man as our tour guide. He took us to the Golan Heights and to the concrete bunkers the enemy had built above the Sea of Galilee. He told us the Israeli farmers took the mufflers off their trucks and tractors and shut off their lights then headed toward the Golan Heights with engines roaring and lights flashing; the enemy thought they had hundreds of tanks, so they fled and ended up losing the battle. Our guide said the Israelis had only one cannon and tried to lob a shell into the Sea of Galilee in order to get the sight of the cannon set properly. To the Israelis' amazement they had made a direct hit on the enemy and ended up winning the war. We told our Jewish guide that this was God's intervening and helping His people to win.

Our trip was very special and helped us to be knowledgeable about the major sites in Israel that tourists would visit. I was asked to preach the Sunday morning message at our worship service by the Sea of Galilee before returning to Toronto. It was with thankful hearts we returned home from the Holy Land determined to share the message of God's love and light to a dark and dying world.

MARCH 2–12, 2009

This trip was made up of thirty-five people from our church in Florida as well as family and friends. My brother Alan and his wife Grace had about a dozen people. We had three flights, two from Florida and one from Toronto. Our first flight, with only eight on board, left first for Israel a day earlier. An amazing thing happened when our son-in-law Bruce Fitter was selling a high-priced Corvette in Calgary. In the course of the sale, involving a Jewish man, Bruce mentioned his in-laws were going to Israel with others. The prospective buyer knew Israel's Prime Minister and the man in charge of the Temple Mount. He arranged for the eight of us to go places seldom seen by tourists. We saw the foundation of the first temple and one of the stones weighing five hundred and forty tons. The guide explained how they were hewn and moved. There was glass covered areas showing earlier civilizations remains below us and long tunnels and we wore headphones as they showed a film explaining artifacts in display cabinets. When our regular guide heard where we'd been, he couldn't believe it, as he'd never been allowed down there. As we went to the Wailing Wall and toured the old City of Jerusalem, we had a guard with a gun in front and behind us because of our V.I.P. designation. We had a great view of the old city, the Temple Mount, and the Dome of the Rock. We were shown the army barracks where all Israelis

2009 March - Bev at Dead Sea

have to serve in the army; men for two years and women for one year. We saw ancient olive trees on the Mount of Olives, with cemeteries of Jews and Muslims, hoping to be raised when the Messiah returns. We had a moving experience as we visited the Garden Tomb, known as Gordon's Calvary. We saw the traditional site of the Upper Room on Mount Zion where the last supper took place. Downstairs was the tomb of King David. We toured government buildings, the Knesset and the Holocaust Museum, which was very moving, honouring six million Jews killed by the Nazis. We visited Bethlehem, the birthplace of Jesus, now under the control of Palestinians. The town was dirty, but going into the Church of the Nativity, the oldest church in the world was special. We saw ruins of Jericho, the oldest town in the world with drip irrigation date palm, fruit trees, vegetables and grains in abundance. At the Dead Sea, with thirty-five percent salt (versus three to five percent salt in oceans), the world's lowest point, we floated in water Many coated themselves with mud which apparently aids in making peoples' skin look younger.

We visited Masada; the Jewish fortress built by slaves. It is located high above the desert and the Dead Sea near where Sodom and Gomorrah used to be. We saw Bedouins, who are nomads and mainly Arabs. Masada is where the Dead Sea scrolls where discovered by a boy in 1947. On Sunday morning, at the King Solomon Hotel where we stayed in Jerusalem, I spoke on "Mountain Top Experiences". We studied the Mount of Temptation (Mt. Quarantania), the Mount of Teaching (Mt. of Beatitudes), the Mount of Transfiguration (Mt. Hermon), the Mount of Torture (Mt. Calvary), and the Mount of Triumph (Mt. of Olives). We travelled north to Beth Shan in Galilee; a recent archeological discovery of an ancient city that is still being excavated. A funny incident took place when our guide asked for three strong fellows and three of us followed him to a stone structure where he had us sit down on what turned out to be an ancient latrine; just then all our friends appeared and the laugh was on us. We visited Nazareth where Jesus grew up, and ancient synagogues, then on to the Sea of Galilee where we took a boat ride across to Capernaum where I spoke on the "Danger of a Shallow Faith" based on Christ and the disciples and the storm. We went to the Mount of Beatitudes where Jesus taught the Sermon on the Mount (Matthew 5-7). We continued our trip to the Jordan River and there I baptized two of our friends, Pam and Gene Hensley from Kentucky. Our trip to Megiddo, with twenty levels of civilization that have been excavated and view of the Valley of Jezreel where the Battle of Armageddon is to take place, was very sobering. We travelled to Mount Carmel, where Elijah fought the four hundred prophets of Baal and won, then on to the City of Herod the Great, on the Mediterranean, with its Roman theatre and Hippodrome and Crusader city. We concluded our trip with a visit to Joppa (Jonah's town), to Jaffa, and then to Tel Aviv on the Mediterranean. Following a great meal and time of sharing, we prepared for bed and an early flight home the next morning.

Baptizing Gene & Pam Hensley in Jordon River - 2009

10

Fellowship Conventions at which I Spoke Across Canada

I spoke at my first convention which was held in Lloydminster, Saskatchewan. The subject of my messages were centered on the theme, "The Nature and Work of the Local Church". This was the FEBCAST region and the acronym means "Fellowship of Evangelical Baptist Church in Alberta, Saskatchewan, and Territories". I enjoyed the opportunity of sharing biblical truths concerning the church and employed lots of illustrations from Bramalea. The pastors and people were very appreciative. I also spoke at the morning church service and, by the way, this church has an oil well that supports them financially. Later, I was scheduled to speak at the Crossfield Baptist Church in southern Alberta; Pastor Priebe of Lloydminster said he had an airplane and would fly me down rather than me renting a car. It was a fun flight and he showed me Three Hills Alberta in the distance, but he had trouble finding the airport which was overgrown with weeds. It was a scary landing, but we made it and afterwards I was told I should have had extra life insurance. I made it home safely with good memories.

I was invited to speak at the FEBCAR Convention in Sackville, New Brunswick. The services were held at the oldest Baptist Church in Canada — Sackville Baptist — and I spoke on Sunday at their 225th Anniversary. It was a beautiful big white church and the theme of the convention was "Evangelism, Discipleship, and Church Growth". These were my favourite topics and the experiences en-

May 1987 - 225th Anniversary Saskville Church N.B.

joyable. Their pastor had been a drug addict and had lived at Rochdale College in Toronto in the sixties, before he came to Christ and became a faithful pastor. The people in the Maritimes were very hospitable and responsive. Paul Kerr was at the convention representing Foreign Missions and he informed me that the Fellowship needed someone like me to give leadership. I believe he spoke to Roy Lawson and this eventually led me to my leaving Bramalea for the Fellowship Baptist Churches in Canada.

I was asked to be the keynote speaker at the Basic Baptist Beliefs Conference in Vancouver, British Columbia. I had to speak six times, along with twelve other speakers, who each spoke once. The topics I was given were "Evangelism, Discipleship, The Mission of the Church, The Pastoral Role in Evangelism and Discipleship, Critical Issues and the Dilemmas in Evangelism and Discipleship, Strategies and Methods in Evangelism and Discipleship, Making Disciples, Baptism and Church Membership, The Uniqueness of Christ, and the Mandate for Evangelism and Discipleship. There was a lot of preparation and all the messages were compiled in a book, which was a good read.

I spoke at the convention in Montreal, Quebec. It was a simulcast with translation and people wore headphones. Occasionally, the translator stopped and laughed at what was called "Silvesterisms," after which I would rephrase my statement and he would continue translating. I always enjoyed my trips and speaking in Quebec. They would listen intently and take all the literature I had — whether in French or in English. Their churches were growing and dynamic and most of their pastors were trained at Sembec; their French training school. My four messages were "Revival and the Church", "Ten Ingredients for Church Growth", "Servanthood the Secret of Leadership", and "Evangelize or Fossilize".

I was asked to speak at a conference in the Lac St. Jean area of Quebec. It was called "Camp Patmos." Bev and I flew to Montreal and went with Gabriel and Nita Cotnoir. The people were hungry for the Word of God, and understood me, despite using Rene Frey as my translator. Pastors, their wives, and their children attended the long sessions (the children were good.). When I concluded seven or eight messages, they wanted more so I had to prepare more messages. It was a great experience for both of us in spite of a hard bed and tiny cabin.

From June 21–23, 1993 I was the keynote speaker at the B.C. Convention for the churches of British Columbia, held at Maple Ridge Baptist Church. They even had a man with an antique Cadillac drive me from my motel to each service. I spoke six times on the theme of "Christ's Church" as it pertained to His leadership and our relationship as members of His body. I spoke on the following themes:

1. The Origin and Purpose of the Church.
2. Revival and the Church.
3. Leadership in the Church.
4. The Edification of the church.
5. Principles of Church Growth.
6. The Church and Evangelism.

As I concluded my ministry, I sensed a moving of God in people's lives and our Fellowship Churches in British Columbia.

11

Mission Trips to Foreign Countries

My first visit was when I was president of the Fellowship in 1976–1977. I was asked to speak to our missionaries to encourage and challenge them, and to observe their ministries. I visited several of the churches they had planted but was especially impressed with the work being done in the prison in Bogota. It housed about five thousand five hundred criminals — many of whom were guilty of murder. Don and Gloria Rendle our missionaries from B.C., were in charge of the teaching, preaching, and music. The Rendles and guards took me through the five sets of heavy locked iron doors into areas where they held Bible studies and church services; a number of the inmates had become Christians and it was amazing to hear them sing. Some approached me to help them get out, for when they heard I was a "president", they figured I had power. I spoke to them about receiving Jesus Christ who alone can free them from addictions, sin and hell. My worst memory was the circumstances in which they lived, they had hardly any clothes and ate food/slop out of a big barrel using tin cans. I saw them fighting each other like animals and bleeding from their injuries, and I was appalled. Many were incarcerated because of drug-related crimes. No wonder the Bible says, "The way of the transgressor is hard."

COLOMBIA, SOUTH AMERICA — SECOND VISIT
The second trip was with Dr. MacBain in order to minister to a number of our

Fellowship Missionaries, primarily in Medellin, where we had about twenty missionaries. They asked me to speak on "Revival" since we had just had forty revival meetings over two weeks with the Sutera twins from U.S.A. at Bramalea Baptist Church and God did a great work of renewal. Dr. MacBain and I also met one-on-one with many missionaries, as well as with couples. We discussed their personal problems and blessings, trying to be of help and encouragement to them. We had to deal with some interpersonal problems too. One missionary said of another, "Their jeep sleeps a lot." (An inference to laziness.)

These missionaries lived in a Finca, a farm that was protected with barbed wire and guards because of the drug trafficking and drug lords with their criminal activities in the country. The city shopping was uncommonly difficult because of the pickpockets; we had to hold our money in our shoes and hide jewelry as they were ever present. I remember drinking a Coke on a hot day in Medellin with Dr. MacBain and in the bottom of the bottle when I was finished the Coke there was an inch of hard mud. Fortunately, I didn't get sick. I especially remember the difficulty the pilot had in landing the plane as this airport is one of the hardest in the world because of thick cloud cover. The pilot had to dive drop the plane down through the clouds and then the short runway appeared between mountains with tall buildings at the end of the runway. Very scary stuff.

COLOMBIA, SOUTH AMERICA — THIRD VISIT

The third trip, I took Bev with me as it was great to have her company. We flew to Miami from Toronto and then on to Cartagena where we noticed the change to Spanish dialogue. Landing in Cartagena we saw soldiers with arms and we deplaned right on the tarmac since the weather was warm. We brought a lot of goods for the missionaries and were afraid we were going to lose some or all of it. The guards opened a couple of our boxes but didn't take anything. Don and Rachel Whiteside (missionaries in Columbia) picked us up in their Jeep truck. We had to stop at a checkpoint and a guard came out and wanted to see what was in the back. Don got out and walked around with the guard to the rear of the vehicle, pretending he was going to open it. Instead he ran to the drivers' door, jumped in, and took off like "Jehu" swerving back and forth in case the guard started shooting at us. I asked Don why he had done that. His answer was that the soldiers would have stolen most of the things we were bringing into the country. This was the beginning of a lot of dangerous trips and exciting experiences. Don Whiteside had been a wild guy growing up — guilty of attempted murder and put in the Kingston Penitentiary for a seven-year sentence. He eventually received a Queen's Pardon and became a believer, before enrolling in Central Baptist Seminary in Toronto. His pardon (I believe the first Canadian to secure it) allowed him to leave Canada to serve as a missionary until he was seventy years of age.

After speaking to missionaries via four messages from the book of Jonah, we headed to Ecuador to visit Dave and Sharon Gast, who were missionaries at HCJB Quito Radio Station. HCJB means "Heralding Christ Jesus' Blessings" and because the station is located on the equator, the signal travels further and faster. We had a great time meeting the nationals and going to their markets.

Later, following our return to Canada, I invited the Gast's to return to Canada. Both of them have remarkable music skills and Dave became our Minister of Music. This led to many years of wonderful music and great concerts at Christmas and Easter — productions which saw thousands in attendance and many coming to the Lord.

Mexico, February 1998

Manfred and Beth Koehler were a young couple who grew up and were married in our church in Bramalea. Following Bible School, they went on as linguists with New Tribes Mission to Mexico. We decided we'd go and try to encourage them and their colleagues in the work of God. We were at our home in Florida and left from there on a ten-day mission's trip. Bev kept a daily diary so I will use an abbreviated version to recount our experiences.

Wednesday, February 17, 1998 — Stu and I went to bed early but couldn't sleep because the adrenaline was flowing.

Thursday, February 18 — The alarm went off before 2am and we were on our way by 2:30 am to Orlando. We parked and a shuttle bus got us to the airport at 4:30am. We left on our American Airlines plane at 6:30am and flew to Dallas, TX, had a quick breakfast and boarded another flight to El Paso, TX. What a surprise when Manfred greeted us at the airport. After shopping for some mission needs, we crossed the border to Mexico. After fuelling his pick-up truck, Manfred and Bev got in the cab and I rode in the back against the tailgate and we were off on a 200-mile trip. We stopped for lunch and took turns riding in the back, all except Bev, who stayed behind since it was windy, dirty and bumpy. I remember taking a picture of an old house where we had lunch and said I'd tell others it was Koehler's house. At night we stayed in a Mission house and picked up Beth; she had a good meal, but we couldn't use the water to brush our teeth.

Friday, February 19 — Following a good night's sleep, a two-hour time change and breakfast we were on our long trip west. The first part was flat and then we got into the mountains and stopped at the waterfall area and for look at a 1000-foot waterfall. Following lunch and stopping for gas and Stu rode for an hour and half in the back but he didn't feel well. Manfred was getting tired of driving on the curvy and bumpy roads with potholes and no white lines. Stu took over the last 50 km. He was a little sick from riding in the back and had his hands full driving with the sun in his eyes. However, we made it safely and had our first glimpse of life in Maycoba. We turned onto a dirt road on the mountains and parked in front of a grey adobe dwelling. It was more primitive than we expected but going inside found a comfortable home Manfred and Beth had made. In spite of cement floors and rough plastered walls, they had a bathroom, cupboards and a little furniture. They depended on solar power, enough to run a computer, but not toasters or hair dryers etc. There was no shower or bath but there was an area where you could splash water on yourself and wash your hair. The house had bars on the windows to keep robbers out, but no glass, only plastic, it was impossible to see out. They had a fridge and stove. We had supper at Candy and Barry Wingo's home (fellow missionaries), practiced amongst fellow missions while travelling.

Saturday, February 20 — Stu and I went for a 3-mile walk at 7:30am and saw mountains, large cactus and 2 churches, a bar and a few houses. Only 45 degrees but hot sun and vegetation, dry because of little rain. Manfred took us later in

Mexico 1998 - Manfred & Beth Koehler & Bev

the day to a rural home with 2 rooms that were dark and smoky. Manfred used pictures to teach Bible Stories and had some discussion with adults as shy children listened.

Sunday, February 21 — Church was at 10:45am at the Wingo's house and a New Tribes video of work in Indonesia was shown. We sang a hymn and Stu spoke on "Defeating Discouragement." We enjoyed a roast beef dinner and then at 5:00pm went out to a ranch for an outdoor service with 12 adults plus children. Stu spoke and Manfred interpreted. We were going to meet a drug dealer for a Bible Study, but he had to take his wife to the city regarding cancer problems.

Monday, February 22 — At 6:15am Beth, Candy, a native lady, Stu and I went for a 3-mile walk and picked up pop tins along the way for the lady to sell for extra money. I helped Beth do the washing on her ringer washer and we hung everything outside. Stu trimmed an apple tree and climbed a small mountain and returned covered in cactus spikes in his pants and shirt. He put a cross at the top but was hardly visible from below. We ate and did a Bible Study and two visits.

Tuesday, February 23 — Stu and I climbed a small mountain and I did schoolwork with a kindergarten girl. Beth and I canned chicken and beef, since stores are far away. Everyone was invited to the Koehler's for a Mexican barbeque. Then we went to the Grainger's bigger house and Stu spoke.

Wednesday, February 24 — Early in the morning we went for a run, but the altitude was too much for me. Stu ran with the two missionaries who were runners and he kept up ahead. We packed, washed hair and the fellows discussed new ways to reach the native people. It was hard to believe our time in Maycoba was coming to an end. After church/lunch we went to meet the bus, which was late. It was a large, but dusty bus and it almost midnight when we arrived in Chichoba. A missionary took us to a missionary house.

Thursday, February 25 — We were driven next day to El Paso, New Mexico and back into Mexico because it was more hassle-free the missionary said. We saw the Rio Grande River, had dinner at Burger King and were dropped off at a mission house, which was beautiful for missionaries to use as they came and left. There were no meals served.

Friday, February 26 — Finally it was time to depart. The hosts drove us to El Paso airport and we had our last look at the dry mountain scenery as we took off. We changed planes in Atlanta, GA and arrived in Orlando, found our car and returned to Port St. Lucie, thankful for the experience and safety in travels.

12

Cottage on Doe Lake
1978–1998

In the spring of 1978, we considered selling the old farmhouse in Burk's Falls. With Lois and Dale now teenagers and Faye not far behind, we realized it would be good to have a place on water. We started to look around the Burk's Falls area with John Darling our realtor. He wanted us to see a place on Doe Lake that was more expensive than we could afford but we looked at it anyway. It was large (eighteen hundred square feet), built in the fifties by a doctor. Facing south on two hundred and eight feet of lake frontage and more than an acre of property, it was fully furnished and very spacious with a large stone fireplace, a twenty by thirty-foot living room, three bedrooms and a great kitchen/dining room area. In addition, it had a bunkie with two bedrooms, a porch facing the lake, and included a canoe, sailboat, motorboat, riding lawnmower, and lots of tools. We decided to look around at other places one week when the girls were at camp and we looked all the way from Lake Simcoe/Georgina Island to Doe Lake, comparing them to the first one we had seen. As there was nothing comparable, we decided to pursue the one on Doe Lake and put a lowball offer in at fifty thousand dollars and to our amazement the vendors accepted. We saw it once more on a gorgeous quiet sunny morning and confirmed our decision before we sold the old farmhouse for twenty-two thousand five hundred dollars as a great down payment. When we went to the cottage with pen and paper in hand to list the things we needed to bring, my paper was blank; they had left

Cottage on Doe Lake - 1995

towels, sheets, dishes, silverware, electric blankets —everything we needed. So, we moved into a fully furnished place in great condition. It had a beach area, a dock, lovely white birch trees, a lawn area for badminton and croquet. We had many happy family times there and we rented our cottage numerous times to family and friends, in order to defray costs.

The girls and their friends, along with us, loved playing badminton in the yard. It was also exciting to have our own boat — a fifteen-foot runabout with a thirty-five horsepower Evinrude engine. The girls learned to water ski and Faye loved driving the boat. Some fishing was done but our neighbour, Barry Fry, was the most successful in that realm. It was fun to take a picnic lunch with us on the boat ride into Big Doe. We loved being on the water—the view, the peacefulness, the sunsets, sitting in the screened-in porch in the rain, and cozying up in the living room with the fireplace on.

In 1980 the seventeenth Silvester-Lanning Reunion was held at our cottage on August 2 with thirty in attendance. It was a hot sunny day with lots of food, fellowship, and fun. Dad and Phyllis were there but Uncle Gene and Aunt Marjorie were out in Chaplin, Saskatchewan, visiting. We had lots of games, swimming and boating and a great time to renew friendships and to be reminded of God's faithfulness over the years. Our first family reunion had been held in 1964 at Benton Street Baptist Church where brother Alan was assisting. We just celebrated our fifty-eighth reunion in August 2018, as I write these memories down; it turned out I was the oldest member present at age 83 and I sure missed Bev who had just died on June 23rd, 2018.

In 1984 we had a church staff retreat at our cottage with nine in attendance. A great time of physical and spiritual renewal was enjoyed by all in a beautiful setting. We also had a retreat for our Board members at our cottage in 1990 which involved studying, praying, planning, and then some boating, canoeing, and attempts at windsurfing. Mike Brandon was bound and determined to stay on the windsurfer and he almost lost his bathing suit, providing comic relief for all of us.

In the mid 1980's we upgraded our kitchen there. Bruce made forty-two new pine doors and drawers in his shop (Hy-grade Carpentry) and we stained them and installed them for a great new look. We also installed a Jacuzzi in our bathroom.

In 1992 I had Bruce design a three-car garage and shop forty by twenty-four feet. Then I did the primary work of cutting down trees and I found men to blast the Muskoka granite so the concrete foundation and block walls could be completed. In 1993, with Bruce spearheading the project we gathered all our family together for a wonderful workday. We all took orders from Bruce, the project manager, and by the end of that Saturday the walls were up, the roof was on, and the windows and doors were in place. We shingled the roof, painted the walls, and put on the siding a little later. An amazing accomplishment by a great family working together.

13

Trip to Oberammergau
and Europe
May 19–June 11, 1980

A Christian friend, Allan Waddell, who owned "Christian Tours & Travel" in Toronto, asked if Bev and I would host the first of forty-four tour trips in 1980, to eight countries in Europe. 1980 marked the 400th anniversary of the black plague and "Oberammergau" was celebrating their survival of the plague (which they had done every four years), but this was the 400th anniversary and it was the highlight of our trip. The eight countries we visited were Holland, Germany, Austria, Italy, Switzerland, France, Belgium and Britain. There were thirty-nine on our tour plus our tour guide Sven and Adrian our bus driver. The majority of the people on our tour were from Ontario and one from the US and another from Scotland, three from Alberta and one from BC. Anticipation became a reality as we met at Toronto International Airport to begin our "Oberammergau 1980 Tour." We boarded our plane for an overnight flight to Amsterdam. During our flight Bev became acquainted with our tour members as well as enjoyed dinner and breakfast on route. Upon arriving in Amsterdam, we were met by our Globus Gateway Guide and transferred to our hotel. After getting settled for our two-night stay we were free to sightsee or window shop. Amsterdam is a walker's paradise — for the whole of its core is like a museum. Few cities have preserved and renovated their old homes, public buildings, canals and squares as well as

Holland & Windmills - Bev & Stu - 1980

Amsterdam. If you are interested in art the Rijkey Museum with its Rembrandt collection is amazing, or in a newer museum we saw the Van Gogh collection. We visited Anne Frank's home and the home of Corrie ten Boom, recounting her book and film "The Hiding Place."

The following day we boarded a glass-topped boat for a cruise through the Amsterdam tree-fringed canals and out into its famous harbour. We went under numerous bridges and past houseboats as we passed the gabled facades of the 17th century "Golden Age" merchant homes as well as famous churches and public buildings. In the afternoon we visited one of the city's famed diamond factories to watch precious gems being fashioned. Unfortunately, there were no free samples. We also visited a shop where they made wooden shoes and Bev purchased a pair as souvenirs only. After we ate breakfast we went south east by bus to Cologne, Germany. On route we passed Utrecht and the World War II battlefield near Arnhem where the Canadians forces fought to liberate the Dutch. By early afternoon we arrived at the Cologne and visited the famous Cathedral overlooking the Rhine River and had time to shop and sightsee. After our early breakfast we drove through the wooded Rhine Valley. Then we boarded our steamer for a two-hour trip on the fabled Rhine River which is the communications link of Northern Europe. We passed quaint villages, terraced vineyards and ruined castles on every hilltop. Shortly after re-joining our bus we arrived in Heidelberg with its medieval houses and university, the setting for the operetta "The Student Prince," often seen in Toronto on TV. We arrived at Rothenberg, the ultimate medieval town with quaint houses and narrow streets; dating from the 10th century around 942. The local citizenry supported the Reformation in 1544. Bombings during World War II did a lot of damage but now its restored homes and magnificent cathedrals are a wonder to behold.

As we traveled south through Germany, Bavaria I spotted a sign that said, "Dachau Concentration Camp." I asked Adrian our bus driver if we had any spare time and he said we did. I inquired how many would like to tour the Dachau Concentration Camp and all but one did. It was a sobering experience to see the site of the torture and death of thousands of Jews. The walls and barbwire were imposing. The government of Bavaria had designated it a "Memorial Site" and had left and restored the main building. They told how the Nazis seized power on January 30, 1933 and how the camp was started in March 1933 and then prisoners started to arrive to help build and be tortured. We were taken into the gas chamber which the prisoners were told were showers, following a hard day's work. But they were gassed — many bodies were cremated in big steel and brick ovens as well as being buried in mass graves. The original camp was to hold 5,000 prisoners but was expanded between 1933 and 1945 with more than 206,000 prisoners being held, tortured and killed. About 6,000 Russian prisoners were executed on the SS Rifle Range and the last 1,230 prisoners who died in the concentration camp of Dachau were buried in the cemetery in the town of Dachau. We left with a feeling of revulsion at seeing man's inhumanity to his fellow man.

Dachau Crematorium - 1980

Austria's King Ludwig's Castle - 1980

Later that day we arrived in Munich, which is Bavaria's capital. Our hotel was near the site of the 1972 Olympic facilities. The next morning, we travelled through beautiful pine forests to the foothills of the Bavarian Alps. We toured King Ludwig's famous Castle and saw his king size bed covered with gold and jewels. That afternoon we arrived in Oberammergau in Germany for a two-night stay and before supper we toured this beautiful mountain village.

The following day we attended the Passion Play which has made the town famous for centuries and which was the raison d'etra for our tour. No other non-professional dramatic performance catches the world's attention as does the Passion Play — Oberammergau. Approximately 750,000 visitors from around the world attended this play in 1980. The performance lasted all day with a two-hour intermission when we returned to our hotel for lunch. The play is done in German but we had the text in English. It has been performed in Oberammergau since 1634. The prelude began with mankind being driven from the Garden of Eden and Act I portrayed Christ's triumphant entry into Jerusalem on Palm Sunday. How Jesus drove the dealers from the temple and then the priests try to win the people over. In Act II Christ prophesied His suffering to His disciples, the Last Supper and Jesus parting from His Mother. Act III The journey to Jerusalem and conversation between Jesus and Judas and Jesus washing the disciple's feet. Act IV Judas the betrayer promises to deliver Jesus to the Jews. Act V Jesus on the Mount of Olives and His final words, prayer and His agony and then taken prisoner. Act VI Jesus before Annas and struck in the face and led through the streets. Jesus condemned to death by council and taken to Pilate and scourged and taken out to be crucified. At this moment I had to restrain myself from going to help rescue Jesus from his assailant because the scene was so graphic and painful to watch. Act VII Jesus seven sayings from the cross and his death and placement in the tomb. Act VIII depicted the guards at the tomb, the resurrection and the women coming to the empty tomb and the play ended with singing He is Risen. Rejoice you heavenly hosts. He is risen. Rejoice you mortals all. Amazing ending.

The next morning, we headed south to Innsbruck, in Austria, where the Olympics were held. Then through the beautiful pastoral scenery to Salzburg where "The Sound of Music" took place. We also paid a visit to Mozart's birthplace and museum. We headed north in beautiful lake country and the Danube River and valley and saw ruined castles and monasteries and arrived in Vienna, where we had a day to explore. We saw the world's largest Ferris wheel, the beautiful Opera House and Imperial Residence where Napoleon stayed. We travelled south towards Italy and next morning revelled in the glories of Venice, including

Stu at Coliseum in Rome - 1980

an evening gondola ride. We visited Florence with its churches, squares and narrow streets. We saw paintings by Michelangelo, a celebrated citizen of Florence. We went south to Italy's most famous city, Rome. The city's central square is dominated by the Vittorio Emanuele monument. The Pantheon was originally a pagan building built in the last decades B.C. and repaired by Hadrian in 123 A.D. and then converted to a Christian church. The Coliseum is the wonder of ancient Rome where gladiators fought and where the early Christians were martyred before an audience of 50,000 people. We visited Saint Peter's, the greatest basilica in the world, founded by Emperor Constantine. The present building was dedicated in 1626 after 179 years of construction. Michelangelo worked for 4 years on his back to paint the creation on the ceiling of the Sistine Chapel.

The Vatican City covers 110 acres and is an independent state headed by the Pope. When I was in St. Peter's and saw the heathen and pagan idols, I was tempted to start preaching God's word like Paul did in Athens. We went underground to the catacombs where believers worshipped and were buried. Bev and I climbed the 300 sloping steps to the top of the Leaning Tower of Pisa. It leans about 13 feet but since has been straightened lest it fall.

We toured Milan with its Majestic Cathedral, which dominates the city and then on to Lucerne and then north towards the mountains and crossed border into Switzerland. We traveled through snowy passes and saw the Keppel Bridge — a medieval wonder completed in 1333. We went up the 7,000 ft Pilates Mountain by cable cars and enjoyed spectacular views. When we left the Alps, we headed to Paris where we saw mountain villagers and picturesque Swiss farms.

We came to the Jura Mountains that serve as Switzerland's border with France. The French countryside with fields of grain and vineyards are very reminiscent of Canada and we passed the fabulous Florentine Belau Palace and forest and arrived at our hotel in Paris. The next morning, we visited the River Seine with its bridges, the Eiffel Tower, the Arc de Triumph and the Cathedral of Notre Dame. Then we visited some of Paris' 90 museums and art galleries, include the Louvre, to see the Mona Lisa. Then we headed north across the countryside of France to see the Canadian War Memorial at Vimy Ridge before crossing into Belgium. It was Sunday and I spoke and we felt an indebtedness to the many Canadians who fought and died, including Norman Silvester and my grandfather Silvester. We spent a night in Bruges Belgium and slept in a "Royal Suite" and certainly felt like royalty. We enjoyed the riverside restaurants and sixteenth century Cathedral and Grand Palace. We said good-bye to the continent of Europe and boarded a ferry to cross the English Channel. When we came in sight of land we were greeted by the White Cliffs of Dover. Our first stop was the famous Canterbury Cathedral; the mother church for all Anglicans.

Upon arriving in London after crossing the English Channel we had a half-day of sight-seeing the famous sights in London. These included the beautiful Canterbury Cathedral, the Thames, House of Parliament, the "Trooping of the Color" parade, Piccadilly Circus, Trafalgar Square. In addition, we visited Westminster Abbey with its royal tombs and then we stopped at Buckingham Palace for the changing of the guard ceremony. This was the final day of our twenty-four-day, eight country "dream trip" and the final photo shows Bev boarding our British Airways plane for home. A long and demanding trip as host and hostess but very educational and rewarding in being able to visit these great countries and see God's creation as well as made new friends.

TRIP TO CALIFORNIA TO SEE CHURCH
FACILITIES — NOVEMBER 1982

Our church sent Bev and me as well as our church business administrator, John Siderius and wife Francina, to see large churches to help us with our building project in 1984-1985. The first church visited was First Baptist in Van Nuys, one of the largest Baptist churches. There were two incidents at this church which stood out in our memories: the first being when we sat in on a Wednesday night prayer meeting which turned into a battle between church leaders over missions and whom they would support. It became a yelling contest and was anything but Christian in what was said and done. It made any business or board meeting I had chaired seem pretty tame. The second incident was the Saturday night Christmas presentation. This church had the first ever "Living Christmas Tree" presentation and it had made the cover of "Life" magazine. The first half began with a "Kick Line" of gals singing and dancing and I had to keep the Siderius' from walking out. The second half was great with guest soloists in the living Christmas tree. We were given cards to evaluate what we thought, and I wrote "I think you live too close to Hollywood".

From there we went to Calvary Chapel founded by Chuck Smith who now has Calvary Chapels across the United States.

The third church was the Crystal Cathedral pastored by Dr. Robert Schuller. We knew we wouldn't be patterning our new facility after the Crystal Cathedral, although it was an amazing building and good service.

The fourth church was Chuck Swindoll of the Fullerton Evangelical Free Church. Chuck had spoken at our church, so I was looking forward to seeing and hearing him again. It was a wonderful experience with several packed-out services in a row.

The last church was Grace Community Church where John MacArthur was the pastor. John MacArthur was away but this was a very informative trip regarding church facilities and ministries, and we ended it by going to the San Diego Zoo on our final day before flying home.

My First Airplane Trip to New York and Billy Graham — 1969
In late June of 1969, a couple of weeks after commencing our ministry in Bramalea my brother Alan and I were invited to go to the Billy Graham School of Evangelism in New York. I questioned whether I should go as I had just led three to the Lord, one being Mac Campbell, who later would become a strong Christian and Board Chairman. I knew how to do personal evangelism, but this school of evangelism would teach me how to train others. This trip would be my first plane ride and quite a thrill on American Airlines, landing in New York City. Alan and I stayed at a YMCA and someone stole my shaver. Every day we went to seminars on evangelism and at night we went to hear Billy Graham at Madison Square Gardens. One of the seminars I especially remember was taught by Dr. James Kennedy of Coral Ridge Church in Fort Lauderdale. It was material which would later become "Evangelism Explosion". As soon as I returned, I started to train people how to share their faith. One thing they told us was to watch how Billy Graham preached. He would start his sermon like an artist by painting a very black and bleak picture of the world and lost humanity. Then he would share God's plan of redemption which alone can rescue lost mankind from sin and Satan. It was thrilling to see thousands responding to the gospel of Jesus Christ. I returned inspired and determined to be bold in preaching and

5 Brothers travel to Saskatchewan - 2006

reaching the city of Bramalea for Christ. It had expanded my vision and knowledge for reaching the lost.

TRIPS OUT TO THE OLD FARM IN SASKATCHEWAN

The first time I returned after leaving in 1941 with our family was in 1959 while on a trip to BC with Bob McGregor. We were travelling in a 1957 M.G. convertible and tried to find our old house south of Ernfold and Chaplin. As we travelled south on a gravel road we stopped and asked a farmer if he knew where Oscar Silvester lived. He said "Yes, just go to the next road and turn east". He said, "There is a Lloyd Silvester who lives across the road from Oscar" and I told him he was my dad and we had left eighteen years earlier. We found the old empty house my grandfather Silvester had built in 1917.

The second time was in 1976 when our whole family flew out to B.C. and a man in our church who owned many RV's offered the use of one free that was in Vancouver if we would drive it home. After a wonderful week on Vancouver Island we headed back home across the prairies. We eventually arrived at Droxford and the old house. What a thrill to see where we had once lived and see some of our old toys and household effects. The grasshoppers were terrible as we drove near the old Bingham Baptist Church. However, the day we arrived they were holding their Sunday School picnic with games, races and lots of food. I entered the young man's one-hundred-yard race and won at age forty-one. Some said I must have made a false start to win against younger guys. I was just trying to follow in the tradition of my dad who was a good sprinter.

The third time was in June of 2006 with my four brothers. We took a trip to see the old house and haunts. It rained most of the time, but it was a memorable trip. We stayed at the Caronport Motel and travelled to Bingham Baptist Church which is now closed; the church was unlocked, and we saw where our family used to worship and the graveyard where many of our grandparents and family are buried. The old house was still standing with veranda missing. We crawled up the rickety stairs and found old toys. The walls were covered with newspaper to try to keep the cold winter blasts out. We all picked up a few mementos of special memories where our mother and father had sacrificed so much and worked so hard to eke out a living. We saw Uncle Gene and Aunt Marjorie's old farm and met the Knutsons across the road, they invited us in for a lovely chicken dinner. Later we met another old couple who had been taught by my mother at Rosneath School. They said she had the most beautiful smile. She did. We asked if they knew what had happened to the school; the man said he owned it and it was over the hill - what a thrill to go inside and see the old blackboard where mom taught for one year.

Grandpa Silvester's House built in 1917

TRIP TO CUBA — 1986

Wally Featherston, who was working for Operation Children, invited Nelson Beckner and myself from our church along with other pastors to take Bibles and commentaries to churches in Cuba. It was just before Christmas so we wrapped the Bibles, pencils, and toiletries as Christmas gifts so they would be less conspicuous to the Cuban authorities. When we arrived in Cuba we had to go through customs and wait in a long line to be searched. My suitcase was packed with Bibles and I tried to lift it as though it was light. Suddenly a lady in front of me fainted and I tried to help her as I believe it was God's way of distracting from me and my bulging suitcase. The customs officer just waved me through and none of us had our luggage searched. The four of us were in Cuba as tourists but our purpose was to smuggle Bibles. We stayed in a beach house and for a couple of days acted as we were tourists; however, the police were watching us and parked cars near our building. Nelson Beckner went to take a picture of me when I had fallen asleep and his flash wouldn't work. He checked it out and found his batteries had been removed. We believed the police did it just to let us know we were being watched.

Wally and I headed across the island in a rented Russian Lada car to visit pastors and churches and deliver Bibles. The car burned oil and we had to

Cuba 1986 - 3 Generations

drive with the windows open. For a week we visited poor pastors/churches and families, most of whom lived in old dark houses. We had to sneak in and out of their homes under the cover of darkness. I spoke many times and the people were very appreciative, although I went out to eat and was propositioned by a prostitute which could have led to problems — the least of which included being robbed. That night I travelled alone by taxi to a Baptist church which was packed with people who had walked miles to hear a Canadian pastor. I was glad I had persevered and didn't get sidetracked. The next day we took commentaries and Bibles to a seminary which had very few books and they were very appreciative of these books. In Havana we saw long lines of people seeking to buy food amidst buildings which were unpainted after years of communist oppression. The cars were all thirty years old or more and one caught my attention, a 1935 Ford and 1950 Ford welded together. The final day we rented motorbikes and enjoyed touring the island; even then the police stopped us, and Wally told them to leave us alone. We left Cuba with suitcases almost empty but with hearts full of praise for protection and the privilege of preaching and sharing God's word with very brave believers. (I bought a blow fish as a souvenir which was like trying to carry a porcupine.)

TRIP TO ZAMBIA TO VISIT THE FREWS IN — JUNE 1989

When I started at CBS in September 1963, I met a young married couple from then Rhodesia, now Zambia, by the name of Keith and Cynthia Frew. In their second year of studying to become teachers in a Bible School in Chezela for the purpose of training pastors. Fast forward about twenty-five years and now they had two sons and two daughters and were heading up a Bible School in Zambia, AEF Missions. When on furlough they returned to Canada and to Bramalea Baptist Church where they were members, and they stayed in one of the homes we provided for missionaries. They had invited me to go and speak at the graduation exercise at their school in Zambia and possibly take a team to build some dormitories for their students; however, unexpectedly we received a terrible phone call from Africa. The Frew's youngest son, Ian, (aged fifteen) had been killed by a crocodile (April 23, 1988). Keith and Ian and two other missionaries took a yearly trip down the Kabompo River and their boat capsized. At one point all four got out of the river, however, Ian was on the far side. He kept diving in retrieving sleeping bags, food, etc. He started to swim to the other side where the men were and halfway across, they saw a swish in the river and a crocodile took off after Ian. They yelled for him to go back and he almost made it with his fingerprints on the side of the bank when the crocodile grabbed him. In a few seconds it resurfaced with Ian in its jaws calling for help. Then it disappeared and Ian was never seen again.

Keith and Gordie Englbretzon decided to cross the river to save over thirty hours of walking home to tell Cynthia and family what had happened. Thankfully they made in safely through the crocodile-infested river. The phone call was to ask me to inform Ian's two sisters, Renee and Nadine, who were attending university in Toronto, that he had perished. It was a difficult time for everyone but with God's grace we tried to bring comfort from the God of all comfort. We held a memorial service at Bramalea Baptist Church with hundreds attending and several folks came to Christ. I spoke from Philippians 1:21. "For me to live and to die is gain." Ian had been memorizing Philippians, and Cindy and Keith were impressed with his spiritual maturity. We decided to get a team together of nine from our church and beyond and. after I had spoken at the graduation ceremonies of Chizela Bible School we built a memorial chapel in Ian's memory along with a library and other facilities. This was all made by hand — thirty thousand hot hand-made bricks which had to be handled with leather gloves. We were there for six weeks building, and I was speaking in the evenings.

However, about the third week an incident took place, as I returned with Cynthia in her Jeep. We were going by a little shed which was used to house some prisoners who had previously broken into the Frew's home. I asked if I could take a picture of places out the Jeep window and she agreed. We travelled back and started taking pictures around the mission, for the next day Bev and I were scheduled to go to Zimbabwe where I was to speak and meet with missionary friends, the Tuckers, from Toronto. Suddenly I saw a police truck loaded with soldiers with AK47 rifles coming toward me. They yelled, "there he is," and I was tempted to run but instead I threw my camera into some bushes because I figured they had seen me take the picture. One big black man ran at me and punched me on the side of my head. It made me see stars and also the writing on his t-shirt said, "Jesus is Lord". (Probably a shirt he had gotten from the missionaries.) I was arrested and taken inside the Frew's home where they started to search our bedroom and demanded my passport. The police found some short-wave radio equipment which had been left by a short-term missionary from Chatham ten years earlier, in a cupboard. They said if I didn't give them my passport I'd be taken to jail. I had seen the dirty jail and let them have my passport. The police said I had to appear before them in the morning on charges of being a spy. In the morning Keith and I headed to the police station and had to face five policemen including the lead one who had been trained at Scotland Yard. They had all the radio equipment spread out and for the next two hours they interrogated me. They said tell us how you use this equipment to spy on Zambia. They had my passport and could see that I had recently been to Cuba and Israel and, since Zambia was under communist control, I knew I was in trouble. It was their word against mine. They argued that I wouldn't take a picture of our parliament buildings in Canada. I said I'd recently been there and taken pictures and they said I was lying. I kept asking the Lord for wisdom in what to say and not to say. Finally, they released me to go outside and be guarded while they questioned Keith Frew. The first thing they said to Keith was, "Silvester has confessed to being a spy". Again, it was their word against his. I learned later that if they had proven I was a spy, their head policeman would be promoted to the Capital in Lusaka. They said I would have to go to the city of Solwezi to appear before the authorities on espionage charges. I was placed under house arrest which meant I couldn't go off the compound to speak as I had been doing. Bev and I had to let our friends in Zimbabwe know we would have to cancel our speaking engagements due to unforeseen legal issues. Within a few days the police arrived, and Bev and I were put on the back seat of a jeep with a policeman with an AK47 guarding me and Keith in the front seat beside the driver. When we arrived, I was taken inside a theatre-type building and Bev and Keith stayed outside. They shone bright lights in my face so I could hardly see and fired questions at me. I had a certain amount of fear and a lot of frustration. After many questions and accusations of spying, the guard took me to the jeep and I headed back to Chizela knowing little except that I was totally at their mercy. After two weeks of questions and no sign of my passport being returned, I knew I was facing a dilemma. Our youngest daughter, Faye, was to be married in a little over a week. I thought of doing a tape recording of the ceremony and sending it home with Bev who decided to hitch a ride with missionaries going to Lusaka and see if she could get some help for me; if not she should head home to Canada and Bramalea.

When Bev arrived in Lusaka the phones were all down and she had trouble getting help. The missionary director had recently died so help was hard to find. Bev went to the Consulate, with little success. I decided to contact Del Tucker in Zimbabwe by short wave radio and she, in turn, phoned Bruce Fitter, our son-in-law to see if he could get help. Bruce had built a home for a former Ambassador, Leslie Samuel, who had been an Ambassador to Cuba and Spain. He intervened by going to Prime Minister Joe Clarke to intercede on my behalf in order to get my passport returned. (In October 1995 I was asked to take Mr. Samuel's funeral as he had attended our church on occasion.) Within an hour I got word that I was to return to Solwezi and the official apologized for delaying my return to Canada. They returned my passport as well as my camera which they had confiscated so they could see the pictures I had taken. The film was still in the camera and hadn't been developed. I was now free to head home, but I had to get to Lusaka. I hitched a ride on the back of a transport truck loaded with young people and bags of seed and, within twelve hours was with Bev, tired, but thankful to God, family and friends for coming to my aid. We were able to buy plane tickets to New York and then to Toronto.

Before we left, I realized I hadn't got any souvenirs so I purchased a lovely boat made out of ivory tusk, not realizing it might be a problem going through customs in the Toronto airport. As soon as we started to fly, I got a high fever from lack of sleep and the pressure I had been under for several weeks. The stewardess gave me medication and let me lie down and sleep. They told me when we arrived in New York, I wouldn't be able to deplane until I saw a doctor. When we landed in New York, within minutes two large New York policemen entered the plane asking where I was. The people around me were wondering who in the world is this fellow? If they only had known what I had endured with the Zambian police. They took me out in a wheelchair and, later I got the doctor's release and was now free to fly home. Keith asked if I would return to Zambia again and I said, "Don't hold your breath." I felt like kissing the ground when I arrived in Canada. In Toronto we had no problem with the said boat which I had put in the bottom of my bag. We made it in time for our daughter's wedding which was a joyous occasion for them and us.

We also got the film developed and there was the picture that had caused so many problems. I was able to show it on the screen at Bramalea Baptist Church when I was asked to report regarding our trip to Zambia.

As I Thessalonians 5:18 says, "Give thanks in all circumstances; for this is God's will for you in Christ Jesus.

It was this trip and building we did in memory of Ian Frew that gave birth in a few months to "Baptist Builders." I said if people are willing to pay two thousand five hundred dollars each to go to Africa why can't we help build a church in Canada for needy young congregations?

Introduction

The following records a summary of the facts and feelings from Bev's Daily Diary for the six weeks of the Zambia trip from her perspective.

Zambia Trip — June 27 to August 4, 1989

We left at 5:00 a.m. with our two big boxes, two big suitcases, and two carry-on bags. Bruce dropped us at the Toronto Airport and we flew to LaGuardia in New York. Moving our luggage was a challenge as straps didn't want to stay done up. At the JFK airport we moved our luggage and registered on Zambian Airlines. We boarded the plane at noon after a two hour wait but were delayed due to mechanical problems and remained on the plane for six hours. They served us food and showed a movie. Finally, we took off and landed in Moravia. Then by 4:00 a.m. we flew to Lusaka, the capital of Zambia. We finally landed after 22 hours on the plane from New York. We missed our flight to Ndola and were booked on one for 7:40 p.m. but didn't take off until 9:05 p.m. Cynthia Frew and Steve, a short-term missionary from England met us and our luggage got through customs at Ndola and we went to a mission's house.

Thursday, June 29 — After six hours sleep and a brief breakfast, we packed our truck and at 8:30 a.m. headed toward Chizela after pit stops and several hundred kilometers on dusty roads. Stu and I dozed quite a bit and we arrived at 6:00 p.m. in time for a dinner of deer meat, carrots, and potatoes at the home of Gordon and Roseanne Englebretsen's. They were missionaries from the USA who managed the farm.

Friday, June 30 — Breakfast at 7:00 a.m. was maize meal porridge with peanut sugar and milk sprinkled on it. Keith and Stu went to a meeting to choose a new spiritual leader. Stu spoke to the students with Keith interpreting on the history of Bramalea Baptist Church and 10 principles for church growth. Stu, Keith and I went for a walk after lunch to see the bricks (25,000) being fired in a kiln. We saw individual farm plots for the students and Stu checked on wood for the kiln and saw the mission airstrips and moved things from one house to the next.

We were all invited to a graduation dinner in the church building. Students sang in Kikonde and then we ate nshima, a corn meal paste. We dipped bread into it along with pieces of chicken which we ate with our fingers. The graduates sat on one side and the teachers on the other and many had babies on their backs, nursing when necessary. Stu spoke on "Servanthood, the Secret of Leadership". Augustus, a teacher interpreted and they worked well together. The lights went out as he finished and lanterns were lit. There was a lot of lively singing which Stu taped, and they wanted to listen to it. We sat up until after midnight talking to Keith and Cindy.

<u>Saturday, July 1</u> — Stu went jogging for half an hour and then we jogged together. I tripped on a root and scraped my hands and knees but continued running. My hands were sore all day but I helped Cindy clean cockroaches out of a closet. Stu took the truck and moved electrical equipment and fed the fire in the brick kiln hauling two loads of firewood from the bush. We went to the Chizela for an English-speaking service. We sang and prayed inside and then half hour moved benches outside and Stu spoke on Psalms 1. There were missionaries and the rest Zambians. In the afternoon the graduation service was held outside with between two and three hundred in attendance, eight men and eight women dressed in blue and white corsages. Stu spoke on Roadblocks from Exodus 14 and all listened attentively and awards were presented. In the evening 20 of us had supper around a campfire and visitors joined us from Mukinge for a sing song and a time of prayer. Stu and I took time out to write letters to our children and Grandpa Silvester.

<u>Monday, July 3</u> —Keith and Stu each took a truck load of students and children as well as possessions and chickens to Ndola on a long dusty bumpy ride. We stayed and cleaned houses for the work team. Our meal that night consisted of rabbits and chickens along with desserts. Dad did his nose trick for the kids and a bush fire provided entertainment as well.

<u>Tuesday, July 4</u> — Both Stu and I worked on various projects to help the missionaries. Stu and I went into town and finally got through to Del Tucker by phone in Zimbabwe, a friend who was a missionary. Stu made another trip to town with a fellow who was going home. It was another bumpy, dirt road.

<u>Wednesday, July 5</u> —The team arrives in Africa today. The houses are clean and a lot of baking done, cookies, bread, and rolls. Stu always seems to come back filthy from working at mud furniture and bricks. Stu and two missionaries went running but his stomach gave him trouble. I did some ironing before the hydro went off and then early to bed.

<u>Thursday, July 6</u> —This morning I went to town with two missionaries who taught Religious Education to grade 7 and 8 students. There were 35 in each class

and the children were very polite. The students had to be good in Health, Math, Geography, History, and Writing before being able to get in to High School. Cindy and I did more housework and preparing food for workers. Stu did a lot of work making furniture, working with brick layers, moving equipment, cleaned two water tanks, and then fighting bush/grass fires. Everyone joined in to stomp out the fires to save the homes. A lot of water was carried and lungs filled with smoke and faces and legs smudged. Stu's cheeks are really red and he's got blisters on his feet from his workouts.

Friday, July 7 — We had our first meal with our team of 10 workers. Keith talked to the group and then toured the mission station. The team unpacked and set up their rooms and worked on the water system.

Saturday, July 8 — Gals prepared a millet pancake and fellows met at 9:00 a.m. to move bricks and drawing up plans on cleared base. They cut through concrete to make way for plumbing pipes. Many wrote letters as mail goes with Keith tomorrow to Lusaka. I baked a birthday cake for Stu.

Sunday, July 9 — It is Stu's 54th birthday today. He is being kept very busy. He spoke at the English service and then in the vernacular service in Chizela. Then given some "Jungle Juice" and a cold dinner and Stu worked on a message for the staff and team for the evening service.

Monday, July 10-12 —Today was the first real working day for the team and

Zambian Team - 1989

Ross, Stu & Scott - Zambia - 1989

they were anxious to get going. They laid several layers of bricks and cement and sand mixed for lintels. Ladies moved bricks and cleaned new brick walls and everyone was weary and dusty by evening and showered. On Wednesday morning Stu loaded two truckloads of sand, hard slugging, and in the afternoon, he laid bricks and he had trouble staying awake. I helped load bricks in the evening. Each load was 1,000 hot bricks and soon the walls were up. Stu spoke at prayer meeting at the Frew's in the evening. By the evening of July 14, the walls were all up to the top of the windows, inside and outside. Stu handled nearly every brick in each load as well as laying some. I helped as much as I could as well as helping prepare meals.

<u>Saturday, July 15</u> — Stu and the team went to the building site and cleaned up broken bricks and cement. The ladies made sandwiches. At noon we left for a picnic lunch at the Kabompo River, the river Ian Frew had been killed by a crocodile. We saw elephant tracks and hippopotamus tracks. We walked through the shallow river to an island and had a picnic. We saw many beautiful birds and a big ant hill. Because it was Keith and Cindy's 28th anniversary, we had a delicious meal and Stu made a poem about them since he knew them from seminary days in the 1960's. Sunday Stu spoke at the English church in town and then spoke at the vernacular service to a much larger number. After a good evening meal Stu spoke on "Encouragement".

<u>July 17-21</u> — We saw steady progress with trusses going up that they made. Saturday was a relaxing day and our last day before going to Zimbabwe for a week of ministry. We packed our suitcases and took pictures. Stu went with Cindy by Jeep and Al Fitzell to make calls to kids in Canada and found out Dale was two months pregnant. As they drove back and went by the school bus prison, Stu asked Cindy if he could take a picture and she said yes and then returned home. Stu came over to the team house to give news from home and that the prisoners had reacted a little when he took the picture. Cynthia thought they wanted money so drove away. The team decided to make a video around the mission property. Suddenly, Ross our team leader called us all together and said we needed to pray since Stu was in trouble. He said the police had arrived accusing him of spying because he had taken a picture of the bus stop prison. Then they searched our bedroom for more evidence. We all stopped on the driveway and prayed. It was an hour later that I discovered all that had happened. Stu had tossed his camera in the grass as the police armed force guys arrived with AK47 Riffles and ran toward him. As they picked up his camera an officer punched him on the side of his face. It was so unexpected that Stu was dazed and said his head rang for a long time. Then all five officers and Keith and Stu went into our bedroom and they tore it apart, bookcase, drawers, suitcases emptied, and beds. In the top of a closet they found a radio transmitter which Keith had never seen before. The police took it and Stu's camera, two exposed films, and two racks with copper in them. They took Keith's and Stu's passports and told them to be at the police station on Monday at 8:00 a.m. On Sunday morning we phoned Del Tucker and had her cancel our plans. We really felt down in the dumps for what had happened. We went to church and we were given a note of encouragement from Matthew 10:19-20, "as a promise". But when they arrest you, do not worry about what to say or how to say it. At that time, you will be given what to say, "For it will not be you speaking but the Spirit of your Father speaking through you." We discussed what tomorrow would bring and Stu wasn't getting much restful sleep.

<u>Tuesday, July 25</u> — Several nationals came before breakfast to pray for us and say good-bye. We phoned Del Tucker and I told her to cancel everything because of our problems but also because borders were closed due to currency changes in Zambia and we couldn't go from Livingstone to Victoria Falls anyways. We were at the police station at 8:00 a.m. but they weren't ready to go until 9:30 a.m. One officer came in our jeep and sat beside Stu and me with gun in tow and another in front with Keith. Their truck had a flat tire which had to be fixed. We waited for instructions and they left me at Clarkes (missionaries). I stayed at Clarkes' reading, praying, and biting my nails, and eating peanuts. The police, Keith, and Stu picked me up at 4:30 p.m. Stu went through more interrogation

and tried to reason with them, but I was told to go back to Chizela. The police would return on Thursday to check the closet regarding the transmitter. We arrived back at 8:30 p.m. hungry and tired. I just cried when I went to bed and I think Stu was upset. He did not sleep well but I did.

<u>Wednesday, July 26</u> — We phoned Waendts at headquarters in Lusaka to see if he could help us by going to the Canadian High Commission and to the M.P. for this area, <u>Mambuso.</u> He said he would. Stu worked painting trusses all day without a hat in the hot sun. The building is almost complete and all trusses up so an excellent day. Two police officers rode in on bikes and saw our cameras and watched us. As they rode away, Scott and Ross ran for their cameras and Ross snapped a picture of the head detective and suddenly he was reprimanded and taken to prison. Even though Scott didn't take a picture, he was seen as an accomplice. They had no supper and had their shoes and jackets removed as well as watches and rings. They were locked in a nine foot by nine-foot cell with three Zambians. It was cold and humiliating. They were released and questioned and police searched and had to appear August 7th after film was developed. We were all feeling horrible — sick.

<u>Thursday, July 27</u> — It seems we have prayed regarding our issues, but things have gotten worse. We all wondered what the Lord was trying to teach us, but we will keep praying. I have tried to keep busy working and cooking, but sleep has been difficult and especially for Stu because of the unknown and barking of guard dogs. We've became a little paranoid and I even had Stu cut out several pages in this diary, wondering if when the police came, they'd find something they didn't like and we'd be in more trouble. Stu burned them as a precaution. The authorities from Solwezi were to come today but didn't show up. Stu continued painting trusses in the heat. Prayer meeting was at the team house and Stu spoke on "Servanthood".

<u>Friday, July 28</u> — More bricks were laid on high walls. Stu, Cynthia and I went to the police station to see if officer in charge regarding being released. He said he'd talk to the authorities in the morning. I tried very hard to let him know how upset I was. I was shaking and tearful. He finally said he'd phone at 1:00 p.m. and did. At 3:00 p.m. he said they'd be here at any time. We don't really believe them and realize the meaning of anytime could be weeks — How Frustrating. I needed my Visa extended and police said come back another day. They finally got it so I could go to Lusaka on Monday. When the mission authorities in Lusaka learned of our problems and the second incident, their response was "What a terrible thing for the mission." When we phoned them, nothing had been done with the High Commission and our release. We were very disappointed at the lack of action on their part.

<u>Sunday, July 30</u> — Stu spoke at the English service. He arrived halfway through the service as he had gone to talk to police regarding him going to Lusaka with me on Monday or going to Solwezi. Police thought Solwezi would be better. Stu spoke on "<u>Depression</u>" using the life of Elijah. There were 19 from CBI and two nationals. We went to a "Game Park" for a change of scenery. We saw seven kinds of animals including Pukus (the most numerous animal), Impalas, Elephants, Crocodiles, etc. At 6:30 p.m. I phone Steve in Lusaka regarding any news from the Canadian High Commission — Nothing. Keith, Cynthia and Stu went to see the governor, who was in bed, but he was sympathetic and Stu was encouraged that he might do something.

<u>Monday, July 31</u> — Robin a single missionary and I left at 6:00 a.m. and seven of us travelled toward Lusaka in a lovely van at 120kph. The road isn't great and I prayed for safety. We stopped for washroom breaks and gals went on one side of the road in the bush and the men on the other side. We stopped at mission house at 12:30 p.m. in Ndola for lunch. We arrived in Lusaka by 6:30 p.m. We ate at a guest house and did our diaries. Word came that Stu and Keith were getting in touch with authorities in Solwezi and would radio through at 10:30 in the morning.

<u>Tuesday, August 1</u> — I was unable to do anything until after 10:30 a.m. radio call and it was so unclear we could hardly hear a thing. Steve who was head of the mission, took me to the High Commission Office but nothing had been done yet. They said they'd contact the police and home bureau and no use calling Canada no matter who we knew. He did say he could get Stu a new passport and get him out of Zambia but might bear heavy consequences on Keith and the mission. I asked if there was anything else I could do and they all said was contact the M.P. Steve tried to reach him with no success. Del Tucker called around 5:00 p.m. for more details regarding contacting church in Bramalea for prayer. She phoned Brandon's and then Faye and family. I did a lot of pacing today and felt so helpless. Some wanted to go to a gift shop and then Livingstone Falls. I said no because of the cost and the uncertainty. I would rather stay in case there was something I could do. I read, prayed and had a bath.

<u>Wednesday, August 2</u> — After washing my hair and breakfast, I met with Steve and radio broadcaster said the M.P. was in Lusaka. I suggested letting the High Commission know. I phoned numerous times with no success. How discouraging. Finally, in the middle of the afternoon a missionary said she'd take me to the High Commissioner and the counsellor said he'd talk to the Commission of Police and Chief of Protocol. They said the case could be solved quickly and new passports issued if necessary. Our flight to New York had been delayed to Sunday at 10:30 a.m. so it gave us a little more time. The Commissioner said

Stu and Keith should come as quickly as possible. On the radio I learned they are planning on going to Solwezi tomorrow as they are panicking for action. Later in the day I learned that Steve Waendt will be in Solwezi and could have Stu back here on Friday. Robin and I prepared meals and ate.

<u>Thursday, August 3</u> — Robin and I were glad to go to the city to shop for a couple of hours. I got my Visa extended. We bought a loaf of bread so we could survive, along with lettuce and two tomatoes. Stu and Keith went to Solwezi early this morning. Stu phoned with the good news that everything had been returned. He'll be hitch hiking a ride on a lorry tomorrow. Finally, the Lord has seen fit to answer our prayers. I phoned Del and Lois to let them know.

<u>Friday, August 4</u> — A missionary took Robin and me to a gift shop. I bought a pineapple and a wire bicycle from a street vendor. We laid in the sun over noon and I got burned. After supper we waited for the lorry to arrive with Stu and team members. We spent the evening catching up on all that had transpired since early Monday morning and showing Stu the things we had bought. It was so great to be together again. Praise the Lord.

14

Key Conversions at Bramalea Baptist Church

MAC CAMPBELL

He was a teacher/principal and the first week of my ministry I went to his home as Pat, his wife, had asked me to come. Since their children were at the house we sat in his red Volvo and Mac trusted the Lord. Later he told me he had been smoking a pipe and hid it under the dash of his car; he was afraid the wiring might catch on fire, but it didn't. Mac became a strong Christian, Deacon and Board Chairman and a very gifted Christian believer. Mac and Pat became our closest friends and we travelled together to Florida and Arizona on several vacations. They are blessed with two children who are strong, grown believers.

ANGELA AND BERNIE HORLEY

This young couple from England started attending church but were not believers. Through our visiting them in their home, they came to Christ, were baptized and joined the church. They grew to be strong believers and following the Share Course and Evangelism Explosion, became soul winners. They retired to Smith Falls and they were at Bev's funeral, and continue to be caring, strong Christians whose love and letters have greatly encouraged me.

PAT AND OWEN MORTIMER

This couple were Horley's neighbours, whom they invited to church. Owen came to the Lord first, but Pat was a strong evolutionist with many books. At first, she resisted the Lord but through prayer, love and God's Word, she came to Christ too. Owen was one of our finest Care Deacons and they both continue to serve God in their retirement years in Cambridge and Florida in the winter.

IRENE AND DON SPENCER

Their children attended a Vacation Bible School and then Bev and Sharon Gast visited their home. Irene was open to come to church and receive Christ. Don, a big man, was very opposed. Bev said I should go to visit him, which I did. He weighed three hundred and forty pounds and he met me at his front door wearing no shirt. When I introduced myself, he said that everyone who went to church was hypocritical. I could have said, "It takes one to know one," but I didn't. "Don you are a big man. Are you willing to accept a challenge?" "What is it he asked?" I said, "I challenge you to come to four of our church services and then see if you still feel the same about hypocrites and Christianity." I poked my finger in his stomach. He accepted the challenge and came. On the fourth Sunday night I preached on "From Adam's Rib to Women's Lib". I was turning off the lights and saw Don sitting in the pew. I went to him and he said "I'm ready now and he was wonderfully converted, baptized (a major challenge), and later he and his wife Irene served God in Christian Camping. He had run a shoe store and they both became strong Christians; their son is still at Bramalea Baptist Church but both Irene and Don have passed away to their reward.

HOWARD CAROLL

One Wednesday evening just before I was to speak at prayer meeting, I was asked if I would meet with Howard Caroll, who was about to join the Seventh Day Adventists. I got someone to speak in my place and spent several hours with Howard who gave his life to Christ. He became a strong Christian serving in our bus ministry. Later he served in another church as a deacon. He and his wife Trudi continue on forty years later as strong Christians.

JACK WALLACE

He was the husband of Betty who was a faithful member of our church and raised her three sons John, Scott and Craig to follow Christ. Jack was a successful businessman and one of our city councillors. He had attended at Christmas and Easter and was a gracious gentleman. In the last year of my ministry at Bramalea he contracted throat cancer and was taken to a Toronto hospital. When I visited him, he had lost a lot of weight and I challenged him regarding the need for faith. He said he didn't want to accept Christ because he might die but said he would call me to visit him when he got home. He later phoned and I went to share God's plan of salvation. He asked Betty to get the Bible which Scott had given him. He said, "Pastor, you may have never seen one like it." It was a red-letter edition. "I've been reading it and Jesus didn't say much in the Old Testament." Betty said, "Jack, He wasn't born yet." I opened my New Testament to share God's plan and he followed me in my Bible and was wonderfully saved, baptized and wanted to serve and give to make up for lost time of selfish living. When he retired, he moved to Huntsville on the same street to which we later moved. He had been so blessed by our men's ministry at Bramalea that he started one at Faith Baptist Church in Huntsville called "Man to Man" and has reached many men. I was asked to take Jack's funeral at Faith Baptist and the church was packed, especially with a lot of men both from his business background and fellows who had come to Christ.

GLORIA AND GEORGE ASHTON

This couple were neighbours on our street and they, like us, had three girls. They weren't attending any church and when we had Vacation Bible School, our girls invited their girls. They attended and on Friday night we invited parents and I challenged them on the importance of following up on the teaching their children had received. I visited their home and both of them were wide open to trust Christ as Saviour and Lord. They were taken through the "Share Course" for new Christians. They have grown as a family and all five are strong Christians today. George became a deacon and Gloria headed up a lady's ministry at Grace Baptist in Alliston when they moved there. The Bible says, "A child will lead them."

DON PELVIN

In the late 1980's I preached on the power of prayer and challenged people to pray for a loved one or friend who needed Christ. Lois Pelvin prayed for her husband Don, that he would be saved. Don worked for a large company in Toronto overseeing their facilities. He got up one morning but didn't feel good so stayed home. Throughout the day he felt even worse and this went on for a week. He didn't know what was wrong. The second week he got in his car and just drove around and he said it was like God steered his car into the parking lot of Bramalea Baptist Church. He went inside and my brother Alan met him and then led him to faith in the Lord. If I remember correctly, he lost his job but found the Lord. His wife's prayers were answered and Don started a locksmith company. Don became very active in our church and a strong spiritual leader, in answer to the faith and prayers of his wife.

CLAUDE AND JOYCE VAZ

My final account of these conversions pertains to the Vaz family. Near the end of my ministry at Bramalea, on Sunday morning a man from India came down from the balcony at the invitation to trust Christ. The next Sunday morning he was in the front row with his wife and she gave her life to the Lord as well. Claude then told me how he watched our new auditorium and facilities being built in 1984-85 from his high-rise condo just south of our church. Claude owned a printing company, but now it was going into bankruptcy and he was despairing. He planned to commit suicide but decided before he did, he would like to see what the inside of the large auditorium looked like. After they were baptized and became members he said, we not only gave our lives to Christ but also our bankrupt company and we along with our company are growing and Bramalea Baptist Church began using their company to print church materials. When I visit the Church Claude always gives me a big hug and thanks me for preaching God's work. I continue to thank the Lord for the privilege of declaring his Word, "For it is the power of God unto salvation to all who believe." Romans 1:16.

YOUNG PEOPLE GOING INTO FULLTIME MINISTRY

There were quite a number of young men and women who left Bramalea Baptist Church and went on to Bible School and Seminary in order to serve the Lord in ministry.

1. **Rick Topping**, a deacon's son, studied in Toronto for his doctorate and was a Presbyterian pastor in Bala, then a large church in Montreal. Presently he is the professor at Vancouver School of Theology.
2. **Steve Jones** came from a non-Christian family and grew up in our church. He attended Central Baptist Seminary and then became the President of our Fellowship Churches in Canada, wherein God has blessed his leadership.
3. **Manfred Kohler** went to New Brunswick Bible Institute and became a missionary with New Tribes Mission. He and his wife Beth served in Mexico and he wrote a book for youth, as well as articles for Christian magazines. He has also pastored a church in Saskatchewan.
4. **Adrian Ninaber,** as well as his four brothers, attended New Brunswick Bible Institute. They have all pastored churches across Canada.
5. **Dave McMaster** attended seminary in Toronto and has been involved in pastoral ministry in Toronto.
6. **Noel McMaster** went to Central Baptist Seminary as a married student and has pastored several of our Fellowship churches, serving with his wife Dor-

othy.

7. **Peter Berg** attended Tyndale in Toronto and worked in youth ministry and fulltime camp ministry in Muskoka.

8. **Jennifer Sadler (nee Kelly)** became a missionary in Japan with her husband, Paul, and served with our Fellowship. She is the daughter of Dave and Marion Kelly, long time members of Bramalea Baptist Church.

9. **Arnie Heineman** was one of four Heineman children who grew up in our church. I married him and Sue. Arnie went to Central Baptist Seminary and has been a faithful and fruitful pastor in Toronto for over thirty years. They have a large family including three biological children and three children they adopted. A quote from an email Arnie sent to me on November 18, 2018 following Bev's death: "We were sorry to hear of Bev's passing. I can only imagine the enormity of your loss. May the Lord continue to bless and keep you. Your example, teaching, and wisdom has meant so much to me. You married Sue and me. You helped me with my first wedding. You buried my dad and even more importantly, you gave me an example of what it looks like to have a passion for the work of being involved in Jesus' Building His Church. THANK YOU...."

10. **Cathy Richards (nee Koehler)** attended New Brunswick Bible Institute where she met and married Barry Richards. They served as missionaries in Thailand with New Tribes Mission. The last fifteen years they have served at the N.T.M. Training Centre in Durham preparing missionaries for service around the world.

11. **Tim Vickery,** son of Mr. and Mrs. Howard Vickery, went into ministry with Evangelical Anglicans in Ontario.

12. **Gerry Robertson** came from Scotland and was a professional soccer player. His wife, Agnes, was a Christian and asked me to visit him concerning his drinking problem and about his need of the Lord. He recently reminded me how embarrassed he was when I visited their home because he walked out of his bedroom drunk in his underwear. I had forgotten the incident but he accepted Christ. He went to Tyndale Seminary and how heads up a humanitarian mission and their son Ryan is also in the ministry.

These are a few of many who left our church to serve the Lord at home and abroad.

Cheltenham House - 1983 - 2005

15
Cheltenham
1983–1995
from Bev's perspective

We had lived in Brampton for fourteen years and the church had grown a lot so that Stu needed a little time and space away. Lois and Bruce lived a little farther north so that Dale was encouraging us to make a move.

We found a lovely house and property in a little town called Cheltenham about twenty minutes north on Creditview Road. It was an older home on seven-and-a-half acres on the Credit River with a great living room that was perfect for entertaining, and an attached family room into which we could extend.

Lois was already married and Dale was at college in Guelph. Faye lived with us, bought herself a car and began working, taking courses at night while she worked in law offices. Dale came home in the summers and later she started working in hospitals in Toronto and Brampton. They both had to do a lot of driving.

Stu enjoyed cutting all that grass with a riding tractor. I think it reminded him of the farm. The driveway was very long and circular, and the lawns were beautiful with three very large gardens. At the back of the property was a large grouping of trees where we got our Christmas trees. I used to pick fiddleheads in the spring and along the fences there were wild grapes from which I made juice. I made a lot of currant jelly from three kinds of currant bushes. There were lots of flower beds and I had to learn a lot about growing and caring for them. It was great to have a greenhouse in which to work starting plants, etc. — a whole new experience for me. You name it, we tried to grow it. In the front we planted lots of pumpkins and zucchini which I took to school in the fall and gave them out as prizes. When Jonathan was little he helped pick and clean the carrots and loved driving the tractor (with help) and riding in the trailer behind it. One year the corn was eaten by the raccoons before we came back from the cottage. The weeding and watering made the garden seem like a lot of work so after a few years we planted a lot of baby trees instead, giving many away as they grew to a good size.

Stu had the privilege of studying one day a week at home, away from the business of the church and that was wonderful for him…he was getting older, you know. The space, the quietness, and the solidarity were wonderful. Stu enjoyed the solitude when cutting the grass with his tractor. That was a big job. He had a second tractor with a plow and a rototiller so he could pretend he was back at the farm again. We were introduced to many birds and had a huge bird feeder on the deck, easily seen from the kitchen and family room. The raccoons visited the feeder at night and were fun to watch, especially when they brought their babies along. It was not much fun when they nested in the attic and we had to get them out. One year it was Dale's idea to raise chickens. The chicks came from eggs I had hatched at school. They grew fast and roamed about the property close to the house until dogs walked off with them one day. Occasionally we saw deer at the back of the property and in the garden area.

Living on the bank of the river also brought beaver and just before we sold the house, they took down about twenty trees along the bank. We were alarmed and got permission to shoot them if we could, and Stu got two of them. One floated down the river and another died on shore. We hung him to bleed and then Ken and his friend skinned it and we had the fur tanned. One day a pheasant flew into one of the bedroom windows and broke his neck but the window did not break.

Half of the time at Cheltenham we were at Bramalea Baptist Church but the last half of our time there Stu worked for the Fellowship at their office in Toronto and Guelph. When Stu changed jobs in 1989, the Fellowship was talking of moving so we looked at homes in many places — first in the Richmond Hill area and then close to the 400. Eventually we bought a lot near Hwy 10 in Caledon. The Fellowship finally decided on Guelph as headquarters, so we sold the lot before doing anything else with it. Then we looked in Guelph and Cambridge; but I would have to find a job in that area and I tried but did not get one so we stayed where we were. It was a long country drive to work in Guelph for Stu.

Almost every weekend he traveled to preach and to represent the Fellowship all over Ontario. He often traveled out west and to the Maritimes, having to raise his own support. I taught school part time at Macville, just outside of Bolton, as Librarian, until the last five years when I worked at Fallingdale in Bramalea fulltime in ESL.

Dale got married in 1986. She was living at home and it was so much fun getting prepared for her wedding. The last five years in Cheltenham we were empty nesters. While Stu traveled a lot and was therefore away it was a little lonely for me and a little stressful getting out to work on snowy mornings and coming home after dark when there were no neighbour's and a dark house. However, I managed.

Stu started training for marathons while we lived here. He ran almost every day for miles. I began to do some and got up to five miles and that was enough for me. The country roads and the abandoned railway were good places to run. An activity I enjoyed for the first time was downhill skiing; Stu bought me skis and I had to go for it. I went to Caledon ski hills and took a couple of lessons then I went on Friday afternoons, mostly by myself and enjoyed going on the chair lift and doing the best I could. It was a wonderful experience, but I never got proficient.

We put in a new kitchen that Bruce built, which was a huge update soon after we moved. Later in the basement, which was not set up as living space, we fixed up a games room with a ping pong table. The family helped a great deal. Just before we moved, we modernized the main bathroom and it most likely helped to sell the house there was only one main bathroom and a two piece at the back of the house.

This was a beautiful house to have Christmas in together as a family. During our time there we were blessed to have seven grandchildren born. They were so cute and it was so much fun to see them grow. (You'll have to look at pictures to see all the fun times we had together.)

We loved having company and had the room to have large groups. We had our former neighbour's for a BBQ, the seniors from the church, a MacLean Reunion, a Silvester reunion, staff parties from the church and the fellowship, Mom's seventy-fifth birthday, many church parties, and lots of family and friend times.

One time when we were at the cottage and Faye was alone at the house, she came home from visiting Ken and was bombarded with fleas. We had taken the dog to the cottage and left the creatures behind to multiply. Ken rescued her to his place and they got exterminators and we were sorry she had to go through this.

Christmas 1992 in Cheltenham

It would soon be time for Stu to retire and so we thought we should get ready to sell the house in case it would take a long time and we were planning to move to the cottage for retirement. It sold in the spring of 1995. The day before moving out, Stu almost killed himself; he had just delivered one tractor to the guy across the road who had bought it and then got on the other tractor to finish the final cutting of the grass near the house. He pulled the lift lever instead of the reverse one because he forgot he'd changed tractors and found himself flying over the bank into raspberry bushes, dodging trees and going over logs. When he realized he might go into the river, he jumped off as the tractor overturned, just missing him. When it came to a stop the motor was still going so he crawled in and turned the key off.

I was not home at the time, so he got Bruce Fitter to come and they got the tractor turned over and winched it up over the hill. Stu got it going again and finished the grass but was somewhat sore from his ordeal…another of his nine lives.

We had to part with a lot of stuff, so an auctioneer came and took it. We didn't get much for it, but it was good to get rid of it. The kids helped us move our stuff to our house in Brampton— a house we bought and rented out. It had room for our stuff in the basement until we would need it in the spring of 1996. On moving day, I backed into Todd's car…yes, there was damage. Nothing is simple, right?

Our house in Cheltenham had a conditional offer on it for a long time and then the interested party did not come through. The house in Cheltenham finally sold for $345,000 and the Brampton house sold after three years. It was a blessing that we had it rented the whole time, but we did lose some on it since prices had dropped dramatically.

We had to arrange where to live from now until we retired then Dale and Todd took us in. They lived in Ballinafad so Stu was a little closer to work and I had a little farther to go. They were so gracious to have us for such a length of time. In the summer we went to the cottage and that summer Lois and Bruce moved to Huntsville so in September we house-sat their Caledon home until we retired in November. Then we went to the cottage for a couple of months. These months were memorable because it snowed continuously. Fortunately, we had our twenty horsepower Ford tractor with a snow blower and chains on the wheels so we were able to keep the driveway blown clean and our cars would heat up in the garage we had built a few years earlier. We also enjoyed some skiing and tobogganing with some of our grandchildren (Bruce and Lois's kids). I kept the cottage warm by putting wood in the kitchen stove and the new insert we had purchased for the big stone fireplace. We were thankful this episode lasted only two months, as we were leaving for Arizona on January 1st until April 1st, 1996. We headed south in our 2004 Maxima and visited friends and a former Greek professor in Virginia (Ted and Marg Barton). Arriving in Florida we learned that our former dear friend from Bramalea Baptist Church, Dick Fraser, was in a coma in the hospital in Boca Raton. When we arrived in Florida, we went to see Dick and pray for him as Marilyn wouldn't go because she wanted to remember him as he was. He was a marathoner and we had run together. He died shortly after and we headed across Alligator Alley, south Florida eventually reaching Alabama and Mississippi. We enjoyed seeing the Alamo with its history and the beautiful river walkways in El Paso. It was eight hundred and fifty miles across Texas and west Texas was dry with tumbleweeds blowing across the highways. We finally arrived in Arizona; it was dry, dusty and we stayed at a motel in Tucson. Early the next morning Stu left for a run as he was training for another marathon. Having run for about an hour and losing his direction he asked people at a bus stop who instructed him to travel east so he did and ended up in a very poor area. He finally stopped at a garage and the owner advised him to leave this very dangerous area. He started running the opposite direction, trying to find his way back to our motel and stopped a police car; a female officer was driving and directed him to get in as she could get him out of the 'bad' area and back to the motel. The only problem was that she asked Stu for the name of the motel, he didn't remember its name. He knew it was just off the main highway, so they started driving. It turned out she had just competed in the Tucson marathon the week before so when Stu explained why he was running so early in the morning, she understood. She was heading to speak at a school and had to call to say she would be a little late because she was trying to help a lost Canadian. Eventually Stu spotted our car and the motel, and she dropped him off. He had been gone for two and a half hours, and I was glad to see him alive as he endeavored to explain his adventure and thankfulness for God's protection.

We have seen the Lord's providential provisions numerous times in our lives. This was the case when Stu was at a convention in Alberta and, as he drove Dr. Don Launstein to the airport, Don asked regarding our plans upon retirement the following month. Stu told him we were planning to go to Arizona for three months leaving January 1st, 1996. He asked if we had a place to stay and Stu responded, "Not Yet." Dr. Launstein said he used to live near Phoenix and had pastored a church; his mother had just died and left him her retirement home at Sun City near Phoenix so that he offered it for the winter and for only two hundred dollars to cover utility costs. The home was cute and fully furnished with a dozen fruit trees. We had three great months of fun in the sun as well as training for a marathon in Phoenix. Our trip home was eventful as we saw the Oklahoma site where the bombing took place; there we also saw the lawyer who had worked on the murder trial of O.J. Simpson. I got a picture of him and his entourage near the bombing site and memorials. By the time we got home we had travelled through twenty-two states and driven about twenty thousand kilometers with no accidents. Praise the Lord.

On April 1st, 1996, we moved our furniture from the basement of the home in Brampton, which we had just sold. We rented a thirty-foot truck and the two of us loaded and unloaded tons of furniture and household items. Fortunately, the next-door neighbor at our new home in Huntsville saw us struggling and came over and helped us get moved into our lovely retirement home at 500 Bayshore Blvd. on Lake Vernon.

16

Fellowship Office in Toronto and Guelph 1989–1995

I will never forget my first trip to Fellowship Office on Bayview Avenue in Toronto. Dr. Roy Lawson wanted me there at 8:30 a.m. so he could introduce me to the rest of the staff. We were living in Cheltenham, north of Brampton, a trip some seventy kilometers away. I left home at 7:15 a.m., thinking I had lots of time, but I found the traffic backed up for miles. I hadn't expected this problem and it took me three quarters of an hour to reach the 401. I still had over thirty minutes and the traffic was hardly moving. Reality started to set in that I was going to be late and I'm the kind of guy who always arrives early. I didn't have a cell phone to inform the staff of my dilemma. The subject of "sanctification" came to my mind as I did a slow burn while creeping along the 401 at a snail's pace. I thought of Romans 5 and the scripture that says "tribulation produces patience and patience experience and experience hope." I thought, "This tribulation won't produce any good patience for me and, as for a hope was concerned, I had given up." By the time I finally arrived at Bayview Avenue and the Fellowship Office it was 9:30 a.m. and the meeting was just concluding. I ran into the meeting room, totally embarrassed, apologizing profusely, and vowing to myself I would never be late again and I never was. My solution was getting up at 5:00 a.m. as I had done on our dairy farm, leaving home at 5:45 a.m. and arriving at 6:30 a.m. before traffic was bad and long before even Roy Lawson had arrived. I was able to get a lot of paperwork done before any meetings and before the phones started ringing. It also meant if I wasn't out of town, I could head home at 3:00 p.m. before the rush hour started.

A couple of years later the head office property was sold for real estate/housing development and a brand-new beautiful facility was constructed in Guelph. Now instead of seventy kilometers through heavy Toronto traffic my trip was only fifty kilometers without one stoplight and mainly through rural countryside. For the next four years I enjoyed this relaxing trip and I didn't have to leave at such an ungodly hour. I have several memories of my time in Guelph: I started there located in a large corner office with glass everywhere and great furniture. In 1992–1993 a recession hit and giving's dwindled. I lost my big office and full-time secretary, moved to an office less than half its size, and by the time I retired, I was downsized again to an even smaller space. However, my ministry across Canada was flourishing, and I was feeling fulfilled and blessed.

The thing I missed most when I left Bramalea for my responsibility as Church Extension Secretary and Church Growth Consultant was the ability to measure whether I was making a difference in the cause of Christ. Previously during my twenty years at Bramalea, I constantly measured progress in souls saved, baptised, new members, increasing budgets and income, larger staff and facilities. It wasn't until 1990 and the introduction of Vision 2000 Canada in Ottawa that denominational heads and leaders were challenged to develop their own denominations goals, vision and strategy. I was asked along with Gerry Kraft from B.C., to head up this undertaking for our five hundred Fellowship Baptist Churches in Canada. We called together our five Regional Directors from B.C. to the Maritimes and brainstormed and then challenged them to set goals for new church plants — a total of one hundred and thirty-five for the next ten years. Gerry and I worked on setting goals for number of conversions, baptisms, and new church members. With these goals in place it allowed me/us to challenge our pastors and churches to measure our progress on a yearly basis. The old adage says, "If you aim at nothing, you're bound to hit it." In the following years we saw a steady growth in all areas, although about thirty percent of pastors and churches were reluctant to send in their yearly reports which I interpreted as a sign of lack of church growth and/or support.

Over the six years I flew thousands of miles and about once a month I would fly to one of our six regions then I would rent a car and travel to as many churches as possible to speak and meet with pastors and church boards. On one memorable occasion I flew to Winnipeg to the FEB, mid region; when I got to the airport in Toronto, the flight was delayed for an hour and I had to change planes.

In the air I got a terrible toothache since I had been at the dentist for a root canal and they hadn't finished their work, so I got Tylenol from the stewardess to help control the pain. When I landed, the pain had subsided, but it was 11:00 p.m. so I phoned the pastor at Rivers Baptist Church where I was to go and preach the next morning to see if I should get a motel in Winnipeg and leave early Sunday morning to preach. He advised to continue travelling and I should arrive at his home by 1:30 a.m. I rented a car and headed west on the TransCanada highway where a farmer had been transporting bales of hay or straw and these were strewn along the highway for miles. It was like a slalom car race, but it helped me to keep alert and alive. It was nearly 2:00 a.m. before I found the pastor's home and ended up at the bottom of a staircase on an old single bed with terrible springs. I finally got to sleep and then at 4:00 a.m. the lights came on and this Home Mission pastor (who will go unnamed) came stumbling down the stairs. He apologized for waking me up but said he was a volunteer firefighter and had been called to a fire. I had just gotten back to sleep when he returned home and then I had to be up and prepared to preach. Fortunately, the Lord gave me a strong constitution and I was able to keep going on little sleep. That evening I had to preach at a church nearby in Brandon, Manitoba. As I drove into the parking lot and got my Bible and some promotional material for the Fellowship, the pastor greeted me and said, "You'll be preaching from the King James Bible tonight." I agreed and walked back to my car and traded my NIV Bible in for the old KJV. I still remember trying to read from the KJV with all its archaic language and couldn't. I had been using the NIV for years and didn't realized how rusty I was in the KJV on which I had grown up and memorized. So that was just a day of the week in Manitoba; however, I want to conclude with a sequel to the story about the bed with the terrible springs.

A while later I left home in Cheltenham and office in Guelph by car. My first stop was at our Baptist Church in Cottam near London. The pastor was Noel McMaster and wife Dorothy who had been members at Bramalea Baptist Church then had gone into ministry. I preached that night and they offered to let me sleep over since I was scheduled to speak the next morning at London Baptist Bible College and Seminary. They said they had a brand-new pullout couch and I'd be the first one to use it. I then told them of my recent bad experience in Manitoba, but they assured me that I should sleep well. I put out the light in the rec room and climbed into bed. I couldn't believe it, but it felt like there was no mattress, just springs. I tried to make myself comfortable and thought maybe I was becoming paranoid. I got up early and left for London. A few weeks later at our Fellowship Convention in Toronto I met the McMasters. Dorothy came over and said, "Pastor I can't look at you." I said, "Am I that bad looking?" "No", she said, "the bed you slept on, we found out that the mattress was underneath and you slept on the springs." I said, "I knew something wasn't right, but didn't want to complain since the price was right." So much for traveling and serving the Lord and making many memories.

When it came time to retire, the celebration was to take place in Vancouver at our National Convention and the great speaker was Dr. John MacArthur from California. This was November 1995, and I was in my sixty-first year. Dr. Roy Lawson had instituted a rule that the senior staff had to retire once they were sixty. I believe he did this because of problems with former staff so I had to comply even though I felt I could continue and desired to serve the Lord.

I, along with Bev, were presented with some gifts including an engraved plaque acknowledging my years of ministry for the Lord. Then Bev and I joined Gerry and Susie Kraft for a week's vacation on the Oregon coast. It was a fun time with our friends who lived in B.C. I had traveled with Gerry Kraft for six years doing many seminars and preparing materials. Gerry was an expert with computers and preparing overhead materials which made me look good, and I did the majority of the speaking and presentations. Susie had been suffering for sixteen years with cancer and died soon after our time together in Oregon and B.C.

About a year later I introduced Gerry to Nancy Barwell who had lost her husband Gord, a professional football player, to cancer ten years earlier. It wasn't long until a wedding was planned and they asked me to assist in marrying them. The ceremony was held in a colourful old stone house in Guelph on January 1st, 2000. We were on our way to Florida along with our dog Misty. It was a brutally cold day, so we brought Misty inside the house and put her in the basement. Just before the ceremony began, I heard her barking, so I ran down and put her on top of our luggage in the backseat and covered her with a blanket. Chuck Ealey, the quarterback for the Toronto Argonauts attended. Our dog survived the cold and so has their marriage.

TRIP TO JAPAN AND SOUTH KOREA MAY 10–26, 1995

This was one of my most memorable trips and my last to a foreign country before I retired. I had just run the Toronto Marathon before leaving on Monday morning to Japan. The purpose of going to Japan was to minister to our Fellowship Baptist missionaries who were serving in Toyama province. I landed in Tokyo and Carl DeBoer met me at the airport. However, when he picked me up, he discovered he had left his keys on the high-speed train and we had to break in the building where we were staying. He got his keys back the following day. I spoke four or five times to missionaries on themes to encourage them. One of the highlights was taking them to a Japanese restaurant where they could eat all the beef, chicken, etc. they desired. This as a special treat since meat was fifteen dollars a pound and they seldom could afford it. Fortunately, the big bill was covered by our head office and not "yours truly". I had to travel one Sunday morning by myself on a train to preach at a church that had been built by volunteers from our Fellowship. My lady interpreter had me go through my sermon with her before I preached so she would know all the words. The Japanese had a meal after the service and were very courteous and appreciative. As I travelled with Carl DeBoer in his Toyota van I commented how nice it was and he said he would have to trade it in next year because he couldn't afford to pay the licence fee since they increase it yearly by thousands of Yen to the point people are forced to trade them in after five or six years. This helps to keep car manufacturers in business and old vehicles are crushed. I was impressed by the beauty and cleanliness of Japan and at the service stations where men served you wearing white gloves. However only about two percent were Christians in Japan and our churches are thirty to one hundred people in size.

My next stop was Seoul, South Korea for the Global GCOWE Congress on World Evangelism. Four thousand five hundred delegates from most countries in the world attended May 17–26. We met in a magnificent auditorium for most of our meetings which held five thousand; as well as a Presbyterian church which had twenty-five thousand members. I attended Choe's Church (Yeoido Full Gospel), the largest in the world with eight hundred thousand members. The auditorium held forty-five thousand people and they held 14 services a week. They held one hundred thousand cell or bible study groups each week and at noon every person was to pray for each one in their group.

Our delegation from Canada had a private meeting with Pastor Choe following the morning service, and I asked him why he thought the thirty-seven million South Korean's responded so well to the gospel compared to the Japanese? He said one hundred years ago there were hardly any believers in Korea. Now one third of the population, including their president and main generals were born again Christians. His answer was that they had been humiliated by their enemies for centuries and when they learned of the love of God and Christ's forgiveness, they quickly responded. From my hotel in Seoul I saw red crosses shining at night and asked what they represented. I was told they were churches that were open twenty-four hours a day and people could go and get food, clothing, money, and counselling.

One of our highlights was going to a "Prayer Mountain", overlooking the "Demilitarized Zone" between South and North Korea, which was owned by Choes Church. People went there to fast and pray, and 1995 marked the fiftieth

Stu & Ladies at Choe's Church, S. Korea

anniversary of the separation of North and South Korea and they were praying for reconciliation as well as praying for lost friends and loved ones.

The Korean Christians entered into little caves with burlap bags covering the doorway. They would fast and pray for days and weeks. There was a restaurant there and a sign said that if you had been fasting for one week or two or three, then this is how you should break your fast and what you should eat. Now we could see why God was blessing the Koreans with the world's largest churches as well as becoming the country sending out the most missionaries around the world. One evening our Canadian delegates met with delegates from Papua, New Guinea for a meal and then a meeting. We had each contributed two hundred dollars to pay for this trip to South Korea. I was asked to speak to them on evangelism and church growth principles. They were all dressed in suits and we were in casual clothes. This reminded me when I was twenty-one and hearing Ray Holley, a missionary from Papua New Guinea telling about the power of the gospel to change the naked cannibals into Christians. God used this to move me toward preparing to serve the Lord. The final night was the highlight when eighty thousand gathered in the site of the 1988 Olympic Games. Each countries' delegates marched in carrying their countries flag like the athletes do and I carried our Canadian flag. The service lasted for three hours and three quarters of the people attending were college age who were preparing to be missionaries. The music and messages were moving. I returned inspired and realizing how little I had accomplished and how my prayer life and faith needed strengthening.

17

Baptist Builders
Quick Build Story

Shortly after returning from a six-week trip to Zambia in Africa where I was speaking and led a ten-member team to build a memorial chapel in memory of Ian Frew who had been killed by a crocodile, I flew to Halifax. It was the summer of 1989 and I was visiting young pastors in Nova Scotia in order to help them with ministry and facilities. None of the three pastors I visited had his own building; one was meeting in a fire hall, another in a condemned building with no facilities, and the other in a school. However, each of them had property to build on but could not afford to pay for a new building. As I flew back to Toronto, I thought of my recent trip to Zambia in which volunteers had covered their own costs. Why couldn't we get volunteers to help build a church in Canada? I came up with eight ideas which would make this possible— if I could get my son-in-law, Bruce Fitter, a builder, to design a church building and then agree to be the project manager. I challenged him with the concept and he said that he would design the building if I could get the volunteers. Building churches was not one of the seven areas of ministry for which I was responsible in our Fellowship in Canada, but it was a very real need. In October I was speaking at the twenty-fifth Anniversary of Bramalea Baptist Church where I had pastored for twenty years; that Sunday night I asked how many of the congregation would give one week of their lives to help build a church in Digby, Nova Scotia and twenty-six people came forward so that became the basis of our team plus a few from the Maritimes. We chose Digby because they had property, were in the condemned building, and had money for building materials. It was the death of fifteen-year-old Ian Frew that gave birth to Baptist Builders Quick Build concept.

1. EMMANUEL BAPTIST CHURCH IN DIGBY, NOVA SCOTIA (MAY 1990)

Bruce loaded his big truck with tools and supplies and he and John Siderius headed to Digby. When Bruce and John arrived at the Quebec border they were turned back because of a truckers' strike and truckers were stopping any trucks that tried to cross into Quebec. Bruce and John went over the bridge at Cornwall into New York State. Their truck wasn't bonded or licenced for the United States and each state would charge funds for licence and bonding. When stopped Bruce told them about the truckers strike in Quebec and he wasn't properly licenced or bonded, the official at the border asked what was in the truck to which he replied, "Food, propane, tools, and materials." The head fellow overheard Bruce and asked him to repeat the story. He then asked Bruce to open the back, checked it and asked him to close it. He made a phone call to another official he believes was a Christian and put a seal on the paperwork and gave permission to proceed. They did and got through several states to Digby and thus begun our first Quick Build. Also, next Bob and Betty Mann arrived around May 24, 1990. When the rest of us arrived, they had building materials on site and had begun to construct some walls on the concrete basement which had been constructed by the church and local builders. With a team of approximately forty men and women the work began in earnest on Monday morning. Mr. and Mrs. Bruce Fitter Sr. were in charge of preparing three meals a day as well as two coffee breaks; they had been in the food business so were God's provision for great food for hungry workers. The wives of some of the workers helped prepare meals. Bev flew in to work on meals and the project as well. The exterior walls were in place by Monday evening and the trusses for the roof by Tuesday when sheeting was going on. Then the rain came but fortunately the building was closed in for electricians, plumbers, and insulators. We had two accidents with John Siderius cutting off the end of his thumb and a fellow from Bramalea Baptist Church falling off a ladder in the basement and breaking his arm. I heard of these when I returned from speaking at their prayer meeting; however, this didn't deter these men or others from working from sunrise to late at night. The mud was deep and I remember lugging bundles of shingles up the ladder as Bruce encouraged the roofers to keep shingling through the rain in order to keep on schedule. By midnight on Saturday evening the church was clad with white vinyl and we even

Digby Building - 1990 Matthew's & Silvester's

had a wheelchair ramp in place. On Sunday morning Emmanuel Baptist Church was quickly filled with expectant worshipers. Pastor Steve Matthews stood to welcome workers and worshipers, and he was almost overcome with emotion. It was my privilege to preach the first sermon in this brand-new debt-free building. A window company donated most of the windows when they heard everyone had volunteered their time and expertise. Don Pelvin, a new convert from Bramalea Baptist came to the project and he and his company donated $10,000 worth of carpet to Digby project. The Best Western in Truro donated fifteen double rooms for a week at no cost. I had arranged for people who flew or drove to get a tax receipt. Little did I know that Operation Digby would be the first of two-dozen church builds across Canada.

Each year our Fellowship had a Convention Project. One year it was Foreign Missions, then French Mission, and then Home Missions. 1991 was the year of Home Missions and I was responsible to come up with a project to assist our new congregations across Canada. As a result the success of "Operation Digby" Roy Lawson, (our General Secretary) and I decided to try and build four churches across Canada. I was responsible to raise two hundred thousand dollars plus enlist hundreds of volunteers. The four congregations we chose were Truro, Nova Scotia; Espanola, Ontario; Bonnyville, Alberta; and Golden, British Columbia. Bruce, my son-in-law, was both gifted and generous, and designed three more church buildings while taking time off from building restaurants across Canada.

2. CROSSROADS BAPTIST CHURCH IN
TRURO, NOVA SCOTIA (JUNE 1991)

This was the first of four church builds we did in 1991 starting in June. We had about fifty volunteers from the Maritimes and Ontario. The first couple of days saw the walls going up, roof going and then we realized that Pastor Peter Pardoe had forgotten to order the windows needed. Bruce said unless some could be found the project couldn't proceed. They called a prayer meeting for some divine intervention and in a couple of hours (they discovered) windows in Halifax that someone had ordered two years earlier but had never been picked up, so a truck was sent to Halifax. They needed two sets of eleven windows for the sides and one large one for behind the baptistry plus two doors with glass on each side. All twenty-three windows and two doors with side lights were there and they gave them to us because they had been paid for by the original purchasers. By that evening the windows were all installed and fit perfectly at no cost. This was truly a miracle and provision from God. Don Pelvin came to the project and his company donated 80 solid oak doors, cupboards and carpet valued at $25,000. The project went well and CBC TV came out to take pictures and interviews because of the unique nature of building a church in one week. The church was located beside an artesian well where they bottled water and we were able to use this to cool and heat the building. Another goal we had was to distribute invitations in the neighbourhood inviting people to the opening of the church. Again, by Saturday evening the facilities were completed and ready except for the painting of the auditorium. As I stood to preach, I marvelled at the miracle of a five thousand square foot building being erected in six days. This got the congregation out of the firehall and into a new facility years earlier than anticipated and with no deficit.

3. CALVARY BAPTIST IN
ESPANOLA, ONTARIO (AUGUST 1991)

In the last week of August, we headed to Espanola near Sudbury for our second project. The weather was especially hot (ninety degrees) and we had to keep the workers well hydrated. In the afternoon I was heading up the distribution of the literature inviting people to the opening of the church on Sunday which put pressure on the volunteers to have the facilities ready. It was the first time I visited homes wearing shorts because of the heat. Our team of sixty volunteers worked tirelessly and, on two occasions total strangers appeared, one to help with the drywalling and another to do roofing in the extreme heat. It was as if God sent them at the right time with the right skills. One of the couples helping from Sudbury owned a nursery business and they volunteered to supply shrubs, flowers, and sod which I helped coordinate on Saturday. It made the church look finished on the outside to the extent that when the quartet came on Sunday for the opening service, they drove by the building believing the church had been there for some time. I remember sitting in the front row near the organ and seeing some plaster which had been done late Saturday night looking like it might come loose and hit the organist on the head. Fortunately, it didn't happen and I had the privilege to share God's word and rejoice with Pastor Bill Hansford, his people and volunteers in seeing the power of God's people being labourers together with God. During this project, the owner of the building company supplying our materials became very ill. We went to see him in the hospital and ended up leading him and several members of his family to the Lord. He was moved by the love and harmony of our workers as he had previously supplied materials for the Jehovah's Witnesses and said they were very difficult to work with. I heard shortly after the opening of the church that the Mayor of Espanola started attending and became a Christian, and a couple years later I was speaking at an ordination service for their new pastor who had married a girl from Bramalea Baptist Church; here I met the mayor and many new people who had come to church and Christ in the ensuing years.

4. GOLDEN BAPTIST CHURCH IN
GOLDEN, BRITISH COLUMBIA (OCTOBER 1991)

This would be our third church project for 1991 and our last as it was October and Bruce couldn't spare any more time from his Hygrade Carpentry Company. To enlist workers for each project, my secretary sent out sign up forms regarding skill set, age, and need for accommodations as well as insurance coverage. From the beginning of this building project some workers didn't want to send their names to the head office in Ontario. It was a political issue, and as a result, instead of eighty workers we ended up with one hundred and twenty. This created logistic problems and food issues as well as a serious accident. I didn't get to the job site until late on Tuesday because of meeting planning department officials in Calgary where I was looking for future church building sites. In an effort to utilize so many workers, Bruce decided to build the roof structure in five sections on the ground away from the building itself. As a result of so many workers, someone inadvertently removed a brace holding up roof trusses and they collapsed. As a result, Ken Preston from London was crushed, breaking his back. They took him by ambulance to Calgary (several hours south) for treatment. We continued on with the project although the beautiful mountain view made it harder for workers to concentrate on their responsibilities and when we arrived early each morning, elk were roaming around. By Saturday the building was finished and they had enough material for a steeple as well. Two interesting side lights occurred: first when we were halfway through the project we were running out of materials. Bruce had done the ordering for all the materials which were needed to complete the project but after doing a little detective work we discovered that the pastor (who will go unnamed) had cut the list in half for fear his deacons might think too much was being spent on building materials. He confessed his 'sin' and we ordered the needed materials to complete the project on schedule and budget. The other matter related to Ken Preston and his broken back. His insurance company insisted that he be flown to London as soon as possible from Calgary. I felt responsible to help since I had personally recruited him. Two members of the Golden Church were pilots and owned several smaller planes, so they offered to fly to Calgary and get Ken then fly him to London. I met them at 4:00 a.m. and we boarded their plane which had a propeller that pushed the plane at about two hundred miles per hour. We had to leave while it was still dark. The pilot asked me to look out the left window while his co-pilot would look out the right one and he would look down and try to follow the truck lights on the highway below. He added that if I saw a shadow or dark object to let him know because it would be a mountain. You talk about nail-biting, but by 6:30 a.m. with the sun coming up we arrived in Calgary at the hospital. They brought Ken out on a stretcher and slid him back beside me. I was lying on suitcases and I stayed beside him as we headed for London. We had to make a stop in North Dakota for fuel and it was very windy, so they had to come in on an angle very carefully. We took off and by 5:00 p.m. we arrived in London. Bev was there to greet me and I was happy to see her and be close to home. I later visited Ken as he recovered from his injury. Praise the Lord. Another Quick Build was completed along with making a lot of new friends and memories.

5. BONNYVILLE BAPTIST CHURCH IN BONNYVILLE, ALBERTA (SUMMER 1992)

We couldn't get this project done in 1991, so we did it in the summer of 1992. Bonnyville is east of Edmonton and Art Hoehne was the pastor. This model was a slab on grade and was approximately one hundred feet by seventy feet wide on one level. One day a tornado was heading for our site but at the last minute changed directions and missed us. There were a great group of volunteers from across Canada and something interesting took place that week besides construction of a lovely large building. The pastor's daughter was a nurse and she was helping on the project with drywalling and insulating, when a single young fellow from Ontario noticed this lovely young lady and it wasn't long before I noticed them working together late into the evenings. (A little like Ruth and Boaz in the Old Testament.) By the time the project was completed and I had spoken at the opening service, their friendship had grown almost as quickly as the building. The result was a romance that culminated in the marriage of a beautiful western gal and great guy from Ontario. Who said you can't walk and chew gum at the same time? With the completion of Bonnyville church it meant we had completed the four projects. Besides this we had raised two hundred thousand dollars from across Canada that was divided among the four churches. We had seen about three hundred volunteers, men and women, young and old, skilled and unskilled, come together with a willingness to work hard and long in order to build four fantastic facilities in a total of four weeks. Many workers told me that they had never worked as hard before, but it was the most meaningful experience of their lives.

6. FELLOWSHIP BAPTIST CHURCH IN KANATA, ONTARIO (SEPTEMBER 1993)

This project took place in the last two weeks of September 1993. I recall meeting with Pastor Colin McKenzie to plan the type of facility that would best suit their needs. By now we had four models to choose from and Kanata was a rapidly growing city known as "Silicone Valley North" near Ottawa. The large model we had built at Bonnyville, Alberta, was chosen and a great two-acre site was available. This was the first project we built in a city and this meant more stringent by-laws which slowed our progress and it took us two weeks to complete. One incident which I won't forget was in the second week when Bev passed out on the job. I wasn't sure if she was going to live or die, and we phoned for an ambulance. As a result of their expertise and prayers (and some panic) we brought her back to health. It was determined it was caused by heat exhaustion and lack of water — another example of Bev's not only helping prepare meals but also working long hours on the construction site. Our hard-working team of volunteers led again by my son-in-law, Bruce Fitter, and assisted by Claire Miller did a great job. Two other key men were Bruce Morrill, lead electrician, and Bert Faber, lead plumber, both of whom took time off from running their own companies. These key men assisted in at least a dozen projects. Bruce Morrill's lovely wife, Chris, was a key person in preparing our meals. Another feature of every project was that I led in devotions following by a prayer time each morning. The opening service was almost cancelled due to a city inspector not wanting to issue an occupancy permit. Following prayer and pressure, they issued it and we celebrated the grand opening with praise, prayer, and preaching of God's Word.

7. CHURCH ON SAUGEEN INDIAN IN RESERVE, ONTARIO (SEPTEMBER 1994)

This would be our seventh project and the first of two we built on Indian Reserves. I will long remember when Bruce and I went to see their existing "church building". It looked more like a chicken coop and on that cold wintery day, snow was blowing in through the cracks. It was obvious they were in need of a better building. Someone had donated a new property and Bruce designed a one level facility of about two thousand square feet. Our faithful volunteers built a lovely facility in a week in September of 1994. This new place of worship was built on a reserve but when Sunday morning came the worshippers were anything but "Reserved" when it came to praising and worshiping the Lord for His wonderful provision.

8. SPARWOOD BAPTIST CHURCH IN SPARWOOD, BRITISH COLUMBIA (SEPTEMBER 1995)

This church is located in Southern British Columbia in a coal mining area in a mountainous region. Bruce and I flew to Calgary and rented a car there and headed south though a rugged area where floods and an earthquake had done some great damage. When we were about halfway through the project, a torrential rain took place, resulting in such floods that we had trouble reaching our building site. It slowed our project down, but some Mormon men came and offered to assist us. We were grateful for their help in spite of their beliefs. I was not able to stay for the conclusion of the project as I had to take part in a convention in Alberta, north of Calgary. When I went to leave the roads we came in on they were all washed out and I had to take a longer route that took me to the west in British Columbia through a beautiful valley which included some of the most spectacular scenery I have ever seen. I finally arrived at my destination and took part in the Fellowship Convention. The special project was completed with the opening on Sunday morning.

9. FAITHWAY BAPTIST IN WOODSTOCK, ONTARIO (SEPTEMBER 22 TO OCTOBER 3 1996)

The building site for this project is located on the north side of the 401 near the hospital. This structure was a large two storey building with brick work at the front. A Christian man who owned an insulating company donated all the needed insulation. New building codes that demanded a double thickness of drywall in all the stairwells slowed the project down. We had about fifty volunteers coming from as far away as British Columbia. The project took two weeks to complete and it had blue siding with large windows. Two interesting incidents took place when I went later to speak at the opening with two hundred people attending: they had a 'Salamander' heater blowing in extra heat because the furnace wasn't functioning. My wife Bev stood in front of the heater which was like a flame thrower. Her lovely green coat caught on fire and burned the back of it. When I got up to speak, I began by saying "My old flame has become a new flame" and used it to make for a good introduction to help break the ice on a cold fall morning. Following the service, I was greeted by Pastor Harry Toews and his wife Rosemary. They introduced me to a couple beside them and the man asked if I remembered him, but I didn't. He said he was the owner of the lumber company which had supplied all the building materials and had visited the site several times during construction. He was so impressed with the project and people devoting their time and skills that he asked Pastor Toews to tell him what motivated people to be so generous. Harry had explained about their and his faith in Jesus Christ and the new nature of love and generosity that had led the man and his wife to the Lord. The man then said that he and his wife gave their lives to the Lord and had just been baptized and joined Faithway Baptist, so the project had quickly born fruit and continues to with multiple services.

10. HERITAGE BAPTIST SEMINARY IN CAMBRIDGE, ONTARIO (OCT. 21 –NOV. 8, 1997)

I received a phone call one day from the president of Heritage Baptist College and Seminary in Cambridge, Marvin Brubaker asking if Baptist Builders would be able to build the thirty-two thousand square foot facility which would include a gym, chapel, offices, kitchen, and classrooms. Our committee decided to accept the mammoth challenge to start October 21, 1997. I started enlisting volunteers from our computer list of about four hundred people. I got forty men for two weeks which we felt might enable us to construct the superstructure but not finish the inside or the outside (which would be stuccoed). When we arrived early Monday morning with our workers ready to go, we found to our amazement that the man who had been in charge of getting the concrete slab laid and some block walls had forgotten to order the lumber. Sounds like Truro with no windows. Bruce Fitter got on the phone and called the Radcliffes, who owned a big lumber yard in Stouffville, and within an hour had a load heading to Cambridge. We lost a few hours but once we got rolling and framing the eighteen-foot walls we made progress. One scary moment was when we were putting in these high exterior walls by hand — the wind funnelled through and almost blew them on us as we were lifting them by hand. The men responsible for the block work couldn't keep up with us and, as a result, I had to phone and cancel the second week of workers and move them and others to a third week. It was amazing how a structure of that size took shape. We used many tons of beams, lumber, and plywood to close the structure in. By the third week and now early November, the weather was cold with some snow flurries. Every morning I would challenge the workers from God's Word (like Nehemiah building walls of Jerusalem) to keep focused and be "labourers together with God". By the end of the third week, (November 8th) we had the entire facility closed in and our goal had been reached with no serious accidents or incidents other than the safety inspectors making sure we all wore hard hats and steel-toed shoes along with safety harnesses for heights. We had a wonderful celebration in the Chapel which holds four hundred, at the conclusion of these challenging three weeks. Every time I am at Heritage and see the finished facilities filled with seminary students, I marvel at what God accomplished through willing workers who received no remuneration. However, one day they'll hear from the Lord's lips, "Well done, good and faithful servants."

11. KINMOUNT BAPTIST CHURCH IN KINMOUNT, ONTARIO (JULY 2004)

This small congregation in Central Ontario was meeting in a former four room school building. They asked if our team of volunteers could come and make it look more like a church so we accepted the challenge. We got about thirty volunteers, with about ten from Pinegrove Baptist in Bracebridge where I had ministered back in 2003 to 2004. This was a different type of challenge and Claire Miller headed this retro type of challenge without my son-in-law. We redesigned the outside roof area and reconstructed the interior as well. By the end of the week we had made a great change in the look of the building as well as making new friends with people who came by from the small town. The congregation was excited with the retro look and rejuvenation of their building, and the Sunday morning opening was one of much joy and praise to the Lord as well as thanksgiving to the hard work of many volunteers. We left with good memories and new friends that we probably won't see until we meet in heaven.

12. VICTORY BAPTIST IN MIRAMICHI, NEW BRUNSWICK (JUNE 1998)

Bev and I headed toward New Brunswick in our 1995 Nissan Maxima, pulling our Baptist Builder's closed in trailer filled with a big cooking grill, pots and

June 1998 Miramichi Church Opening - Bev & I

pans, and sixty by forty-foot eating tent, that we put up at each project in which to prepare meals and eat. We enjoyed the scenic trip through Quebec, where Bev was from, and before we reached Miramichi we could smell it. The reason was that a large pulp and paper mill was located nearby and it created a lot of smell and noise. A large team of volunteers was arriving on the scene on Sunday afternoon from across the country. The model we were to build had a basement and a large upper level that we had to construct in six days and then worship in it on Sunday. By the end of the first day we had the walls up. Then someone (or a company), when they heard no one was being paid, offered to donate all the drywall for the project. What a blessing and it shows how generosity often replicates generosity in others. We had ten wives of workers who provided nutritious meals. Ladies also distributed invitations throughout Miramichi for the grand opening Sunday morning. When the day arrived, the beautiful white church building with over five thousand square feet of space was complete, other than the inside painting which we left for the congregation at each project; this gave everyone a chance to participate and gave them ownership of their church building project. I have two dozen photos of various stages of this project; from the empty lot to cranes lifting walls in place and workers shingling the roof with others installing siding. The two final pictures are of Sunday morning, a crowded auditorium of worshippers, and the other thirty-man choir composed of volunteers and myself. I'm including a picture of Bev and myself in front of the beautiful building and, as I write this story, it is five months since Bev died from cancer and has gone to her Lord and heavenly reward. She faithfully accompanied me to most of our projects across Canada and brought laughter, beauty, and faith in action for the cause of Christ and the glory of God. I miss her.

13. EGANVILLE BAPTIST CHURCH IN EGANVILLE, ONTARIO (JUNE 1999)

This project, an hour and a half west of Ottawa proved to be an exciting undertaking. The building was an L-shaped design and slab on grade. The motel where many of us stayed was just a short walk up the street and the building company supplying the materials was almost across the street. I have twenty-seven pictures documenting the six days of construction with excellent workmen. We had four newspapers competing for coverage of this project; there was the Eganville Weekly, the Pembroke Weekly, Christian Week, and the Ottawa Citizen from one and a half hours away. Every day they sent a reporter a photographer and published almost a full-page account of this project. They titled it "Six Days of Creation" from Genesis and resting on the seventh day. I asked them why they were spending so much time and money, and they said a year previously they had evaluated their religious content and felt they needed to increase it. Then somehow, they heard of our project in Eganville. The four reporters from the four papers were constantly wanting to interview me in an effort to get an edge on their papers. I still have all seven pages from the Ottawa Citizen with seven headings; for instance, on the day we installed the large multi-paned window facing the highway, their caption was "Let there be Light". Secondly the seventh day was "They Rested from their Labours". Very biblical, very creative, and great coverage. One day a local grocery store came with barbecues and four staff, providing dozens of hamburgers and hot dogs at no cost. The project went very smoothly and, when Sunday came, volunteers were tired but inspired by the by-product of "faith and works". I enjoyed speaking at the opening to a full house with enthusiastic singing, our men's choir, and testimonies. An amazing story came to light a year or so following the project. I was working on my antique boat in Huntsville when a reporter came into the building where I and others were working on our old boats. He wanted to take some pictures and then he came over to me and said, "I think I've met you before". Following a brief discussion, it turned out he was the reporter from the Pembroke paper covering the project in Eganville and had interviewed me. He said that he was so impressed by the spirit of love and cooperation that he had come to the opening service with his wife. They hadn't been attending any church and within a few weeks

Eganville Opening - Bev & I - 1999

they came to Christ and joined the church. He said he was a musician and took part in the worship team. Even though he had been transferred to Muskoka as editor of the Muskoka Magazine, they were driving back to Eganville each Sunday to worship and serve the Lord. Last year Bev and I stopped in for a worship service on our way to Ottawa and the church was alive with people; we met two or three who had been volunteers' years before.

14. CALVARY BAPTIST CHURCH IN DESBARATS, ONTARIO (SEPTEMBER,1999)

Desbarats, pronounced Debra is north near Sault St. Marie. The congregation had been meeting in a small white building but their congregation under the leadership of Pastor Smith needed a much larger facility which would be in the form of a beautiful L-shaped structure with brick work at the front of the main building. We had a very enthusiastic crew of willing workers. One older man told me at the end of the project that he had worked-out to get in shape for the demands he would face. He said he had difficulty keeping up with the speed at which we worked but said it had been the most meaningful week of his life. We even built a fireplace in the lovely lounge area. I have nineteen great pictures of the Desbarats project in an album which my late wife Bev had created comprised of all our projects across Canada. The whole week was characterized by harmony, joy, great food, hard work, and a spirit of Christian love. By Saturday evening this beautiful church facility was ready for Sunday services and what an honour to share God's Word again in our fourteenth Baptist Builder's Quick Build. A couple of years ago while phoning pastors in Ontario on behalf of Heritage Seminary, I found myself talking to a young pastor in Sudbury. He said, "I know who you are. My dad was the pastor of Desbarats Church when you came in and built us a great new building in one week. I was ten years old and it left an incredible impact on my life and it seemed like a miracle took place in front of my eyes. Now I'm serving the Lord with two other men on staff 'Praise the Lord.'"

15. FELLOWSHIP BAPTIST CHURCH IN COLLINGWOOD, ONTARIO (JUNE 2000)

When it came time to build our largest church model in Collingwood, my son-in-law was in the hospital and for the first time unable to be the project manager. Our advertising was out and volunteers were coming so we couldn't cancel the project. Fortunately, I was told that in the past, there was an experienced builder by the name of Bruce in Collingwood church who was able to stand in the gap and help us. However, we did have a serious accident happen that wouldn't have if Bruce Fitter was on site because of better supervision. We were constructing all the roof trusses on the ground to spread out our workers. I had just rung the bell calling everyone for our noon meal when I heard a loud crash. About ten trusses collapsed with workers on top and two underneath. One man, Harry Wahl, got his leg broken and back injured, and several others had cuts and bruises. The person in charge didn't have enough bracing in place to strengthen the roof trusses. It was a scary time and Harry ended up hospitalized for several days; however, by the end of the week we had the building closed into the place where we were able to have our Sunday service. The outside brick work and some interior painting and finishing was done in the following weeks. A serious situation developed during this project that we had never faced before. A married gal drove all the way from the Maritimes in an R.V. to work on our project. Bev and I first encountered her early Monday morning when we arrived on the site. She was sitting on a lawn chair on the cab of her R.V. and singing. She was tall with dark hair, and very attractive. She came with a tool belt and ready and willing to work. It wasn't long before she started flirting with some of the younger guys and offering to give them back massages. As we were preparing to eat and I had just spoken, she ran up to me in front of everyone and tried to hug and kiss me, but I fought her off in front of everyone. This gal was dressing in shorts and a halter top and I had to get her to dress more appropriately. It was obvious she was there to do more than help build a church. When it came time for the opening service, she came to me and said she would like to sing a solo. I told her our program was planned and refused her offer. Bev and I headed home Sunday afternoon and that evening I received a phone call from Pastor Rob Elkington saying the gal had talked one of their members to take her for a plane ride which he willingly did. When the fellow's wife found out she was livid and the pastor ended up in a counselling session with the gal and the fellow and his wife. Later I had to have a meeting with this gal's pastor and ban her from any future projects. So, as you see these projects can be challenging and one needs the wisdom of Solomon to make wise decisions when Satan endeavours to disrupt God's work.

16. HOME ON SAUGEEN INDIAN RESERVE, ONTARIO (FALL 2000)

There was a poor lady and a member of the Saugeen Baptist Church who I believe gave the church land for building on in 1995. She lived in an old shack of a house so Baptist Builders decided to build her a bungalow as a way of saying 'Thank you' for your generosity and faith in the Lord. It was completed in the fall of 2000 in a week and was a very meaningful and rewarding project.

17. LIVING WATER BAPTIST CHURCH IN SHEET HARBOUR, NOVA SCOTIA (SUMMER 2001)

I was not able to be a part of this project. Bruce Fitter was the project manager of this small model that was greatly needed by the people of Sheet Harbour. He told me the story of prison guards from a nearby prison coming and asking if some of their prisoners could work on the building project. He said they could as long as they were guarded. He told how he was working with one of the prisoners and started witnessing to him; before long he opened his heart to the Lord and came to Jesus Christ. He said they were stuccoing the exterior and by the time he led him to Christ, the product had hardened and it left a gap in the exterior, a reminder that a prisoner worker had lived a sordid life and was separated from God was now united to Him through faith in Jesus Christ. So, another church building was completed in one week, our third in Nova Scotia, thanks to the selflessness of dozens of volunteers; tens of thousands of dollars were saved and the new building made available years earlier because of Baptist Builders Quick Build.

18. WILLOW LAKE BAPTIST CHURCH IN ANZAC, ALBERTA (SEPTEMBER 2001)

It was the week following 9-11 that we were scheduled to build a church on an Indian Reserve in Anzac, Alberta, the second last week of September 2001. There were six of us from Faith Baptist in Huntsville that were flying together on WestJet from Hamilton. We had a lot of power tools and equipment to take with us and it had to be taped shut for security reasons following 9-11. We had a good flight to Edmonton and rented a vehicle to travel several hours towards Fort McMurray and the tar sands. I found out that the pastor of the Anzac Church had been sent as a missionary from Canton Baptist Church in Ohio. which I had visited in the early 1970's. Also, Gerry and Nancy Nadeau, who attended our church in Florida, were members there; so, it seemed we had connections. As we worked on the project, we found our work boots became covered with oily tar which oozed out of the ground, very similar to the tar sands. The former church on the reserve was twenty feet by thirty feet and the new one would be forty feet by sixty feet with two levels. The project proceeded on schedule with about forty volunteers. The six of us from Huntsville booked a cottage on a nearby lake and we enjoyed fun times as well as long hours of labour. By Saturday night we had progressed to where we could hold a worship service on Sunday in the Willow Lake Baptist Church in Anzac. Pastor Art Hoehne's son had helped on the project and he took the six of us to the tar sands site in Fort McMurray where he worked. What a thrill to ride in great electric/turbine powered trucks that carried four hundred tons per load. They were processing over one million barrels a day. We flew home with a new appreciation for the world and gratefulness to God for a safe and successful project.

19. RAYMOND BAPTIST CHURCH IN RAYMOND, ALBERTA (2003)

I especially remember this project for two reasons: the first was that it was located in a strong Mormon region. The Mormons had kept us from purchasing property for several years and had made it difficult to even find a place to rent. After a lot of prayer and perseverance, a property was bought as the church had outgrown a rental facility. The other issue we faced was that Bruce, our project manager, was unable to assist us. Upon arrival I found a great spirit, adequate workers, and a pastor with some construction experience. We ran into a little opposition from the Mormons as newspaper reporters seemed to be Mormons; however, by the end of a busy week a new church building was constructed to the amazement of church members, volunteers, and the Mormons. Before I flew back to Toronto the facility was opened and dedicated to the glory of God and the salvation of souls. A few years later I heard they had outgrown the building and had to expand in the heart of Mormon country.

20. CALEDON HILLS BAPTIST CHURCH IN CALEDON EAST, ONTARIO (SEPTEMBER 2005)

This project would prove to be the largest and most difficult of all our church buildings. Located on about forty acres north of Brampton, and pastored by Bill Henderson, a friend of Bruce Fitter since their teen years. Bruce and Lois had assisted in this church plant and personal friends from Bramalea (Arnold and Elaine Adams and sons) had become key leaders. When we arrived, the ten thousand square foot concrete basement was in place. Our goal was to construct a ten thousand square foot superstructure in two weeks with a smaller work crew than usual, since we had a project in Lake Echo, Nova Scotia, for which we were responsible at the same time. So, our volunteers were split between these church builds. We had to construct ten separate sections for the roof on the ground and then lift them with a massive crane. Each section weighed many tons and required exacting work to build. A couple of the sections weighed over ten thousand pounds which the crane had difficulty lifting into place. When the final section was "boomed" into position, it would not fit down into place. I went up to the southwest corner of the building, twenty feet above the ground; Bruce

Caledon Hills Baptist Church - 2005

directed us to chainsaw which I pulled up with a rope and cut the corner of the roof structure that was stopping the section from fitting into place. Having used chainsaws since I was a teenager I did, the necessary 'surgery' and the final piece of the puzzle fit perfectly. When I was speaking at the opening of the church, I said I didn't know if the architect who designed the building was present and had to confess, I had done a little "chainsaw surgery" on his design. When this very demanding project was closed in, it made a very spacious and beautiful place of worship and ministry. Bricklayers were hired after we had completed the framing of the structure and were doing the drywall, electrical, and plumbing. There were a lot of weary workers at the end of two weeks (including yours truly) but this major challenge had been conquered. Our volunteers had worked hard and harmoniously and they included my wife Bev. A beautiful card was given to Bev and me from the pastor, elders, and deacons. Inside they wrote, "Thank you for your inspiring and edifying devotionals, your resolve and workmanship, your fellowship in the kitchen, and the contagious love of God that both of you shared with our church family." Such words of appreciation to us and the other volunteers made the cuts, bruises, and tired bodies a distant memory compared to the "labour of love" of which the Lord had allowed us to be a part.

21. LAKE ECHO FELLOWSHIP BAPTIST CHURCH IN LAKE ECHO, NOVA SCOTIA (SEPTEMBER 2005)

The same time we were building in Caledon East, a team of our volunteers went to another church in Lake Echo, Nova Scotia, to build an addition on their facility. The workers were from Ontario and the Maritimes — a small crew because of the large Caledon East project. The work went well without any serious incidents along with typical Maritime hospitality and lots of lobster and fish so that everyone was well cared for.

22. SANNICH BAPTIST CHURCH IN SAANICHTON, BRITISH COLUMBIA (MAY 2008)

This project was unique in a couple of ways. The church was founded in the 1880's about ten miles north of Victoria, near Butchart Gardens. The heritage building was donated to the heritage society and the congregation purchased two acres. With the cost of servicing, it totalled half a million dollars. Also, it was located in an earthquake zone which required us to do all nailing by hand and three inches apart instead of the usual six inches apart. We had to put on over one hundred Johnson brackets on all the walls at the bottom of all partitions. Bev and I flew in and worked on the project for two weeks along with about twenty-five volunteers. Progress was slow and tedious because of a municipal ban on the use of nail guns. Bev and I stayed with a retired pastor and his wife and enjoyed good fellowship. By the time we left for home the structure was being closed in but weeks from completion. Eventually the facility was completed and opened to be used by this growing congregation. We were able to tour Butchart Gardens before flying home to Toronto. This was the last project that Bev and I worked on together. We had both been retired for twelve years so were thankful for the extra years God gave us to be together and serve Him.

23. MADOC BAPTIST CHURCH IN
MADOC, ONTARIO (JUNE–JULY 2017)

I received a phone call from Pastor Harry Toews at Madoc asking me if I would help plan and promote a Quick Build for them. He had been the pastor at Faithway in Woodstock in 1996 when we built for them. I was a little hesitant at first at age eighty-two regarding whether I should accept the challenge or not. After Bev and I visited their building site on a return trip from Arnprior after visiting her brother Keith, I felt I should try and assist them. It was almost ten years since our last project and we didn't have secretaries and Fellowship office to advertise so we had to pick forty to fifty Fellowship Churches within a sixty-mile radius and try to find volunteers to assist. Fortunately, there were several capable contractors in the Madoc Church and, with planning help from Claire Miller (age ninety) we began this major project. Once the slab on grade concrete was poured and a thousand square foot basement completed, the forty-five foot by eighty-foot facility was ready to be tackled. We started with between forty and fifty workers and a lot of energy. The walls were constructed and erected in about two days. The large roof structure made up of large trusses was prepared beside the concrete floor; it took a week to get the roof structure finished and boomed into place using a large crane. Each day I spoke to the workers prior to eating great meals provided by the ladies and local stores. I had to leave after one week but was able to return for three days, a couple of weeks later, to help finish the dry walling in the main auditorium. The entire project took several weeks because of a lack of workers; however, the finished project was beautiful with a steel roof and lovely siding. The congregation is growing steadily and the Town of Madoc is being impacted by the gospel and witness of a vibrant congregation.

18

Vacation Trips Abroad

Cancun — Bev's 50th Birthday (1991–92)

I surprised Bev on her birthday with plane tickets to Cancun. We had a great time touring Inca ruins one day. Also, great swimming and beaches accompanied by some nudity from Europeans, to which we weren't accustomed. The natural scenery was beautiful and the food was delicious. It gave us time to relax, reminisce, and renew our relationship away from people and the pressures of work, family, and ministry responsibilities.

Arizona — with Pat and Mac Campbell

On two occasions we spent March break with our close friends from our church. Dean Brown at the seminary said we shouldn't have close friends at our church, but we found it both physically and spiritually beneficial to do this. Mac and I played golf, and all of us played tennis. We enjoyed fun and fellowship with people of similar age and interests. Our friendship with the Campbells continues to this day, having just returned from visiting them in Kelowna, B.C.

Arizona — to Shuttleworth's (1994)

Our friends George and Joan Shuttleworth retired to Arizona in the early 1990's. He had been the minister of music at High Park Baptist in Toronto and also with Don Holiday in evangelistic work. We spent a wonderful week in March at their lovely home in Pecos Ranch, in Chandler near Phoenix. We climbed mountains together, hiked, swam, and ran. Both he and I were into marathoning. We at-

Bev's 50th Birthday Cancun - 1991

tended a Baptist church where George was on staff as well as looking at homes as they were encouraging us to retire to Arizona. We decided it was too far from Ontario and later chose to buy in Florida where our girls and families could join us and travel by car.

BOAT CRUISES WE ENJOYED

Bahamas — Our first cruise was a surprise I planned when Bev had flown home from Florida for the birth of a grandchild. When she returned, I told her it was a Valentine's trip. We went to Fort Lauderdale and ate a scrumptious breakfast, then headed out even though there were strong winds. As a result, everyone got seasick and, for the first time in fifty years, I vomited. I didn't see Bev for a couple of hours as she was lying on a bench in the middle of the boat where there was less rock and roll. It took us eight hours to reach the Bahamas and we could stay only a couple of hours before heading for home. To make matters worse it turned out to be a "Gambling Boat" which was why the cruise cost less. We were finally able to enjoy a meal on board before we landed in Fort Lauderdale. I remarked to Bev as we drove home that this was two cruises for the price of one … "Our first and our last." My surprise treat for Bev did not turn out as I had hoped but we had some good laughs and lifelong memories.

Alaska (September 2000) — This was the year of our fortieth Wedding Anniversary, so we took three weeks and first flew to Vancouver where we and visited our friends, Gerry and Nancy Kraft. We borrowed Nancy's car and drove to Kelowna for the wedding of Laurie Campbell, Mac and Pat's daughter. Upon return to Vancouver we set sail on the Sun Princess for a seven-day cruise up the inter-coastal, stopping at Ketchikan, Juneau, the capital of Alaska. We enjoyed sightseeing, shopping, then took a helicopter ride and saw black bears; landing on a big glacier, the pilot turned out to be a pastor's son (and a Christian). We continued cruising north to Skagway and toured old buildings, travelling by train to White Pass where we saw the "gold rush" trail of 1898 which led to the Alaska/Yukon border; there we noticed old grave markers where hundreds of miners had perished in their pursuit of gold. From the ship we viewed mammoth glaciers — some up to sixteen miles long and two miles wide, with a thickness of eight hundred feet. We watched 'calving' the breaking off of large pieces of ice making big splashes. Since it was the year of the Olympics, they, had ping pong tournaments, and Bev and I competed against younger couples. We won the gold medal in the mixed doubles, Bev won the silver in ladies singles, and I won gold in the men's singles. When our cruise ended, a bus took us to Anchorage where we rented a car and headed north to Fairbanks. We panned for gold in an abandoned mine and had mine mounted in a necklace for Bev. We saw beautiful scenery including Mount McKinley which is twenty thousand feet high. We also saw wildlife including, moose, mountain goats, and grizzly bears. We returned to the lovely City of Anchorage for site seeing before flying to Vancouver and then home. It was a wonderful vacation as we enjoyed seeing God's glorious creation and spending quality time together after forty years of marriage and a lot of busy years of ministry.

Caribbean Cruise (November 2005) — Bruce and Lois surprised us by planning a Caribbean cruise for Bev and me, and our three daughters and their husbands. This was partially triggered by Bev's triple bypass surgery in 2003 and also for our forty-fifth wedding anniversary. We were already in Florida and met the other six family members at Fort Lauderdale to cruise on the Royal Caribbean ship called "Voyager of the Seas". We had a lot of fun and fellowship. The only negative note was when I went to dress up for the "Captain's Dinner" I had forgotten my suit, shirt, tie, etc. I had laid them out on the bedroom floor so I wouldn't forget them. Dear Bev, hung them up in our closet so they wouldn't be wrinkled and we both forgot them. You can figure out who was at fault. Bruce came to the rescue and rented a tuxedo, much better than I've ever worn so that "all things worked out together for good". Romans 8:28

Florida Keys and Bahamas (2006) — Three of our closest friends/couples in

Stu' & Bev at Mt. McKinley - 2000

Florida from our church decided to take a trip to the Florida Keys and Bahamas; this included John and Roseanne Fenwick, Gene and Pam Hensley, and Stan and Pat Lehman. We travelled to Fort Lauderdale by limousine and then began our cruise to the Keys. The Keys are the most southerly part of the United States and come within ninety miles of Cuba. There are historical homes and stores, and many noted writers and artists. Our cruise ship took us to the Bahamas with all its beauty where we enjoyed touring, shopping, and eating. There were magnificent hotels to see and beautiful homes to admire. These are idyllic islands and it would be easy to want to retire to this lovely oasis that God created and that man and money have developed. We returned to Florida and eventually to our home with many memories and gratefulness to God for the health and resources to travel.

FISHING TRIP TO BRITISH COLUMBIA IN JUNE 2001

My good friend Gerry Kraft who was the President of Outreach Canada, a mission that assisted churches and denominations in strategic and long-range planning, invited me on a fundraising fishing trip. It was to be held in the Queen Charlotte Islands at St. John's Fishing Lodge, which was located on a retro-fitted ferry. The cost was three thousand five hundred dollars plus airfare, and I had trouble spending that much money for five days. Gerry had a close friend from the U.S. who had just sold a computer company and purchased a sixty-three-foot yacht. His name was Chuck Ramey and I had met him in Florida at a boat show. He told Gerry he wanted me to come and paid the three thousand five hundred dollars and so I flew out (on Air Mile points). Approximately 40 Christian businessmen from Canada and the United States registered and we flew in a large plane up the B.C. coast. Then we had to transfer to small planes that had pontoons on the wings. These planes had been used to rescue downed air men in the Second World War. About eight of us fit in to a plane and we flew to the lodge and then landed on the belly fuselage of the plane in the water and it felt like we were going to go under.

We had an evening of great fellowship, singing, and a challenge from God's Word. We all slept on the floating Lodge and in the morning about twenty-five fishing boats with Honda motors were lined up with rods and bait etc. Everything was first-class and two of us went in each boat, which were equipped with "fish finders". Not being an experienced fisherman, and not overly patient, I wasn't very optimistic about the outcome. However, it wasn't very long before I had a large Chinook salmon on my line. There was no braking system on the

Gerry Kraft giving Stu Briefcase - 1993

38lb. Chinook Salmon - June 2001 B.C.

reel and you had to use the palm of your hand to control the line. After forty minutes of trying to play the large fish out and not to mention myself, I landed a thirty-eight-pound Chinook, which turned out to be the largest of the day for all of us. The following day, Benjamin Loch, an American, caught a forty-pound fish. By nature, I'm competitive so I asked a professional guide if he would go out with me and try to land a bigger one. He agreed and took me to a nearby island by boat where he knew there was a large one that nobody could land. Twice we caught this monster Chinook salmon, estimated to be sixty to sixty-five pounds, but both times it broke loose and we returned empty handed. Once back at the lodge, they had facilities and people to clean, package, and freeze each person's catches. I ended with over one hundred pounds of frozen fish, the most of any person and the two large boxes were shipped on Air Canada back to our home in Huntsville. I greatly enjoyed the fun and fellowship as well as the fresh fish Bev and I and family enjoyed for several months. In my den I have a beautiful duplicate of the thirty-eight-pound Chinook salmon and plaque as a reminder of this once in a lifetime experience.

19

The Ministry of Marriage and Weddings and More Weddings

Following my ordination in 1967 I was issued a licence by the Ontario Government which permitted me to perform marriages. My first wedding was in Toronto and it was bilingual. Pastor George McAlphine of Oakwood Baptist Church did the French part and I did the English. Everything went well as we alternated between the two languages until it came time to kiss the bride. I did the English but Pastor McAlphine couldn't remember how to say "The groom may now kiss the bride" in French. After sputtering around he finally said, "Just do it." in English.

My first wedding at Bramalea Baptist Church was May 23, 1970, when I married Sam Reynolds and Doris Archambault, and I was assisted by Pastor E.C. Wood. It was Sam's second marriage and he became one of our deacons and both served faithfully for years before moving up to Muskoka. Later I had the privilege of taking Sam's funeral at Faith Baptist Church in Huntsville. Don Reynolds (Sam's son) and his wife Trudy are our friends and live at M.B.C.

Bev prepared over thirty albums of pictures covering many facets of our life and ministry. She did one entitled, "Church Weddings". It has pictures, dates and pertinent information on one hundred and fifty weddings I performed at Bramalea. However, the three most memorable were when I married our three daughters, Lois, Dale, and Faye. I had never thought that one day when our little girls grew up, they might want me to do the honours. They all met and married

Wedding of Lois & Bruce - 1982

fellows from our church.

Lois our oldest gal married Bruce Fitter on September 25th, 1982. I do remember saying if Dale was ready to get married, we could do the two together for the same price or make sure they spaced them out two or three years. I did say on one occasion — regarding the cost of weddings and after paying for everything — about the only thing I had left to give away was our daughter. We had two receptions, one for everyone who attended, which were hundreds and then the invited guests at the Holiday Inn. I brought Lois to the church in my 1933 Ford Coupe at her request and it was a memorable experience for her dad and pastor.

Dale married Todd Heywood on May 3rd, 1986, in a lovely ceremony with many family members and friends in attendance. The reception was held at the

Royal York in Toronto which she had requested, which provided a lovely setting for celebration and pictures. What I remember the most was my driving Bev and myself home about 1:00 a.m. in my 1985 Chrysler: the car was still decorated with streamers and I was going up Highway 10 just north of Brampton, heading home to Cheltenham when I came to a light just as it was turning red and kept going. I was really tired and Bev and her mom were asleep. I kept going, fighting sleep myself and maybe weaving a little when suddenly a police car turned its flashers on and pulled me over. Immediately I reached for my driver's licence and insurance slip and hoped it said "Pastor Silvester" on it, but it didn't. The OPP officer asked for my licence and he said, "Pastor Silvester, you haven't signed your licence and that's a criminal offence. Have you been drinking because you were weaving some and at that red light, you should have stopped — Pastor Silvester?"

Wedding of Dale & Todd - 1984

I finally said, "I don't know who you are but evidently you know my name." He started to laugh and said, "You were speaking at your brother Alan's induction service at Bethel Baptist in Fergus last week and when I pulled you over, I recognized you and thought I'd have a little fun. You better get home and get some sleep." No ticket, just some laughs at my expense — but there is a sequel to this story for about six years later I was working at head office in Guelph and took several youth pastors our for lunch and, as we waited for our food we all told stories of being stopped by the police. I shared this story and everyone laughed. When we went outside this tall Dutch fellow pulled me aside and said, "I was the OPP office who stopped you back in 1986." He had left the police force and gone into the ministry. I said, "Why didn't you say something at the restaurant?" He answered, "I didn't want to embarrass you." — a thoughtful person and pastor but he wasn't quite as kind as a police officer.

Faye, our youngest, married Ken McKenzie on August 19th, 1989. It was a beautiful service with lots of people, flowers, love, and pictures taken. The reception was held at the King Edward Hotel in Toronto. There is an aside connected to this wedding as well. Prior to the wedding I was to meet Bev and Ken's parents at the King Edward to make sure it was suitable. That afternoon I was making hospital calls at the Toronto General Hospital and had parked on Bloor Street. As I got in my car and headed east looking for a parking place since I had more calls to make, I spotted a parking place on the north side of Bloor, put on my blinker, and made a left turn and suddenly I was hit broad side by a TTC Street Car which blew out my side windows and did significant damage. I had thought I was on the inside lane but I wasn't. They had been shooting a movie and had all the cars removed on my right side and so I thought I was over on the left lane. It was right at rush hour about 5:00 p.m. and the streetcar driver tried to stop but slid on the wet tracks. By the time the police arrived there were about ten street cars backed up. Fortunately, there were no charges laid so I hung a blanket over the broken windows and drove to the King Edward. I actually arrived on time but didn't say anything about the accident. We had a lovely dinner and approved of the hotel then I offered to pick up the tab. Mr. McKenzie said, "I'll get this one, you can get the next one." Thanks, and I paid thousands for the wedding reception.

I had a lot of interesting wedding experiences. I said once to Bev following a wedding rehearsal which had twenty attendees and everyone with a different idea regarding where to stand, "I find funerals less pressure than weddings since no one is trying to tell you what and how to do it."

At one wedding when the ceremony was over, the flower girl wouldn't move off the platform; the reason was she had wet and didn't want us to see the pud-

Wedding of Faye & Ken - 1989

dle under her long dress. Another time in the middle of the ceremony the ring bearer sat down and started taking of his new black shoes which were hurting his feet.

MARRYING SEVEN GRANDCHILDREN

The first of our grandchildren to be married was Katelyn Fitter to Rob Niemi, whom she met at Liberty University. The ceremony was on August 11th, 2007, at Bruce and Lois's lovely home on Fairy Lake. It was very hot as I stood on a rock beside the lake. The reception was at Bigwin Island and everyone enjoyed the great facilities, food, and fellowship.

The second of our ten grandchildren, Jonathan Fitter married Summer Neff, whom he met at Liberty University. I performed the wedding on August 30th, 2008, in a Baptist Church south of Lynchburg, followed by a fun reception.

The third was Amanda Heywood to Peter Simpson on July 14th, 2012, at a beautiful golf course setting north of Toronto. Amanda and Peter used my Ford Thunderbird for pictures and for a great time of love and celebration.

The fourth was Megan Fitter to Danny Barnett on July 6th, 2013, at the Norway Point Community Church on Lake of Bays. Megan arrived in a Rolls Royce driven by her dad. It was a very hot day and one groomsman fainted. Following the service, I was approached by two church elders who liked my biblical devotional and as a result I've been asked to preach twice a year ever since.

The fifth wedding was Gregory Heywood and Alyssa Oliver on June 24th, 2016, in a lovely outdoor service near Ajax, followed by a reception at the golf course banquet hall.

The sixth wedding was Brendan Fitter to Tessa Harrower on February 4th, 2017, at Deerhurst Resort in Huntsville. It was a cold weekend and I did the official marriage on Friday evening; the large celebration was on Saturday with many guests. The hall was decorated with pine trees and it was a time of tears of joy.

The seventh was Laura Heywood to Brandon Crump, held just north of Toronto on August 18th, 2017. The wedding and reception were held outside on an idyllic setting at the Crump's family home/ranch and everyone enjoyed tasty food, speeches, and dancing.

What a privilege to be asked to perform our grandchildren's weddings. There are still three more grandchildren (Faye and Ken's) but they are younger and all going to university or college so their weddings may be at a time when I'm out of circulation or too old.

FUNERALS CONDUCTED

Over my fifty years of ministry I have conducted scores of funerals. I will include some of the most memorable and meaningful ones.

1. My first one was at Forward Baptist in Toronto in 1965 —that of a baby. It was very difficult and I used the text from Matthew 18:1-3, "And Jesus called all the little ones to Himself," except you be converted and become as little children you shall not enter the kingdom of heaven. Jesus was Creator (He made them), He loved them (Friend), He died for them (Saviour).
2. Grandpa Hamilton, my mother's father died at age ninety-three. I led him to the Lord in Milton a few months before his death. My brother, Alan, and I took his funeral in Orangeville and I was thankful he had trusted Christ when he did.
3. I ministered at Bramalea Baptist for several years before I experienced a

death and funeral. I remember speaking on "Immortality" one Sunday morning and saying, "We hadn't had a funeral yet". I said, "When we promise them eternal life, we really mean it." On the way home from church, Bev said to me "Maybe you shouldn't have said that". Guess what happened? The next day, Mrs. Hammond, an elderly member died. I remember saying, "If I hadn't said that when I did, then I could never have said it."

4. In November 1978, Paul Mitchell was killed in a car accident, which also resulted in the death of two other teens. Parents Ken and Mae had just become Christians in late October. I remember going to the morgue at Peel Memorial Hospital with Ken and the other girls' father. The mortician took one father at a time to identify their sons and I accompanied them. The first dad identified his son but when Ken was asked, he said it wasn't Paul, his son. The mortician covered his son and then waited. Ken and I looked again and finally, through many tears, Ken recognized the mangled body of his son Paul. This funeral with three young people dying was very difficult and heart-wrenching.

5. On October 4 1988, I conducted the funeral for eighteen-year-old Tara Myles who was killed in a car accident. She was one of our vibrant young people. Tara's parents, Barb and Henry, didn't want the service to be sorrowful but a celebration. Tara's favourite verse was "This is the day that the Lord hath made; we will rejoice and be glad in it". The service and her life had a great impact on scores of young people's lives.

6. My brother Alan and I conducted my father's funeral on September 16, 2003, at Temple Baptist Church in Sarnia. He was in his ninety-ninth year and had lived a full and fruitful life. In my eulogy I talked of seven dimensions in Dad's life.

a. *Careers* — Included wheat farmer; foreman; dairy farmer; sawmill business; real estate agent for twenty-five years in Sarnia.

b. *Sports* — Track and field, baseball, soccer, hockey, and boxing.

c. *Creative* — Wind charger to lighthouse in Saskatchewan; designed sawdust burner to heat our house.

d. *Hobbies* — Oil painting; woodworking (fourteen grandmother clocks); hunting, and fishing.

e. *Musically* — Violin, accordion, singing with Mom, and organ playing.

f. *Personality* — Outgoing, caring, letter writing (over one hundred letters to editors), generous, strong conviction and handshake.

g. *Faith* — Sunday School Superintendent, and Pastor's friend.

7. Ed Montangue was a member of our church in Florida. While having his

teeth cleaned by the dentist, he inhaled a crown off his tooth into his lung and within two weeks he died from infection. Several hundred attended the funeral of this fine Christian man and father of Pam Hensley, our close friend. Ed's wife, Kaye, received a large financial payment as a result of his death which enabled her to move into Harbour Place, a beautiful high-end retirement centre. Then because of her life and influence, we were given a large conference room where we were able to hold our worship services — an amazing provision of God. (Romans 8:28.)

8. Our great grandson, Koa Fitter, was born prematurely and died after only a few hours. Seeing Jonathan and Summer carrying the little casket into the funeral service was heartbreaking. This was the hardest funeral I have ever conducted. I thank the Lord; he has blessed Jonathan and Summer with two daughters and two sons. Bev and I were at the hospital all night waiting for the helicopter from Sick Children's Hospital to arrive. However, it was too foggy and they had to relay the equipment on three ambulances, but by then it was too late. I had to preach at Riverside Baptist in the morning with no sleep and my topic was "God's Remedy for Damaged Emotions". One of my points was "Let God Relieve my Grief" and my text was II Samuel 12 where David and Bathsheba's baby had died. How ironic was this?

20

The Retirement and Moving to Huntsville 1995–1996

In the fall of 1995, Bev and I prepared for retirement following very busy and blessed lives of teaching and preaching. After twenty-two years of being a teacher/librarian, Bev retired in October of 1995. She was given a wonderful send-off with speeches and gifts with friends and family present. She gave a great speech of which I was proud and I realized maybe she should have been the preacher. The staff gave her a lovely cabinet which she used as a 'pulpit' for her speech.

My retirement took place in November in Vancouver at our National Fellowship Convention. Lovely gifts were presented and I was toasted/roasted by my friend Gerry Kraft who had travelled with me doing seminars across Canada. He told about the time where I was driving the rental car and I suddenly stopped right on a busy highway. He said, "Why did you stop?" I said, "For the red light." There was no red light, but maybe I had seen red because my eyes were almost shut from lack of sleep. Gerry and his wife Susie, along with Bev and I following retirement spent a weeks' vacation on the Oregon Coast in a small cottage right on the Pacific Ocean giving way to wonderful memories of God's goodness and many undeserved blessings. Susie was suffering with cancer and died shortly after this then Gerry flew to Ontario to visit us during his time of loss and sorrow.

We sold our lovely home on seven and a half acres on the Credit River in

Bev's Retirement - Oct 1995

Cheltenham after one and half years on the market. We had purchased a home in Stonegate in Brampton earlier but never moved into it. We had it rented until we sold it just before moving to Huntsville. We had to leave our Cheltenham home and needed a place to live for several months. In September we lived with Dale and Todd in Ballinafad, and Bev drove to Bolton to work and I drove to Guelph. Then Bruce and Lois moved to Huntsville and asked if we would move into their home in Caledon Hills for a month since it was sold and available for October, so that's what we did. We were like gypsies living in five different places in 1995: this included Cheltenham, our cottage (July and August), Ballinafad, Caledon Hills, and our cottage (November and December) before heading to Arizona for the winter.

While at our cottage it snowed constantly and fortunately, I had a tractor with a snowblower. We skied some and kept warm with our fireplace and wood stove. In early January we headed to Arizona for three months in the sun and

My Retirement - Vancouver 1995

travelled through twenty-two states in total. In Virginia we stayed with Ted and Marg Barton, (Ted had been my Greek professor at CBS.) then on to Charleston South Carolina and visited with Steven and Melissa Silvester, our nephew and his family. We toured historical areas of Charleston and Myrtle Beach then on to Florida and saw Mrs. Fitter at Nettle's Island. Travelling to Boca Raton, we visited Dick Fraser, a former church member at Bramalea who was dying, and saw his wife Marilyn before we headed across alligator alley in Florida; north to Pensacola and Tallahassee, and into Alabama and to New Orleans and the French Quarter. Eventually we arrived in Texas at San Antonio and saw the Alamo. After eight hundred and fifty miles in Texas and El Paso, we arrived in Tucson, Arizona. We stayed at a motel and I was training for a marathon and went running about 6a.m. I got lost and into a dangerous area and a garage owner told me to get out ASAP. I flagged down a police car and I told the woman police officer I was lost. Fortunately, she was a runner and had just run the Tucson Marathon so was sympathetic. She was on her way to speak at a school, but said she'd take me to my motel. I didn't know its name or location since we had arrived at night and I'd left running in the dark. We drove up and down the highway and eventually I spotted our car. She had to phone the school to say she would be late because she was trying to help a lost Canadian runner. Bev was sure relieved to see me and I was happy to have survived the ordeal.

We arrived at Whispering Winds Motel on Apache Road in Tempe and stayed for two weeks. We spent time with our friends, Joan and George Shuttleworth, who lived at Pecos Ranch west of Phoenix, saw the Rose Bowl Parade, and went to a colosseum and heard noted football coach, Tom Landry, before we climbed a mountain. Then we went to Sun City and to Youngstown, to see our rental house which the Lord provided for only two hundred dollars for three months. I was taking part in a convention north of Calgary and was asked if I'd drive Dr. Don Launstein, (the convention speaker and friend) to the Calgary airport. He asked me what I was doing when I retired the next month. I told him we were going to Arizona and he asked if we had accommodations. I said no and he said his mother had died recently and left him a home. He wanted Bev and I to use it for $200 to cover the cost of utilities. It had lots of fruit trees and was a great provision from the Lord. We had a lot of time playing tennis, golfing and I ran a marathon. We attended several great churches and were physically and spiritually renewed. Faye and Ken (our youngest daughter and husband) flew in for a visit and we took a trip to Los Vegas, Sedona, and the Grand Canyon and toured the Hoover Dam.

Mary and Murray Pipe visited us and we went to the Boothill Cemetery. Our friends Mac and Pat Campbell from Bramalea days came to visit as well. We went to the Grand Canyon, which was spectacular to see, and we also went to Palm Springs California, to visit my cousin Roy Morden, a musician. We headed home through New Mexico and saw a petrified forest. On our way through Oklahoma, we visited the site of the Oklahoma bombing. While touring the memorial site we say Johnny Cochran and his bodyguards of O.J. Simpson fame. We were told he was considering suing the fertilizer company that sold fertilizer to the bomber which resulted in many deaths and great destruction.

We arrived home the end of March, safe and sound, and grateful to God for His protection, having travelled twenty thousand kilometers. Now we had to move our furniture into our new home on Bayshore Boulevard in Huntsville. Our furniture was stored in a home we had purchased several years earlier but never moved into. We had it rented and they allowed us to store our furniture for six months in the basement. The home sold two days before moving to Huntsville. Perfect timing. We rented a thirty-foot truck and, with some help,

Stu & Johnny Cochrane - Oklahoma City - 1996

loaded our earthly possessions into it. We headed north on April 1st (April Fool's Day) with Bev following me in our car. When we arrived, the snow was gone and there was only Bev and I to unload that packed full truck. Fortunately, our next-door neighbour, Ted, saw our dilemma and came to our rescue. This was the start of twenty-two eventful years living on the water in the Muskoka's. Our home had been custom built eight years earlier and with three thousand square feet we had lots of room to roam and to entertain our growing family as well as a growing number of friends. Bev loved to entertain and so we were never lonely and enjoyed many trips in our boat.

On two occasions we entertained all our tennis friends with a picnic/barbeque with lots of fellowship, food, and games. We were also blessed in having numerous Bible studies and some games nights with our 'Small Group' which grew to thirteen couples.

MEMORIES OF LIFE AT 500 BAYHORE BLVD., HUNTSVILLE (FROM BEV)

We so enjoyed the many birds we saw while there. The chickadees, goldfinches, blue jays, bluebirds enjoyed the feeders while the mourning doves, and juncos picked the seeds from the ground. The chickadees would feed out of our hands.

Huntsville Home - Autumn 1995

The colourful flickers were often looking for insects on our lawn. The wood-peckers found the seeds on occasion as well. The water attracted the loons, the kingfisher, and the large blue herons, as well as several kinds of ducks —the mallards, mergansers, and a few I couldn't name including a black bird with a large white circle on each side of its face.

Many mammals visited over the years. Deer regularly ate our plants in the front and backyards but were always a joy to see. On our walks we often saw deer and fox but my most memorable time was seeing a large buck on the side of the road up on a grade, just three doors down the way, with his rack looking so stately. He was huge. One day a bear was standing in the turnaround of the driveway. What a surprise that was when I went out to water the plants.

One evening our dog Misty's growl woke us up as there was noise in the kitchen. Two raccoons had torn the screen of the open window and were helping themselves to the dog food; they had opened the bread drawer, but the sliding lid was still on. It was a challenge for Stu to get these visitors out the door. From then on, we never left the kitchen (floor) window open. Sometimes we watched raccoons on the opposite shore with our binoculars.

Beaver chopped down the willow at the water's edge, but we did not see them. I think they also cut down the birch at the water. Otters would run across the dock on occasion. Groundhogs were seen on our deck stairs. A fellow who was living at our place for a time met a moose on his walk just down the way, but we never saw one. Chipmunks and squirrels were abundant, and we enjoyed the tameness of the chipmunks as we fed them.

The sunsets were to die for. We never got tired of watching their variety of colours and hues. Seeing the movement of the sun from north west to west from spring to fall was interesting. Watching the weather when on the lake is wonderful; the winds portrayed in the waves; the rain coming across the lake; the formation of the ice and its melting with many large ice flows floating by and the crashing into the docks on the way; the many trees and logs that were caught up in the spring runoff going by all made life interesting. One winter we had a beautiful swan come up on the ice and snow-covered lawn, and we fed it with gloves on. It was banded and beautiful.

Most of the time the waterfront was beautifully quiet. In the winter there were very few snowmobiles because the gas line running under the water prevented a good hard freeze. However, in the summer especially on weekends there was much activity on the water. Yes, sometimes it was rather noisy and we added to that with our boat as well. It was interesting watching the wide variety of boats, canoes, sailboats, paddleboats, kayaks, and sailboards. Sometimes there were long distance swimmers, boat races, people in trouble, and even float planes landing and taking off. Lois said when we first bought the house that this would be our entertainment in our old age and it was.

Our lot hosted many trees. The huge pines were predominant and gave us many needles to rake up before the deciduous leaves dropped. We had them thinned out in 2015 to let more sun in and open the driveway up. There were three lovely cedars at the road for a long time but one winter when we got home from Florida, they looked really strange as they were bare from above the snow-banks to as far as the deer could reach from the snow piles. They were rather deformed and had to be removed as the needles do not grow back quickly, if at all. However, right behind them were birch trees which now could be shown off, so we just enlarged the garden at the road, and it looked presentable. There was one unusual tree, an olive, on the front lawn; it never produced fruit, but we kept it because it had biblical 'roots'. There was a sugar maple that we planted near the road that was beautifully red in the fall and a huge oak that produced many acorns each year, making happy squirrels and chipmunks. We planted an apple tree, but the birds seemed to get the apples before we did. However, the last two years we were able to collect fifty to seventy-five apples. Near the water there were four white birch, but the beaver destroyed them, so we replaced them with a red maple. In our early years we planted four small spruce, two blue and two green and they grew into beautiful large trees at each corner by the lake. The willow that the beavers cut down grew back and we covered the trunk with fencing. I guess it will be bound into the trunk as it grows; it gave us lovely privacy while sitting on the dock.

There were ten garden areas to maintain. At the road there were numerous perennials and shrubs. Along the side of the driveway we planted a maple and, as it produced more shade, we put ferns. On the right-hand side of the garage there were hostas and hydrangeas while in front of the house there were many bushes and flowers: including hydrangea, blue thistle, turtleheads, and phlox. On the waterside were three areas with bushes, perennials, and two miniature spruce. Near the water for a time, we had another garden, but later put it back to grass. Somewhere under some pines in the backyard near the water, little Misty is buried.

ADDITIONAL HIGHLIGHTS FROM
500 BAYSHORE BLVD., HUNTSVILLE

In the spring of 2016, Bev encouraged me to consider selling our home on the lake. She said you are getting older, and we've both had cancer and maybe it's time to down-size. With her gift of discernment I believe God led her to this conclusion. We listed our home in June of 2016 and in early July purchased a home in Huntsville with a fall closing. We had over thirty showings but no offers. We were doing a lot of praying and then on September 29, 2016 we had a call from a realator named John Fincham. When he came to our door, he asked if I knew a Stu Silvester. I led him along and asked what he knew about him? He said when he was ten this Stu had given him a ride in his 1966 Mustang convertible in Burks Falls, and he'd never forgotten it. I told him I was Stu but I had sold the Mustang. We knew his parents who were Christians. God used him to sell our home within two hours that day; a big return after investing a few minutes in a ten year old boy's life!

When we moved into our home at 23 Kendra Cresent in Huntsville that fall, we had the kitchen up-dated and a stone fireplace built in the great room. Bev enjoyed the lovely gardens. We looked forward to spending years together, but it was not to be. Within a year her cancer returned, and we had to have Pallative care nurses come assisted by our daughters. On June 1, 2018 we called the ambulance to take her to Grace Hospice in Huntsville. When Bev was carried out of our home for the last time it was a sunny day. As she lay on the stretcher before being placed in the ambulance, she said she could sun-bathe. This was Bev, my amazing wife; always positive and never complaining, and exhibiting the fruit of the Holy Spirit, Galatians 2:22-23.

Before Bev died, she made a list of the following things that were special to her/us on Lake Vernon.

1. BIRDS – They included Chickadees, Gold Finches, Morning Doves, Mallard and Merganser ducks, Loons, Woodpeckers, Blue Herons, and Kingfishers, not to mention Robins, Crows, and Sparrows etc.
2. ANIMALS – We saw a moose, black bear, deer, raccoons, skunks, otters, groundhogs, beavers, rabbits, squirrels, and chipmunks.
3. TREES – These included Oak, Maple, Red Maple, Blue Spruce, regular Spruce, White Birch, Olive Tree, Cedar, several kinds of Pine trees, and an apple tree.
4. SKY – On clear nights saw shooting stars, big and little dipper, bright scarlet sky and beautiful sunsets.
5. BERRIES – Stu primarily picked the many raspberries and black berries that grew on or near our property. I made pies, jam and jellies from them.
6. GARDENS – We both loved flowers and bushes and had ten flower beds which produced beautiful blossoms and beautified our lovely property.
7. BOAT MEMORIES – One night when Stu was away on a trip, someone tried to start and steal our Dural motorboat and I heard the noise and turned on a light and called out and they took off in their boat. We saw and heard numerous boats with big noisy motors, and small quiet ones as well as canoes, kayaks, paddle boats, airplanes with pontoons, and fisherman and swimmers in races etc.
8. IMPROVEMENTS —We installed a lovely 40-foot aluminum and wood dock for our two boats. In addition, we built a sunroom facing the water in 2006 which was greatly enjoyed. We also installed a central air conditioner, new gas furnace, water purification systems, and electrical line into the lake.
9. EXERCISE – Stu and I ran and walked the 2.2-mile loop starting down Bayshore Boulevard, south on Airport Road (Float Planes) and east to Lakewood and home hundreds of times. I also walked it numerous times with Lori Brown from our church enjoying great talks and fellowship.

21
Interim Church Pastorates 1996–2010

TEMPLE, SARNIA

In 1996 after returning from three months in Arizona, our first interim pastorate occurred. I received a call from Temple Baptist in Sarnia to see if I'd be willing to become their interim pastor, following the ministry of Warren Kimball. It was to be for six months — a long time when we'd have to drive five hours each way every weekend. We agreed to go and arrangements were made to stay with brother Ernie and his wife, Sharon. There were two services each Sunday that were well attended by nine hundred in the morning and about five hundred at night. Soon the leadership was looking toward putting in a balcony and they asked if I'd consider becoming their pastor. However, having family in the church, having just bought a house in Huntsville, and being retired from ministry, we did not feel led to go there on a permanent basis. I did a long series on "Spiritual Gifts" (fifteen weeks) which was well received. Then I got a lead from the seminary on a good pastor by the name of Dr. Greg Curtis, who ended up being called and responded positively. Unfortunately, due to burnout he was unable to stay very long. In 1998 I was asked again to fill in, so I returned for another six months — from May to October. We thank the Lord for the privilege of ministry as well as safety on the highways while traveling thousands of miles. We had a chance to reconnect with many friends and family, whom we hadn't seen much over twenty-five years. We lived in Huntsville but hadn't sold our cottage yet, so we were renting it out. On Saturdays we would go twenty-five miles north to clean the cottage and cut the grass then leave for Sarnia, a five-hour drive. We would stay over at Ernie's Saturday night and a few Sunday nights. Sometimes we'd get halfway home and stay at Dale and Todd's, then come home the next day. The church was very generous with the pay schedule as they included preparation time and travel but I asked them to cut it back when I came the second time.

WILLOW CREEK, MIDHURST 1997

This work had started as a daughter church of Emmanuel, Barrie. The first pastor was Dan Schurr, who a few years before I had interviewed to be our youth pastor at Bramalea. Upon hearing his preaching and maturity, I encouraged him to leave youth for the pastorate. Now ten years later, when he resigned after a very fruitful ministry, Cliff Topping, board chairman and formerly a deacon's son at Bramalea asked if I would be their interim pastor for six to eight months. I was happy to accept the challenge. One thing I especially remember was that they were sixty-five workers short and I said I would preach on serving the Lord if they would list all the areas of ministry needs within. A form listing all of the areas to serve was prepared and printed. These were given out at the start of the service and received following the sermon. We ended up with sixty-five responses and we all thanked the Lord — a great time then and I've enjoyed ministering there several times since.

BETHEL BAPTIST, ORILLIA 1999-2001

This church is an hour's drive south of Huntsville. Each of the three years I ministered Sunday morning and evening as well as two weekdays. I was first called in after the prior pastor experienced moral failure and I had to deal with a lot of raw emotions and hurt church members. Former members from Bramalea Baptist Church, Martin and Tony Shaw were very active at Bethel. Two vivid memories remain with me from Bethel: the first was a phone call from Arnold Nogy, a member and noted artist who said his wife was expecting a child but she had a large tumor in her abdomen and their doctor said either the baby or his wife would die, as they couldn't operate. He asked if I would come and pray for her. I said I'd get two deacons and we'd fast and pray for twenty-four hours and then come. We met with this couple and read from James 5; we anointed her with oil and prayer fervently for healing. I received a phone call a week later and Arnold said they'd been to their doctor and to his amazement the tumor was gone. A few months later a beautiful healthy baby boy was born. The Nogys had

Bev and I to their home for dinner and presented us with one of his paintings of Elora Gorge as a 'thank you' gift. I also purchased a painting of an Owl called "The Noble" for which he had won an award in New York. Both pictures hang in our home as memories of God's power and faithfulness.

The other incident was my forgetting my Bible and sermon notes. I was preaching on "Dealing with Bitterness" in the morning and it was hard not to be bitter. Fortunately for me I had run off a sermon outline and it was in the bulletin. At night I was speaking on "The Quartet that Raised the Roof" and I could remember my points from the story of men bring a paraplegic to Jesus and lowering him through the roof.

PINEGROVE BAPTIST, BRACEBRIDGE 2003–2004

Pinegrove was in need of an interim pastor as Pastor Cooper had left to do mission work in Africa with ABWE Mission. I was asked to preach mornings and evenings for two six-month periods in 2003 and 2004. This church had five great men who served as elders. My responsibility was primarily preaching each Sunday and meeting with the board to assist in ministry strategy and to seek a full-time pastor. The church had great musicians which helped to lead in worship. We greatly enjoyed the fellowship as the people were very appreciative and responsive to the preaching and teaching of God's word.

Several years later, ten couples who had left Pinegrove because of pastoral concerns and problems asked me to do a ten-week preaching series. They used the Salvation Army facility in Bracebridge where we did a preaching and teaching ministry to help serve these fine folks in a time of transition in their lives. We still keep in touch with many of these faithful Christians.

RIVERSIDE BAPTIST, HUNTSVILLE 2002 and 2012

My ministry was two days a week and started May 1 to October 30. The attendance had declined to thirty and I tried to encourage the struggling congregation with visitation, biblical teaching, and preaching. Our attendance grew to one hundred by the time I was ready to leave and return to my ministry in Florida. As I met with the deacon's board, they were looking for a pastor but didn't know many of the names given to them. Don Brubacher's name appeared and I encouraged them pursue him, as he had just left Shenstone Baptist in Brantford and was considering Calvary Oakville. He responded in the affirmative, as it seemed Riverside was just what he felt prepared to lead. Subsequently, he was there ten years with a fruitful ministry.

WEST HIGHLAND, HAMILTON 2006

When I was working at head office I had spoken at West Highland on several occasions. When their pastor resigned to minister in Mississauga, Murray Pipe encouraged their board to call me. I preached Sunday mornings and evenings for seven months from June through December. We left early Sunday morning and after preaching at both services we headed home arriving close to midnight in Huntsville. The morning service was streamed on the internet and I enjoyed the challenge, seeing God work in lives and meeting former friends and making many new ones. John Mahaffey, whom I'd known as a seminary student and pastor at Churchill Heights in Scarborough, came as pastor in January 2007.

GLENWOOD CHAPEL, MUSKOKA 2009

I preached at this church for only four or five Sundays. I was delighted to meet Dr. Ev Moller from Forward Baptist Church since he had a cottage nearby. We also met Terry and Jean Fitter and other friends from Bramalea days as well as friends from the Huntsville area.

GREENWOOD BAPTIST, NORTH BAY 2010

I enjoyed a three-month ministry in this university city church when Pastor Hawman went on sabbatical. The majority of the two hundred and fifty people were university students who faithfully took notes on my thirteen messages. We made some great friends and pastor Hawman, who is also an artist, gave me a lovely painting as a "thank you" gift.

SHORTER PREACHING STINTS

These included Emmanuel Baptist in Barrie, North Broadway in Tillsonburg, Chetwyn Church near Burk's Falls, and Norway Point Church on Lake of Bays.

Chaplaincy — Muskoka Landing

In 1989 when I worked for the Fellowship, one of the aspects of the ministry was oversight of chaplains across Canada. At that time, I never expected to be a chaplain myself. Our granddaughter, Megan Fitter, was working at Muskoka Landing part time and when their chaplain, Bill Finney retired, she suggested that I could take on that responsibility. I took the job for two years, in the months we were home from Florida, during 2011-2012. When I first went, I asked if I could use the Bible and talk to the residents about heaven and the administration agreed. The gal in charge first took me to meet their most obstinate patient at that time. Fred was lying on his stomach and was not responding to anyone around. I told him I wanted to be his friend and he gradually rolled over and was willing to talk to me. He was very open to discussion of life and death and he responded by accepting the Lord that day. The authorities asked me to tell them what I did that resulted in Fred behaving so differently and I said that I had led him to faith in the Lord. He wanted to die but he wasn't ready. Now he is ready, but he doesn't want to die. He went around in his wheelchair with his Bible and Daily Bread and attended every Bible Study I had once a week. He was the nicest fellow and his father owned a funeral home, and he did the embalming, so he had lots of music from the funeral home in his room. Within three years he died, but we know we'll see him again someday.

One day a lady asked me if I had ever lived in Brampton on Banbury Court. When I acknowledged, we discovered that she had been a neighbour on our street whose children had played with our girls. She was Doris Short, who had encountered a degree of Alzheimer's but had not forgotten me. I gave up my job there to another fellow who needed the work and money more than I did. I had enjoyed what I did, visiting about forty seniors each week and having a Bible Study, but two years was enough, especially since we live and work with seniors all winter in Florida.

22

Silvester's Nine Lives

My start in life was shaky and would be perhaps a foreshadowing of some of the things I would face along the way. My mother was unable to nurse me and I was not eating the formula the doctor prescribed (corn syrup and milk). I lost weight and my Dad said I looked like a wrinkled old man. At times they put me in the oven to keep me warm; possibly I came out half baked. My parents decided to remove the corn syrup from the milk and I began to improve.

1. At the age of eleven, I and my brother Roger climbed the highest maple tree near our house at Rich Hill Farm south of Shelburne, Ontario. Uncle Roy and Aunt Margaret Hamilton were visiting us at that time from London, Ontario. Aunt Margaret was standing at the bottom of the tree when Roger and I decided to have a race to the bottom. Unfortunately, I stepped on a dead branch; it broke and I plunged to the ground, hitting other branches along the way. I was stunned if not partially knocked out. However, I won the race. Some say I have been stunned ever since.

2. While attending Shelburne High School, my class took a trip to Toronto. Our bus driver was Mr. Waters who unfortunately drank more than water. On the way he stopped at the garage where he worked. Unknown to us he had been drinking liquor and brought more onto the bus and hid it under the seat. As we headed down Highway 10 toward Orangeville, the bus started to swerve. I was sitting in one of the rear seats and I noticed we were on the wrong side of the road. I still remember cars going into the ditch to avoid

us. We made it past Orangeville, but he was still weaving and we knew we were in trouble. We were just at the brow of Caledon Mountain when the flashing lights of a police car forced the bus to pull over and stop. The driver was arrested and taken off the bus while we waited for a new driver. We were so fortunate not to have had a serious accident for that hill was incredibly steep and his speed could have made the problem worse — possibly deadly.

3. When I was about eighteen, we were working in the bush cutting trees and hauling them out with our International tractor. I was hooking a chain around a huge log and dad was backing up the tractor so I could hook on the chain. As he backed up, the slope of the ground caused the tractor to go further than he expected. I was crushed between the log and the back of the tractor. I collapsed with the air squeezed out of me. Dad quickly put it in forward, but he thought he may have killed me. Thankfully I was okay and from then on, we worked much more cautiously.

4. One Sunday afternoon when my parents returned from visiting friends in their 1950 Studebaker, my Dad mentioned that the brakes were soft and advised me to be careful as I was planning to go to young people's meeting in Orangeville. After I finished milking the Holsteins in our milking parlour, I changed my clothes and jumped into the car. When I stopped at 20 Side Road, the brakes were fine. I was heading east toward Highway 10 for about three miles on gravel road, but I didn't need to use my brakes until I got to the highway. I could see a steady stream of traffic heading south from Wasaga Beach. When I touched the brakes, the pedal went right to the floor. I had to think quickly. It was a stick shift with overdrive and that made it freewheeling as I could not get it to slow down by shifting gears. I started swaying the car from side to side to try and slow it down but knew if I did it too much, I could send it into the ditch. I was still going about forty miles an hour as I crossed the highway. I crouched down and ducked my head and as I went through the intersection with horns blasting. I was hoping God would part the traffic like He did the Red Sea. I coasted for about a quarter of a mile before coming to a stop. I sat there realizing that God had spared my life. I abandoned my plans to go anywhere else but home and very slowly made my way back without brakes.

5. When I was youth pastor at Forward Baptist Church in Toronto, I was asked to lead the sports program at Youth Week at MBC in August 1967. Warren Kimball, who later became the pastor of Temple Baptist Church in Sarnia, was the speaker. We decided to add some excitement and announced at the noon meal one day that the Ladies from Cyprus Gardens were putting on a water ski show. Warren and I, with limited skiing experience, were the

"Ladies". Harry Beer was willing to use his high-powered boat to pull us. We dressed up as the fancy ladies with long dresses and hats and sunglasses. I had a belt floatation device in case of problems. (I am not a swimmer.) My dress had long tight sleeves and wrapped itself around my legs. As we came up the Muskoka River and into Mary Lake there were many kids on shore watching the show. We went around a couple of times at pretty good speed with the young people cheering. Warren finally let go and I decided to go around one more time. In front of everyone I flew over a wake around the last curve, lost my balance, and fell. Because I couldn't move my arms or legs well due to the tight dress and only had a belt float, I was in trouble. Marg Beer realized I was floundering and dove in after me. I pulled her under and fortunately she knew what to do and got me safely to the boat. The Lord wasn't finished with me yet. Bev, who was seven months pregnant, was nervously watching on shore with our two little girls. Right away, without the dress, I went out again behind the boat to overcome my fear. The years have not improved my swimming skills, but I continue to be around the water in the Ditchburn boat.

6. In 1959 while working at Polymer Corporation in Sarnia the Atomic and Chemical Workers Union went on strike which lasted for ninety-six days. For all that time striking we only got two cents an hour more. We lost about one thousand five hundred dollars in wages during that time. For strike pay we got fifteen dollars a week and free haircuts. I decided to work for a friend who was also on strike but owned a small farm. I blocked (thinned out) sugar beets and got fifteen to twenty dollars a day. My friend Bob McGregor who also worked at Polymer suggested that we go on a trip to British Columbia together in a 1957 MG convertible that was for sale on his father's car lot in Petrolia. We packed our clothes, stove and a tent and headed out. The first day we got a speeding ticket in Michigan and our battery died. We stopped in Wisconsin and Bob who was a good golfer played a round of golf and I was his caddy. In Montana we pulled into a car lot because Bob knew some of the cars would be unlocked. We slept in one overnight and left before anyone arrived in the morning. There were no speed limits, so we drove fast. In Idaho the Rockies came into view. Bob was driving when suddenly he said, "Look at those beautiful mountains." At the same time, he drifted over to the left lane and a logging truck was heading toward us. I grabbed the steering wheel and yanked it and we skidded, just missing the front of the truck. Bob yelled at me for trying to kill us, but he hadn't even seen the truck. We were lucky to be alive. We met a couple of gals in British Columbia who had an identical car and we had lunch with them. We soon

discovered that the one I was sitting with was married so didn't pursue them any further.

7. For approximately two years I had been heading up FBYPA, working a day a week, while pastoring at Bramalea in 1970. As the ministry grew, we saw the need for a full-time worker. It was decided that Roy Lawson would be a good prospect so Mike Brown, Jack Hannah, Jim Watt and I, (all graduates of CBS), headed to London to interview him. Following a supper meeting and a good interview we decided to head for home quickly because of freezing rain forecasts. In retrospect we should have stayed overnight but I had a speaking engagement at the Seminary chapel the next morning. It didn't take long to realize we were in a bad storm. The 401 was very slushy and icy and as we neared Woodstock with Mike driving his Olds Cutlass, he decided to pass two transport trucks hauling Massey Ferguson equipment. I was sitting immediately behind him and realized the danger we were in as there was so much slush from the trucks. We got by the first one and part way past the second when our wheel dropped of the north side of the highway. I said that he would have to be very careful when he came back up on the icy road because when you come back up on the highway, the car would have a tendency to turn sideways. Sure, enough when it came up, he lost control and we skidded sideways down the highway in front of the first truck. The truck hit us on the rear fender and spun us around and up over the snowbank and guard rail. We started to come down in front of the second truck and from my vantage point we were going to go right under the second truck and we would be crushed. Suddenly the car stopped moving and the second truck raced by our front bumper. The rear bumper had caught on the guard rail. The second trucker stopped to see how we were. I jacked the car off the guard rail and still have a scar on my left hand caused when the jack slipped. The truck that had hit us had a double-depth bumper that saved us from going under the transport and then the guard rail saved us. A tow truck coming toward us on the 401 stopped to see how we were as they had seen the whole thing and were sure they'd find us dead. It was 4a.m. when I arrived home and was at Seminary for morning chapel, very thankful to be alive. We told Roy that he better take the job because we had risked our lives to interview him.

8. Driving to Fellowship Office in Toronto one morning at 6 a.m., I left Cheltenham and went west to Airport Road. I headed south on Airport Road and was up to eighty kilometers per hour when suddenly in the dark I saw headlights on one side of the road and brake lights on the other. Then I noticed a yellow florescent strip across Airport Road in front of me. I knew

something was strange and hit the brakes, skidding to a stop. There within ten feet of my car was a long flatbed transport trailer right across the road trying to turn around. Another second and I would have been decapitated as my car would have gone under the tractor trailer. I thanked the Lord for quick reactions, good brakes, and His having kept me alive to continue to serve Him.

9. At our cottage on Doe Lake near Burk's Falls, we often had electrical storms, but never like this night. In the middle of the night I got up to see what was happening. I went out to the back porch and opened the outside door. A terrible flash of lightning and a loud crash of thunder scared me. It knocked me to the floor and I believe I was knocked out briefly. When I came to, I had a cut on my head, but I don't know what I hit. I believe the lightning struck the standpipe where the hydro came into the cottage and had blown out the fuses and our water heater. I don't know exactly how I fell but I had cuts and scrapes on my face to prove it. This was another close shave.

10. On our last full day at our Cheltenham house in 1995, I had just sold our Gravely tractor with snow blower and delivered it to our neighbour. Then I jumped onto our other tractor to finish cutting the grass around the house. However, when wanting to back up, as I got to the top of a cliff, I pulled the lever to stop the tractor, forgetting I had changed machines. Instead the blade lifted and it kept going. I went flying through raspberry bushes, trees, logs on a steep slope. I realized that I'd be in the river if I stayed on, so I jumped off the tractor as it rolled over. The tractor had capsized and the motor was still running and gas was leaking out so I crawled under and turned the key off, thankful to be okay and just shaken up.

11. My latest incident was in Florida in 2013, while riding my bike at a fair rate of speed. Suddenly I decided to make a turn to go visit someone. I skidded and made a five-point landing with my forehead being the last thing to hit the pavement. I was a little sore all over and my face was bleeding badly. Fortunately, I did not suffer a concussion. I wonder why Bev will not let me clean out the eves on the second level of our home at age eighty-two.

23

Sports

My father had played a lot of sports, so he encouraged his five boys to so the same.

TRACK AND FIELD

In Grade 9 I won the Jr. Boys Championship with six events: 100, 220, high jump, broad jump, triple jump and shotput.

In Grade 10 I won the intermediate championship in the same six events plus the one hundred yard and the two hundred- and twenty-yard races against Orangeville High School, beating my cousin George Phillips from Orangeville. I ran all my races in my bare feet. The only race I ever lost was when I tried to run with running shoes and I stumbled and lost the race. I trained for the mile in 1954 when Roger Bannister from England and John Landy from Australia first broke the four-minute mile at the Commonwealth Games in Vancouver. I used to train behind our tractor with dad driving it. It went fifteen miles per hour and that's the speed I had to run for four minutes; it was good discipline, but I could only keep up for three minutes. My best time was about 4:30 as far as I could remember.

BASEBALL

The Junior Farmers had a ten-team league and my brothers Roger and Grant played as well. Twice we went to the Ontario finals at the University of Guelph and we were the runners-up when Grant pitched and I caught for him. I also played fastball under the lights in Orangeville when I was twenty and twenty-one. One year I remember averaging one homerun per game in both leagues.

In Florida I played slow pitch for several years but broke my thumb from a line drive, while playing shortstop and I had to fly back to Toronto to get it fixed. Following that incident, I quit playing and became an umpire for a few years. It was less dangerous (unless I made bad calls). One player incident I remember was the coach calling me out for swinging at the first pitch and not letting it go by. I finally informed him that I had just hit a homerun and a triple so not to complain. He told me to keep quiet and follow his instructions. I found that hard to do.

HOCKEY

When I was seventeen, I played in Shelburne on the Juvenile team. In the 1953–54 season we won the championship in the Central Ontario Hockey League (COHL). I played forward — either center or right wing — and Hugh Maguire, who married my cousin Marietta, played defense. One of the funny incidents in one of the games for the championship in Markdale arena was a bench clearing brawl. In an effort to bring things under control they turned off the lights in the arena. When they turned them back on, I was on top of a Markdale player and a priest in his black garb was trying to pull me off. I felt a little embarrassed, but I won the fight. We won the game and the series championship the next week in Shelburne so what more could I ask. The Bible says, "Whatsoever you do, do with all your might."

When I moved to Sarnia in 1966 while working at Polymer, I played in the Industrial League which was very rough and tough. The first time Bev saw me play, I was crashed into the boards head first with no helmet and split my skull at my temple so that blood came out of my ear. I went to the hospital but, even though they wanted me to stay, I didn't want to worry my Mom who was ill with cancer, so I drove myself home. Another time in Chatham, our goalie was sick and they needed a substitute. I volunteered and they didn't score any goals against me. The main reason was because a Chatham player got a breakaway early in the game and I moved out to poke check him with my stick and he tripped over it. The blade of his skate came up and hit me over my left eye. It bled profusely so I was taken to the hospital to get stitched up and I never played goalie again. While playing at Forward Baptist Church league, one of our players was Bob Sheffield, a former American pro, and whenever we needed an extra goal, we just sent him out. He was so fast that he was heading back after scoring when we were still heading toward the net. At Bramalea I played some for our church team. I remember warming up for a game and I was skating behind the net. Cliff

Marathon in Toronto - 1995

Topping took a slap shot and he missed the net. The puck came right at my head, so I put up my glove hand to stop it and my head was saved but my hand was broken. The next Sunday I had to baptize several people and I put a plastic bag on my hand to protect my cast with the result was that when I finished with the baptisms, I had a bag full of water. I had tried to keep the cast dry but at least I was able to get the people baptized.

MARATHONS

In the 1980's I started running distances to get myself in shape and to strengthen my right leg which I had broken in 1979. One of our church members, Dick Fraser, who weighed two hundred and sixty pounds and was having some heart pains, had started to run and ended up running marathons. I thought if he could do it so could I. He encouraged me and so occasionally we ran together. When we moved to Cheltenham in 1982, I started running six days a week, seven to eight miles a day and twelve to fifteen miles on Saturdays. After approximately one thousand miles of training and strict diet, (losing about twenty-five pounds) I entered the Toronto marathon in 1990. I completed it in four hours, five minutes, and six seconds — finishing in the top third of my age category. Some of my family (The Heywoods and McKenzies) were there to cheer me on and held up signs to encourage me to keep on running. I completed the Niagara Falls Marathon in four hours, fifteen minutes and the next one in Phoenix, Arizona. My knee swelled up and I was advised to quit at the twenty-two-mile mark. Bev, Faye, and Ken were there to cheer me on. In the next Toronto marathon, I wanted to save some time so lined up with the elite runners. The problem was I got caught up with those who were running six-minute miles and it was hard to slow down and see everyone passing me. After an hour and a half, I had finished half of the marathon and I was really tired. Then I spotted Bev, Dale, and her children, and pulled over for a break which was a big mistake because I never got going again. The next day I was flying to South Korea and Japan so I think I would have been very uncomfortable if I had finished the race. When on the airplane I got a Globe and Mail newspaper and there was a picture of the start of the marathon and there I was in the midst of the elite runners. It made a great picture, but unfortunately quitters never win. The upside was that I was able to walk and complete my two-week mission trip.

GOLFING

When I started playing golf I was living in Sarnia and played at Bright's Grove the home course of Mike Weir. At first, I got so frustrated trying to hit the ball with my woods and irons, I ended up just using my putter. Fortunately, I persevered while pastoring at Bramalea and I used to get free golf at the Mississauga Golf and Country Club. Although I never had any lessons, by reading and watching TV I started to improve. When we retired to Huntsville, I joined the North Granite Ridge Golf Club and tried to play three times a week. While a member there I won two men's tournaments in a row then I played the Jack Wallace Tournament at Grandview and won the low men's score. This was special because I had led Jack to the Lord before he moved to Huntsville where he started the "Man to Man" ministry. He died of cancer and I had the privilege of taking his funeral which was attended by scores of men. When we retired to Florida, we lived on a golf course and I was fortunate to get two holes-in-one which I and others attribute to divine intervention. Golf can be frustrating at times but fulfilling too, and a game that can be played in old age — in my eighties now.

TENNIS

I first started playing tennis at March break in Florida and gradually learned

Richling's & Bev's & I in Ping Pong Tournment in Florida

how to play fairly well. When we retired there in 1987, Bev and I joined the SC tennis club and played two or three times a week; mainly doubles. We won a few mixed doubles tournaments, but it is not always easy playing with your spouse. Bev and I won the Muskoka Seniors tournament twice and we both belonged to the Huntsville Racketeers Group. Tennis is a great game to keep your legs and lungs strong and now twenty years later we are still playing regularly and competitively.

PING PONG

Since high school days I have enjoyed playing ping pong. While at seminary I played an hour at lunchtimes and played a tournament against Ontario Bible College. I was down twenty to ten and fought back to win twenty-two to twenty. While Bev and I were on a cruise to Alaska to celebrate our fortieth anniversary we played ping pong on deck. Since it was an Olympic year, they had ping pong tournaments, so we competed against a number of younger people and won a gold in doubles; I won a gold in singles and Bev won the silver. More recently in Florida a ping pong club was started. We played a couple of times a week. I was the best player the first year until a Florida champion joined (Jim Richling) and even though he was older I could not beat him in singles. Jim and I teamed up to win gold in the Florida Seniors Games. Here is a quote from Savanah Club Voice in 2011, "This year the Table Tennis (Ping Pong) Senior Games for Florida were hosted by King's Isle. There was a large turn out with players coming from as far away as Miami and north to Melbourne dressed in their team jerseys, and I am proud to say our matches were very competitive, with players in singles, doubles and mixed doubles. Jim and Marcia Richling along with Bev and Stu Silvester came away with a total of six gold and silver metals. Jim and I also qualified for the State Championships held in Lakeland, Florida."

We all went to Lakeland for the State Championships. Jim and I competed in the finals with hundreds of players; the best we could do was a bronze medal. Many of the competitors had their own coaches and expensive paddles. The moral of the story is that no matter how good you are there is always someone better. I enjoy playing against our grandchildren, but it is getting hard to win now. Thanks to grandson Brendan we have a great new ping pong table and hopefully Bev and I can play for a while yet.

CARS

When I was twelve, I designed my first vehicle. The engine was a Briggs and Stratton taken from our washing machine, when we got hydro on our farm in 1948. I took two bicycle wheels and an airplane tire for the front and built a three-wheel tractor type machine. Using a gear box and belts I produced a drive system and had fun with my mechanical creation.

My first car was a 1930 De Soto I got for $15.00 from Harold Hamilton, a cousin of my mother's. I used it around our farm and then cut the body off behind the front seats and made a truck to haul seed and fertilizer etc. on our farm. I had seen an article in the Mechanics Illustrated magazine on how to make a roadster out of a '32 Ford. I decided to try the same with the 1930 De Soto. I removed the body and lowered the motor and I sat between the propeller shaft and the frame on boards about four inches in from the ground. One day as I drove it across a field to get our Holsteins I hit a dead furrow and it twisted the frame and my seat let go and I found myself being run over with my back against the rear-end and I finally reached up and put the car out of gear before I was run over. A lot of fun with little investment.

The first real car I owned and drove on the highway was a 1939 Mercury Coupe, painted pink and grey. My brother Roger purchased it in Sarnia and I paid $125.00 for it and this was in 1954. It was fast and we later discovered it had a three-quarter race V8 engine that had been in a stock car. In 1955 when my dad bought a new Ford, my car could actually beat it in a drag race. I put on many miles going to young peoples, church, courting, and selling chickens in Dufferin County as well as going to Sarnia in December of 1955 with it. It got crushed between two other cars in an ice storm in Sarnia when I was selling Fuller Brushes. I took some of the parts, including, front and rear ends, the dash and transmission to be used in my next car project. I purchased a 1931 Model A Roadster body and decided I would build a "Hot Rod". I rented space in a garage and welded up parts and chopped and channelled the body and put on cycle fenders. I got a 1953 Rocket 88 V8 Oldsmobile engine from a wreck in St. Thomas and it became the power plant. With chromed valve covers and special headers and painted "Tropical Rose" a Ford colour it looked pretty sharp. I had a white convertible top and the car would go 0-60mph in six seconds. It was fast, fun and no one ever beat me in a drag-race, even going against motorcycles. I belonged to the "Rod Benders" club in Sarnia and went as far as St. Thomas but mainly used it around Sarnia. One incident happened to it at the quarter mile speedway in Sarnia. They would let me in free if I used my roadster as the "Pace Car" for all the races. One night I was pacing eight cars in the A-class and as I came around the final corner and the flag man waved me to get going, my car sputtered and the cars were roaring up behind me. He yelled at me and just in the nick of time my car took off into the pits. After the races my brother Roger, who had been in the grandstand said he saw sparks coming out by my right rear wheel and he thought I was going to get run over. We decided after the spectators were gone to run my roadster around the track again. As I came around the final corner at about 60mph in second gear it started to sputter again. Then a big explosion in my trunk where my gas tank and battery were and the car died. When I opened the trunk, I saw what had happened. I had a spanner wrench between the gas tank and battery and when I went around the corner at high speed, it tipped over and welded itself between the positive battery cable and the car frame and blew the top off the battery. (I remember going to the Canadian Tire store and getting it replaced). My brother had to tow me home behind his 1956 Ford. While still on the farm I had purchased a 1932 V12 Cadillac Brougham Coupe for $75.00. It had come from Guelph and had been chauffeur driven. It had power brakes, dual carbs, adjustable ride control, and dual exhausts. I used to use it on the farm to go and get the cows, but I never licensed it. When we sold our farm Roger and I towed it to Sarnia. It weighed 5,600 pounds. Eventually I sold it for $500 in order to buy a better car for our honeymoon and more furniture. A Cadillac dealership in Caledonia bought it and restored it and today it is probably worth $75,000.00.

1954 Studebaker Commander Coupe — This was a fast V8 car and I had it for about two years. It was the car I took Bev home in from YFC in September 1959. It was actually in this sporty car that I proposed to her since it was the only place, I could get some privacy. Not overly romantic but cars had been a part of

My Racing Stable of 3 Cars - 1959

my life for a long time before she came along.

For our honeymoon I sold my 1954 Studebaker and bought a beautiful 1955 Pontiac hardtop. It was two tone brown and had a big V8 with a floor shift and was fast. Then a year later I bought a 1955 Ford Thunderbird which had two tops and was aqua green. It was the ninth T-bird made. We enjoyed this car and Bev learned to drive on it. The month after we were married, I bought a 1940 Ford coupe for $40.00 from the original owner. It was a good second car but burned a lot of oil. I loaned it to my brother Alan to go to Kitchener and by the time he returned he had to put in six quarts of oil. Later I took the Olds V8 out of my roadster and put it in the 1940 coupe which I had painted jet black. Ernie purchase the 1931 Ford roadster as his first car.

Another special car I owned was a 1964 Studebaker Grand Turismo. It was white with red interior and had an R-2 Avanti supercharged V8 engine. It would pass everything but a gas station and had a top speed of 150mph according to the manufacturer. In 1972 I bought a lovely 1966 Ford Mustang convertible which had been owned by Dave King of the Toronto Maple Leafs and Los Angeles Kings. We had many enjoyable trips, car shows, and after almost 40 years sold it for more than five times what I had paid for it. Ernie had totally rebuilt it in 2000 so it was still in good condition when we sold it to a car collector. One special car I owned for almost fifty years was a 1933 Ford three window coupe. We found it in a farmer's field near our old house at Burk's Falls. Between 1972 and 1976 I worked on it at my brother Ernie's body shop in Brigden. I would take a Monday a month off and work on the car and he would do the finishing, painting, etc. By July of 1976 it was completed; painted tan with red wheels and leather lined rumble seat. We made many memories as a family in this antique car and I sold it in 2006 to a car collector for $32,500 and since the car was given to me free and it cost me $7500 to restore it turned out to be a great investment.

The final two vehicles I still own that are special is a 2002 Thunderbird which I purchased in Florida and shipped up to Ontario. It is red with two tops and a fun car that Bev and I have enjoyed driving and travelling together in. The last one is a 2005 Mustang convertible I've had in Florida for use as my winter car. It is burgundy with a tan top and tan leather interior. Our kids enjoy driving it when visiting in Florida. So, you can see cars have been a part of my DNA since I was a youngster. My regular car is a 2016 Lexus Hybrid which is economical and enjoyable. I purchased this car from Mike Brandon just prior to his death. Mike was the chairman of our board at Bramalea Baptist Church.

Gail & Don Thorne - 1933 Ford Coupe - 2004

BOATS

This may seem like a strange sport for a pastor, but boats played a major part in the Bible: the well-known story of Noah and his adventures in Genesis and in the N.T. Jesus travelled often by boat on the Sea of Galilee. When we purchased our cottage on Doe Lake in 1978 it came fully furnished including a small sailboat and a fifteen-foot motorboat. However, in a couple of years I decided we needed a more powerful one to pull water-skiers.

While in Florida one March break I looked for a better boat and I found it at a marina in Jensen Beach. It was a twenty-foot orange and cream-coloured one-owner boat powered by a four-cylinder Volvo inboard motor.

It was available for a reasonable price and included a trailer. I had two major problems: I didn't have any money with me, so I called my brother Roger who had just sold a nursing home in London and graciously lent me what I needed. The other issue was that we were driving the 66 Mustang convertible that didn't have a hitch, so we had to have one installed. If I had known what lay ahead, I might have forgotten the whole thing.

We left early Friday morning with our new acquisition being filled with our luggage and lots of grapefruit and oranges. The car had a 225 V8 engine so lots of power but the radiator had a pinhole leak and under pressure, the anti-freeze started leaking. As we travelled north it got worse. I purchase numerous kinds of radiator products that promised to stop any and all leaks and they worked for a while but as we progressed north and into Kentucky, I looked in my rear-view mirror and noticed the trailer looked very low at the front. Sure enough, the trailer hitch had bent under the weight of the boat. I left Bev and the boat and looked for a welding shop in the Kentucky hills to find someone who could add a brace to hold the hitch in place. That fixed, we continued our trip north but the rad remained a problem. I had to stop and get water numerous times from ditches. We decided not to go to a motel but to keep driving all night. By early Saturday morning the car's rad was so bad that I couldn't go any further. Somehow without a cell phone I was able to get a tow truck to haul us into a city in Ohio. By midafternoon a garage had installed a new radiator for twenty-two dollars and we were on our way. Just before the Canadian border I hit a pothole and it knocked the fender off the trailer, but I recovered it. After paying our customs fee we arrived at Ernie's at midnight; however, we could not stay because I had to preach at 8:30 a.m. and 11:00 a.m. in Bramalea. Bev started to drive so I could sleep since it had been thirty-six hours since I had slept. However, it was snowing hard and Bev couldn't keep her eyes open, so I drove through the snow and arrived home at 4:30 in the morning.

We were sure thankful to have made it safely. I used to call the early service "Warm up, Wake up" and I'm sure many of the people wondered why I wasn't more rested after a good holiday. Fortunately, I had prepared my sermon before I had left for holidays. So much for buying a boat in Florida but it was half the price of one in Ontario and we got a lot of pleasure out of it once we hauled it from Sarnia to the cottage. A couple of years later I traded the boat in for a ninety horsepower one, but I was never happy with it.

When I returned from six weeks ministry in Zambia where I had gotten into trouble with the authorities, I was so happy to be home that I decided to treat myself with a new boat; it was a 1990 Doral bow rider with a one hundred and seventy-five horsepower motor and it was two-toned blue and white. It was called "Spirit" so like John in Revelation I was in the "Spirit" on the Lord's Day. We enjoyed this boat at the cottage and then at our house in Huntsville. When we got our antique boat going, we then had two boats for a while but realized that Faye and Ken could use a boat with their kids at their cottage, so it went there to be enjoyed the whole time they had the cottage. Once in a while Bev and I would enjoy boating with them on Bay Lake.

1937 DITCHBURN SPORT MODEL

In 1968 while working at MBC camp with young people I was asked to go across the Muskoka River to see some new property, formerly the Acadia Lodge, which MBC had purchased for Camp Widjiitiwin. I spotted this old boat in the mud and then noticed the Ditchburn plaque on a cobweb- covered dash. I knew I was related to the Ditchburns through my great grandmother Stoneman. I was given the old boat for moving it out of the mud and in November, 1968, Ernie and I loaded it on a trailer he had built for me and in pouring rain used a borrowed Ford tractor, got it out and moved to our old farmhouse in Burk's Falls. We pulled it with my 1964 Studebaker Gran Turismo and the supercharged R2 Avanti until the engine caught fire; we were able to extinguish it quickly and didn't lose the boat or car. The next year only I was able to get the four-cylinder Buchanan engine going. I put two coats of varnish on the upper half and deck and painted the lower half white to cover the metal which had been installed earlier to keep it from leaking and sinking.

Bev learned to water ski behind it and we used it for a couple of years, taking it once to Lake Cecebe when our friends Pat and Mac were with us. We laughed as she was sinking as the boat was taking on more water. One morning I went out of our cottage and the Ditchburn was three-quarters under water including the motor. It was then I decided to store it and endeavour to restore it when I retired and had more time and money. We even pulled it all the way to Sarnia

Launch of 1937 Ditchburn Boat in 2008

for a family reunion at Lake Huron. I was crazy enough to take our family and Bev's Mom and Dad down the St. Clair River. We passed some large ships and I am not sure if it was faith or foolishness. One day we pulled the boat behind our car to Huntsville, put it in the Muskoka River, and went through the locks all the way to MBC. We had a great day as the girls took turns steering while I was at the back of the boat siphoning water so we wouldn't sink.

I stored the boat in our garage in Bramalea for a while. Bruce Fitter was going to do some woodworking on it but we only got two or three boards replaced before he got so busy building restaurants that we never got back to doing anymore.

When we retired to Huntsville, we hauled the Ditchburn to the cottage where I planned to work on it in the new three-car garage and shop that Bruce and the family had helped build. However, in 1998 we sold the cottage and I moved the Ditchburn to Huntsville. Some fellows helped us, headed up by Tim Doyle, who was trying to open a boat museum and asked if I would donate my boat to the museum if they allowed me to use it some. At first, I agreed and then later decided I wanted control of the restoration and use of my boat. For a couple of years, I worked on it in a facility north of the hospital along with other fellows who worked on their boats. Then in 2001 I moved it home and started to rebuild it with new mahogany, oak, and ash. I made new frames using the old ones as my templates; however, the problem was that the old ones were warped. I was replacing the old ones but even with new planking, when we tried to fare the sides, they couldn't be fared properly. Finally, I realized I needed help from an experienced boat restorer. Don Allman was recommended and I took my boat to his shop about three miles away on Old Ferguson Road. For the next six years, part time, he and I worked on the Ditchburn for approximately three thousand hours. No power tools were used and all was done by hand to eliminate circular marks by sanders. A new V6 Chevy motor and velvet drive transmission was installed by High Performance Marine in Gravenhurst. By June 2008 it was finished with eighteen coats of varnish, new upholstery, and all new chrome. It took twice as long to complete as I envisaged and also cost much more by including a trailer, travel cover and electric boat lift. I decided to name the boat "Born Again" since it was totally renewed and also was a testimony. I had a professionally made boat storyboard with pictures and story of its life and why I called it "Born Again". Bruce's men made a beautiful stand for it. I was hoping I could win one trophy but the first year I won four and by 2014 I had twelve from American and Canadian boat shows. Numerous articles have been written in magazines as well as features on CBC radio, CBC, and Global T.V. during the G-8 meetings. (The boat judges appraised it at two hundred and fifty thousand dollars in 2008). There will come a day when we'll have to sell our home on Lake Vernon and our boat, but until then Bev and I will take it on cruises as often as possible, continuing to enjoy it as long as we can. In 2016, after selling our home on the Vernon Narrows, Bruce, our son-in-law allowed us to move our boat to their new home on Peninsula Lake. The condition was that I buy a solar-powered boat lift so in 2017 we started using our Ditchburn boat about once a week and took a number of our family out for cruises. Using a remote control, the boat can be raised and lowered in about thirty seconds, so it is quick and very enjoyable.

24

Church Planting in a Foreign Country – Florida, U.S.A.

The closest I got to plant a church was when I was called to Bramalea in 1969 as their first full-time pastor. I was often credited as the one who started it but several students from CBS including my brother Roger and another pastor worked part-time including Bill Hiltz who proceeded me helped plant it in 1964. However, when Bev and I retired in November 1995, we decided to go south to Arizona the first year and then to Florida the years following. Once we settled in our new home following a busy life of travelling, meetings, speaking and people, I wanted to enjoy myself. I played a lot of golf and tennis as well as baseball. Everything was going great until one day playing shortstop, I got hit with a line drive on my right thumb and it was broken in six places. It was going to cost twelve thousand dollars in Florida to reconstruct it. My insurance wouldn't pay that much so I flew to Toronto and went to East General Hospital for half the price. My insurance company wouldn't fly me back to Florida, so I got a ride with Dale, Todd, and family. (This was over the winter of 1999–2000.) With a cast on my thumb and stainless-steel protruding, I wasn't able to play ball, golf or tennis. I started feeling sorry for myself and I sat on the sidelines for most of the winter. As I "stewed" in my own juices, God started to speak to me regarding my self-centered lifestyle. Savannah Club where we lived was expanding rapidly with hundreds of snowbirds moving in. The only spiritual emphasis was a weekly Men's Bible Study and I realized many snowbirds like ourselves had no church

2005 Mustang & Florida Home - 2009

home, so I did a survey regarding the possibility of starting a worship service in the clubhouse. I did a survey and found at least twenty-five people who were interested in a non-denominational church service. For the first four years of retirement we spent January through April in Florida.

So, on January 6th, 2001, after some advertising, we held our first worship service in our Fairways Club House and thirty-three people attended. We had Ian and Marg Crawshaw, professional musicians, as our special music and people started coming in from a next-door restaurant. The next week we dropped to twenty-five and I realized I needed to do more follow ups and advertising. By the end of April, we had grown to one hundred. My plan was to shut it down until we returned the next winter. However, the people said I couldn't shut it down as it was their new church home and wanted it to run year-round. Jim and Esther Tobias, a wonderful Christian couple from Bible Town in Boca Raton, said they could get speakers to fill in until we returned. They also wanted me to lead and preach from November 1st for six months. The attendance kept increasing and I would visit every person who attended and a monthly fellowship night was started. Our friends from Ontario, Stan and Pat Lehman, both fine musicians, provided vocal and instrumental music on trumpet, flute, guitar, and keyboard. Our auditorium was filled to the max and beyond. Suddenly with no notice the

Board of Directors called a meeting and said they were going to shut our services down. The Treasurer of the Board, Judy Robbins who attended our church, immediately tried to contact me but I was out so she got Jim Tobias and he went to the directors and arranged for a meeting the next day with two of their leaders, Jim, and myself. They said we were getting too big and were creating traffic and congestion so that golfers weren't able to find parking. We reasoned with them and said we'd get people to use golf carts and they allowed us to continue on a couple of months. New charges were made that we were a 'cult' trying to make Savannah Club into a Christian Community. More allegations were made that I wasn't ordained and that we were taking widows' houses. By 2004 there were two hundred to three hundred people attending and several came to the Lord and were baptised and the attendance continued to increase. When we returned in November 2004, letters were being circulated in Savannah Club that the four SCHOA board members and their wives would have to move away or be killed by Jim Tobias and me.

Detectives got involved to try and find who was behind these lies. I appeared before hundreds of people to try and defend our ministry and said that whoever was behind the threats would not only answer to me, but to God.

Other accusations included that we had building plans; we were sending money to Canada to buy drugs; we had a bank account in the Bahamas, and that we were a 'cult' turning Christians against Catholics and Jews.

The next step was to check everyone's I.D. who came to our services and then the board members started to videotape all of our Sunday services. At least they were hearing the gospel and enjoying Christian fellowship. I invited all board members to come and some did, admitting they couldn't find anything wrong except we were getting "too big and influential". Letters were written to the local papers and the Voice publication in Savannah Club. Then television stations came in to interview us and others regarding the controversy but rumors and lies persisted. We tried to overcome evil with good. Their stated goal was to block us from using the Fairways Club House. We sought legal advice and the Board was prepared to spend hundreds of thousands of dollars in insurance money to attack us and take us to court. The Christian lawyer handling the problem was David Gibbs, from Tampa, Florida, who came to our aid. One of the lawyers lived in our home for a couple of months while we were in Ontario. The board demanded that I fly down in July to be deposed by their lawyers. For eight hours the board and their lawyers grilled me with countless questions. One was "Have you ever gone through anything like this before?" My reply was, "Once in Zambia, Africa where I was accused of being a spy and held under house arrest — in a communist-controlled country." Our case went to court in Miami and we took a bus load of people along with our lawyers. The charges we were making were 'religious persecution'. Our lawyers decided to go with only a judge and no jury which I feel was a mistake because we had to prove three points to win. After we waited three weeks, the opposing lawyer said because we still could go into the Club House to use the bathroom or library, we weren't blocked out.

On that technicality he said we weren't totally blocked out and we ended up losing the case. It was disappointing and it led to the SCHOA board's giving us four weeks to use their facilities before we'd be shut out permanently. We met at Eagle's Landing for three services and the final one was in the small cove facility. Earlier that week we learned that Bev had serious heart problems. While jogging Bev started to have pain in her arm and I noticed she was very pale when she returned from running. Tests revealed blocked arteries and the doctor in Florida wanted to put in stents. However, our doctor in Huntsville who was our neighbour had given us his personal number, so we phoned him and he recommended for Bev to go to the heart specialist in Newmarket. So, with this information we decided to stay for our last service in Savannah Club facilities. The small cove facility where we held our monthly socials was opened to us, so we jammed one hundred and fifty people in and Ernie and Sharon Silvester provided special music. Board member Rich Paul was videotaping the service and ironically, I had planned to read a letter his wife had published in the Voice regarding her appreciation for my visits to her in the hospital and her home following a car accident. I desired to show that contrary to accusations of divisiveness we were having on this community at least one board member's wife felt differently. That morning I spoke on the theme "God's Purpose for our Problems" from 1 Peter 4:19. "Those who suffer according to God's will should commit themselves to their faithful creator and continue to do good." Consider five ways God uses problems in my life:

1. God Uses Problems to Direct Us
   Proverbs 20:30
2. God Uses Problems to Inspect Us
   Deuteronomy 8:2 & John 23:10
3. God Uses Problems to Correct Us
   Psalms 119:21 & Hebrews 2:7–11
4. God Uses Problems to Protect Us
   1 Peter 3:17 & Isiah 4:1-10
5. God Uses Problems to Perfect Us
   Romans 8:28 & Galatians 5:22

We all had lessons to learn from our problems — including persecution from the Savannah Club — and we prayed for God's direction now that we were banned from using any club facility. I often quoted Matthew 5:11-12 regarding Persecution to my congregation during our time of testing.

The Savannah church board and members decided to worship outdoors and not give up; they used carports of church members and a tent was erected in the backyard of Tobias' home. For the next four years we carried on worshiping with Dr. Glen Clifton speaking in the summer until we returned. November through April, despite some opposition and threats, we only missed one service in four years due to a hurricane. Our numbers declined somewhat to around one hundred people as some didn't want to be connected to controversy and the less-than-ideal conditions. After four years of worshiping outdoors, one of our members, Carl Allem offered to buy a large triple wide home on an oversized lot so we could use it as our "church home". We removed some walls and for, the next four years, we preached to one hundred worshipers and held many great services. We continued to reach people, even though we had been banned from advertising. Carl became ill and died. I took his funeral and his home had to be sold. As a church we could have purchased it but decided not to. The Lord opened a new door for us outside of Savannah Club at the beautiful "Harbour Place" retirement centre south of us. One of our members, Kaye Montangue, had gone there as a result of her husband Ed's death. He was planning to take all his extended family on a lovely cruise and went to have his teeth cleaned and a cap came loose; he inhaled it into his lungs. He had warned the dentist and they said they could retrieve it. They tried several methods and he got an infection and three weeks later he died, January 2003. His wife received a generous settlement allowing her to move to Harbour Place and they said we could use their beautiful facilities at no charge. The funeral for Edward was attended by two hundred family and friends, and God used testimonies and music and a biblical message I was able to share with Christians and non-Christians.

Again, we saw the hand of God using the death of one of his family to open a new door and location for our worship services to continue for the next four years and beyond. When Bev had endometrial cancer in 2013, we weren't able to come to Florida so it seemed a natural time to conclude oversight of the worship service; it was turned over to Glen Clifton Stu to continue on giving leadership to the remaining folk from Savannah Club and Harbour Place for as long as he was willing and able. About fifteen folks along with us began to attend Grace Emmanuel, an Evangelical Free Church with a great biblical pastor and a caring congregation. They asked me to speak at men's meetings. The only ministry I continued to carry on was a Men's weekly Bible study with about ten men which we had in our home along with a Women's Bible study, and these have produced some good fruit in these seniors' lives. However, these were discontinued in 2017 due to Bev's cancer returning and having to return early to Ontario.

To end on a positive note, I want to tell of the conversion of our neighbour named Jan. Her husband had left her and she was trying to survive on her own. My wife Bev befriended her and loved her, playing games and listening to her hurting heart. Jan started attending our church services, yet she remained bitter against her estranged husband. She had become strong and stubborn in order to survive. One Sunday evening we had Jan to our home in an effort to love her and lead her to Christ. I said, Jan you will die a bitter woman unless you give your life and bitterness to the Lord and allow Him to transform you. That evening in our sunroom she surrendered her life to Jesus Christ and was wonderfully converted. She went home and told us she had laid on the floor for two hours and poured out her feelings to God. Later her next-door neighbour asked me what has happened to Jan because now instead of yelling she was singing. I told him she gave her life to Christ and he transformed her life completely. Bev took her through a follow up course and now she is active in a local church welcoming new folks.

25

Bev's Health Challenges

The winter of 2004–2005 in Florida was to become a very challenging time. We were being evicted from all the facilities in Savannah Club, as a congregation, in spite of much prayer and assistance from Gibb's Law firm in Tampa. Then Bev started to have pain in her arm and back while running. I noticed her cheeks were pale and not pink and we knew something was wrong. I took her to a heart specialist and he said she had blockage in her arteries she needed a stent and he could do the procedure the next day. We immediately phoned our doctor in Huntsville who lived down our street and he said to head home as quickly as possible and he would arrange a place for her at the Heart Hospital in Newmarket. This was a Saturday in early March and the next day, being Sunday, marked the final Sunday we would be permitted to use the facilities in Savannah Club. I decided to stay and preach on the topic of "God's Purpose for Our Problems." As soon as the service ended, we said goodbye to our people and lawyers who were present, and we headed home to Ontario. We arrived in Newmarket in about thirty hours and immediately Bev was examined and tests run. Doctors found three arteries had blockages; one 100%, second 95%, and third 85%. They hooked her up to heart monitors immediately. Since it was March Break the doctors were on vacation in — guess where — Florida. It would be a week before she could have her triple bypass surgery done. I stayed between our daughter Faye's home in Whitby and Dale's home in Uxbridge. Bev got to know a man who was waiting for heart surgery; she played games with him and discovered he owned a computer company and was a Jehovah's Witness. His surgery was the day before Bev and his heart exploded so that he died on the operating table. I trust what Bev said, as well as her love and kindness, helped him be ready to meet his Maker.

The next morning, when I was at Faye and Ken's in Whitby, I received a call from Bev saying that she had been moved up because the other patient scheduled before her had eaten breakfast. I jumped in my car and grabbed Misty our dog and headed to Uxbridge at high speed in order to leave Misty there. I crossed the backroads to Newmarket in record time, parked, and ran up to Bev's room but she was gone. The nurses said I just missed her and the doctor was preparing her for surgery. A cleaning lady overheard our conversation and she said she knew where they took her. We ran down a long hall, down several flights of stairs and she pointed to a door and said, "She's in there." I knocked on the door and the surgeon, dressed in his green garb opened the door. I said, "Doctor, I'm her husband but I'm also her minister. Could I have a few minutes to pray with her and say goodbye?" He agreed so Bev and I hugged, kissed, and prayed and said goodbye trusting Bev would survive this open-heart surgery, in which her heart is stopped and a machine takes over. Following many hours of meticulous surgery, it was over and she was taken to a recovery room. When my daughters and I saw her, she looked like an astronaut with all the tubes sticking out of her. Following a week of convalescence in the hospital she was able to go home to Huntsville. It took many weeks of rest, exercise, diet, and perseverance before she recovered enough to function normally. The many prayers of God's people and excellent medical staff were used by the Lord to bring healing. Two side notes: first Bev's heart problems were due to heredity since both her parents died in their early seventies from heart disease. Secondly, the French doctor operating on Bev said, "You have nice legs and I don't want to leave long scars from taking out the needed veins." So instead he made a small incision and removed the vein with no visible scar. From that time in 2005 until her death in 2018 her heart never skipped a beat, except maybe when I came to her and said, "I love you."

We acknowledge the ultimate heart surgery is done by God as noted in Ezekiel 36:26 "I will give you a new heart and put a new spirit in you. I will remove from you the heart of stone and give you a heart of flesh." This is divine surgery and the ultimate spiritual heart transplant.

2013 CANCER CHALLENGE

In the early summer of 2013 Bev knew something wasn't right physically. I took her to Princess Margaret Hospital in Toronto following blood tests which revealed the possibility of cancer being present. The test results verified the presence of endometrial cancer. Princess Margaret worked in concert with Toronto General Hospital and on July 13th, 2013, Dr. Joan Murphy, a top cancer surgeon and noted lecturer was assigned to perform the operation. She met with us (and Lois and Dale) and said she might use a robot. It wasn't available the day of the operation, so she performed the operation herself. Dr. Murphy met with us immediately after the operation to tell us it had gone well.

Once back in Huntsville chemotherapy treatments began and these caused a lot of side effects; including Bev's losing her hair. Following months of chemotherapy, we prepared to go to London for radiation treatments. We left on November 14th, for Brampton, as I had to conduct the funeral of John Siderius, business administrator of our church. Bev couldn't attend and stayed with the Fitzells to keep her quarantined. Following a standing-room-only service, internment and fellowship time, we headed to Faye and Ken's. For the next six weeks I took Bev each morning to Victoria Hospital for about twenty-five radiation treatments. It was a very snowy and cold winter (a lot different than being in Florida); however, Faye and Ken made us feel at home and we stayed until December 30th, 2013. Everything had gone as scheduled and we looked forward to returning home. As we arrived home, I was glad to see our driveway had been blown clean with six-foot banks on each side. I drove into our garage and, as we walked into our home, it was freezing since our furnace had "given up the ghost" and hadn't worked for over a week. The water pipe to the lake was frozen solid. I lit a fire in our airtight stove and tried to melt snow and ice. I phoned the furnace man and, within two days, we had a new furnace. I encouraged Bev to go to Lois and Bruce's home since they were in Florida. Bev felt we should make a game out of it and pretend we were camping. What a gal. She never complained. I spent over two thousand dollars getting our pipes thawed out but within twenty-four hours they were frozen again. I carried water through deep snow from a nearby spring and finally, after ninety-six days, I got a new heated line installed and we had water again to drink, cook, shower, and flush our toilets. During this long siege we went twice a week to Lois and Bruce's home to shower and wash our clothes. By now it was April and spring would soon come. It was a very trying time for Bev and me, but we grew closer together as we trusted the Lord for strength and protection. It was nothing compared to what my parents went through in the winters in Saskatchewan with forty to fifty degrees below zero temperatures and three stoves and still the water would freeze. In the summer of 2016, we sold our home on the lake with Bev's encouragement and moved to 23 Kendra Crescent in Huntsville. It was a lovely home and we remodeled the kitchen, added a fireplace and looked forward to spending many more years there.

Then Bev had to face another round of chemotherapy at our local hospital. Hours of IV's and a lot of discomfort was faced by faith that her cancer would be defeated and become a distant memory. We prayed for God's grace to take us through this testing time and also for His will to be done.

BEV'S 2017–2018 CANCER CHALLENGE (FROM BEV)

The cancer journey started not knowing what I was dealing with. In October 2017, I had my regular semi-annual cancer check. The bloodwork showed normal numbers but slightly elevated. Dr. Presnell suggested since it was my fifth year since chemotherapy, I could skip the next checkup as my numbers were so good. I was not comfortable with that so scheduled it as usual then we happily took off for Florida. In November 2017, I was coughing regularly and it gradually got worse. At one point I got a cold as well, so I went to a walk-in clinic at the end of November and was given an antibiotic for bronchitis or possible pneumonia. A couple of weeks later I went to ER at the hospital and another set of antibiotics was given but still no change and a dry cough. Another trip to ER and supposedly resolution by changing my high blood pressure medication. Still no change so I went one more time and was told I had pleurisy and didn't need medication. In December I just didn't feel right but in January I had no energy and was staying home and lying on the sofa. I didn't want to make meals or eat much. During this time, I contacted our doctor in Huntsville who said we should come home as now Lois gave warning that possibly my cancer had come back. On January 23rd, 2018, we flew to Detroit to a clinic, had an x-ray which showed abnormalities in my lungs and the doctor said we needed a CT scan as we had planned on having one in Florida. Our doctor said we couldn't get a CT scan in Windsor but the doctor in the clinic arranged it for us. We flew back to Florida the next morning and planned to drive home the next day, but Lois and Bruce talked Dad into flying home; so we did on January 29th. Dale picked us up at the airport and drove us home. Now the medical 'circus' started once again. My oncologist in Barrie arranged for a consultation with Dr. Gazala, a thoracic (lung) surgeon who came from East General and we arranged for surgery on February 20th, after a pre-op in Barrie. This was to be exploratory surgery of my right lung and to remove several nodules including two blocking my windpipe; the procedure was more involved than I thought with five openings into my lung and throat. Without this I would have been in distress much earlier. I stayed in the hospital overnight and was uncomfortable for some time. Lois drove Dad and me to Toronto the night before and Dale met us at the hospital. Stu and Lois went to Dale's overnight and the next day I was discharged and Lois drove us home. I don't remember much but was glad to get into my bed and it took a few weeks to recover. On February 28th, I started taking Intervenus vitamins, administered by naturopath Brian Knapett in Huntsville, and weekly visits to Gunn Sikk in Weston, Toronto. It turned out this man had been a pupil at Gulf Stream School where I had taught from 1963 to 1965 when Stu was attending seminary. His office was next door to the school. Very ironic and it brought back fifty-five-year-old memories.

Upon returning home from Florida at the end of January 2018, it became evident that Bev's battle with cancer was becoming a greater challenge. For the next four months we utilized a variety of medical approaches in an effort to save Bev's life, as well as many prayer's being offered. I endeavored to care for her as she grew weaker, and my three caring daughters responded wonderfully. Dale a nurse along with Lois and Faye spent many days with us. I am also very grateful to my three caring son-in-laws Bruce, Todd and Ken for their love and support. Friends brought food and flowers along with their love and prayers. We had Palliative Care nurses come who were a blessing as they provided counsel, medications and needed supplies like oxygen. The time came when Bev needed 24-hour care and a Hospice was the answer. When the ambulance arrived, she was placed on a stretcher and taken outside. It was a beautiful sunny day and Bev said she could get a suntan, before being placed in the ambulance. She knew she would not be returning to her/our home, but with a joyful spirit was ready for her heavenly home. Bev was taken to Grace Hospice where she received loving care for twenty-two days.

BEV'S FINAL FIGHT WITH CANCER

June 23rd 2018, was Bev's last day on earth. She had been in Grace Hospice in Huntsville for three weeks. Our three daughters, Lois, Dale, and Faye and I had taken turns sleeping beside her on a murphy bed. I slept beside her the final night before she died. I tried to keep an eye on her during the night since Dr. Gerry Forestell said she didn't have long to live. She was heavily sedated, hadn't eaten in several weeks, and was unable to drink any water because she would choke. We had music playing on the iPad and the girls stayed close by. In the early afternoon I went out of Bev's room to be in the sitting room. A friend from the church, Wayne Reid, came to encourage me and pray with me. His wife Diane was the head nurse in the hospice which, was providential. When he headed home, I went back into Bev's room to see how she was doing. I had asked the doctor what would take place before Bev passed away; he said her breathing would become irregular and gradually her body would shut down. I had been monitoring her breathing which was laboured but was remaining the same. I went over and raised the bed up so I could hold her in my arms. I held her close and hugged and kissed her. The girls slipped out of the room as they saw I was having an intimate time with their mom. I told her how much I loved her, said she was the best gal, wife, mother, grandmother, and pastor's wife. I asked her to forgive me for where I had failed her for sin of omission or commission. Through tears I said to the Lord, my wife is suffering and she wants to die and needs to die and yet she lives on.

Then with Bev still in my arms, I turned and said to the Lord, "In case you have forgotten, my wife's full name is Beverly Ann Silvester and you need to take her home to heaven now," and she stopped breathing immediately and died in my arms. She went from my arms to the Lord's arms at 4:30 pm. I laid her down and ran out of the room and called our three daughters and said "Mom just died" and has gone from here to heaven. We cried and prayed together, and in this bittersweet moment thanked God for hearing our prayers and freeing her from her suffering. She heard and He heard my desperate cry and now she was absent from her body and present with the Lord. That was Saturday and they lit a candle in her memory (and some pictures were taken).

We left to finalize Bev's memorial service and an evening of visitation at Billingsley Funeral Home on Tuesday, June 26,2018. Bev and l had planned most of the details of her service. It was her desire that the service be honoring to the Lord, and not too long or about her. I feel we accomplished her first wish but didn't do so well on the last two. Bev wanted our three daughters and ten grandchildren to be involved, as well as her brother Keith if he was willing. On Tuesday evening the immediate family met at Billingsley Funeral Home for a time of fellowship and prayer and view Bev and say our good-byes. Scores of people came and shared their condolences. The hardest time was when I assisted in closing Bev's casket and seeing my lovely, loving wife for the last time on earth. The funeral service was held on Wednesday, June 27, 2018 at Faith Baptist Church in Huntsville at 11 am. I was there an hour early to make sure things were in order. People were arriving early and the slideshow was in progress and being enjoyed by many. The auditorium filled with over four hundred people-the largest attendance for a funeral that they had seen at Faith Baptist Church. The music led by our grandson Gregory and assisted by Jillian McDougall was inspiring. My brother Alan led the service as well as sharing a challenging message from John 11 on suffering and God's comfort. Our three daughters, Lois, Dale and Faye gave moving eulogies in memory of their mom. Jonathan, our grandson led in prayer and scriptures were read by granddaughters Rachael, Lauren and Megan. Amanda gave the granddaughters remarks and Laura read the poem, "If you could only see me now". Katelyn shared the tribute l had prepared in memory of Bev. Bev's brother Keith gave a fine tribute filled with funny incidents as they grew up. The hymn, "How Great Thou Art" was a fitting conclusion to a very moving and powerful service in memory of my wonderful wife, mother, grandmother, great -grandmother and friend. A lovely luncheon was served, allowing the many folk who had come from near and far, including over one hundred from Bramalea Baptist Church (our former church), as well as many pastors and their wives. Our three son-in-law's, Bruce, Todd and Ken and three grandsons, Jonathan, Brendan and Matthew were pall bearers. The internment for about thirty of the immediate family took place at the Hutchison Cemetery in Huntsville. Alan, Jonathan and l led the graveside service, followed by a time of testimonies and tears. Then we went to the "Local Restaurant", to a room we'd reserved for a meal and a time of fellowship. Faye announced she had a final Communique from Bev to me. l broke down and cried and didn't open it until l was at home alone. I discovered she had gotten Faye and Ken to get several Father's Day cards, and she picked out a beautiful one for me. Although by now she could hardly write, she wrote some of the most loving and lovely thoughts. It is a special keep sake and memory which I'll cherish forever.

Bev's Grave Stone in Huntsville - 2018

Appendix A
Memories of Christmas
Before 1960–Stu's

Out in Saskatchewan I was waiting for Santa and they said he had to come by airplane. I can only remember getting an orange. Dad made a barn with wooden animals for us boys when there was no money. It was probably difficult to find wood on the prairies to build it with too.

At Sunday School and church, I remember lots of music. Uncle Roy brought us gifts one year and someone stole them out of his car so he went and got new ones for us; those would be the only gifts we got that year (1942 in St. Thomas).

At the Weatherhead company where dad worked there was a Christmas party where we got the biggest gifts we'd ever had. We walked to Hiawatha Baptist Church because gas was rationed and we would go along railway tracks as a shortcut, probably over a mile.

In 1946 after moving to Shelburne when I was eleven, we got a Christmas tree from our bush. We had lots of special things to eat but not many presents. At Whittington United Church they had concerts that we attended. The Lannings were close by and many Christmases were spent together. There was always lots of music mom played the piano, dad the violin and sometimes the accordion, and Uncle Gene played the violin and the bones.

I remember one Christmas going into a variety store in Shelburne and buying six gifts for my brothers and mom and dad. It was one stop shopping. I made money by being the caretaker at the school from the time I was age fifteen. I got fifteen dollars a month as payment for cleaning it and lighting fires in winter. When a teen, I went to YFC (Youth for Christ) activities, dinners, and musical programs. I was going with several gals I had met at YFC and our church in Sarnia ('57–59) before I met Bev.

At a store buying a Christmas gift, I couldn't remember the girl's name when the sales lady asked. I did finally come up with the right name. Possibly it was this embarrassing incident that helped me settle down to dating only one girl (Bev) and saved me making the same mistake twice.

MEMORIES OF CHRISTMAS — BEV'S

Christmas's growing up in our little apartment were cozy. Putting up the Christmas tree was always fun and as I got older, I took over getting the tinsel on just right (at least I thought so.) I was always excited about Christmas and the gifts I would get. I remember a tin doll house and dolls, roller skates, and ice skates. It was always a time of having company, friends of mom and dad. Sometimes they had children who came too. The adults played cards, drank beer, and smoked cigarettes and pipes. Dad sometimes drank too much and was not too pleasant to have around. I never got used to that. Stu's first experience with that in 1959 was a shock to him and I was so embarrassed.

After we got married, on our first Christmas, we were invited to my mom and dad's for dinner along with Stu's parents. Mom always used her good dishes and silverware at Christmas and had a big turkey with all the trimmings, including turnip, a ribbon salad made with jello, mincemeat pie, ice cream, fruit cake, and sometimes Christmas pudding.

Every Christmas dinner was at mom and dad's, and Stu's dad was nearly always there because his Mom died in our first year of marriage. When our children arrived, they enjoyed the fun they had with their Uncle Keith who had no choice but to love being awakened early to play. He was about fourteen when this first started. Our children have good memories of the fun of Christmas morning and, as they got older, they enjoyed the hidden gifts that Santa had left. How fortunate they were to have Christmas with their grandparents and Uncle Keith and all the attention that that brought. Until they were older, we always went to Sarnia to celebrate Christmas.

Thanksgiving Celebrations At Our Home

As our family of three daughters, their husbands, and grandchildren increased to a total of eighteen, "Thanksgiving Day" became a special time. Prior to our retirement in 1996, we would meet at our home in Cheltenham or our cottage on Doe Lake. Bev loved to host this annual event which included scrumptious food, turkey, vegetables, pumpkin pies, and all the trimmings. Once we retired to our home on the lake in Huntsville, we would gather for this annual celebration. Bev planned "candy tosses", hikes, and games so everyone from the youngest to the oldest had lots of fun, food, and fellowship. As we gathered around food-laden tables, with children in the kitchen and adults in the dining room, we would each thank God for blessings in the past year. It helped us all to remember that every good and perfect gift came from above. Often family photos and group pictures were taken on our lawn by the water and as time went by the members increased, including several dogs and the little grandchildren grew into teenagers and young adults. Since moving into Huntsville and less space, Lois and Bruce's spacious homes on the lake became our meeting place. As I write, our numbers have increased to over thirty including spouses and great grandchildren. Bev is no longer with us, so my three lovely daughters continue on this tradition.

Family Picture at Huntsville Home - My 70th - 2005

Appendix B
FBYPA
Fellowship Baptist Youth

I was twenty-two and living in Sarnia when I first heard of FBYPA through Temple Baptist Church. I left in my Dad's new 1957 Ford for MBC (Muskoka Baptist Conference) in Huntsville, ON. I remember he gave me his credit card in case of trouble. It was a good thing he did because I forgot my wallet and had no money, so had to borrow from other young people. MBC was originally started by the Young People's Association and each Labour Day Weekend had a week for college and career young people. This was my first introduction to FBYPA as well as to a girl named Helen from St. Thomas whom I dated for a while.

FBYPA held large rallies at Stratford Shakespearian Festival periodically as well as at Niagara Falls. When I was in seminary, I was asked to be on the FBYPA executive. This led me to be involved in speaking at retreats following graduation from seminary and when I was youth pastor at Forward Baptist Church. Our rallies grew and attendances reached up to two thousand, with busloads of young people traveling to these exciting events. Shortly after moving to Bramalea in 1969, I was asked to become the first paid worker for FBYPA. This involved one day a week; with my publishing a monthly newspaper, conducting rallies, and speaking at many youth retreats across Ontario and even into Winnipeg, Manitoba. I traveled by car and occasionally by plane, and for two years I planned youth week at MBC for college and career students.

I especially remember one year when I was sports director and Warren Kimball was the speaker. To add some excitement, we announced that after dinner we would meet down at the beach to see professional water skiers who had come from Cypress Gardens in Florida. Warren and I dressed up in women's dresses and hat with sunglasses and got behind Harry Beer's fast motorboat and headed off from his cottage on the Muskoka River and headed into Mary Lake. About one hundred young people were waiting at the beach. We circled near them at increasingly higher speeds. Warren let go of his rope and I motioned for the driver to go around one more time. That was a mistake for as we went around the waves tripped me up and I took a spill. I only had a small lifebelt on and a dress that clung to my legs right down to my ankles. I came up sputtering and yelling for help since I couldn't kick my legs due to the dress and I couldn't swim. I went under and came up sputtering and yelling for help. The boat had disappeared but returned. Marg Beer dove in and rescued me. All this time Bev was watching with Lois and Dale by her side and very pregnant with Faye. She was up on the hill so fortunately didn't know exactly what was happening until it was over. Once safe on shore I went back skiing without the dress. Even then, it was not wise because my swimming skills were limited. This was a very scary incident but there would be one more during my work with FBYPA.

In about 1972 as a result of FBYPA growing it was time for a full-time worker. Bramalea Baptist Church was growing quickly and I needed to give all my attention to it and resign from FBYPA.

We approached Roy Lawson in London and he said he'd be open to a move. Four of us on the executive headed to London; this included Mike Brown, Jack Hannah, Jim Watt and me. It was winter and we met Roy at Central Baptist Church where he was Pastor. As the four of us headed home along the 401 there was freezing rain and treacherous driving conditions. Mike was driving his 1968 Old's Cutlass and pulled out to pass two long tractor trailer trucks. His left wheels went onto the shoulder and I warned him to be careful getting back up on the highway once past the trailer. Sure enough, he started to slide sideways and the first truck hit us in the left rear quarter panel and spun us around and up the snow bank going backwards. Then we started to slide back onto the 401 and the second truck was coming toward us. I was in the back seat behind the driver and I was sure we were going to go under the transport truck. Then the car's bumper caught on the guard rail post which kept us from being run over and possibly killed. A tow truck driver coming west on the 401 said that they saw the accident happen and thought the car was going to be crushed and its occupants killed.

The only damage was to my hand when I was jacking the car off the guard rail and it slipped and injured it. The car suffered a dented fender and we pulled it out and continued home — more slowly and grateful to God to be alive. I arrived home in Bramalea at 4 a.m. Bev was up when I arrived home, naturally worried, as I was so late. I had to be at Central Baptist Seminary to speak at chapel at 8:00 am so didn't get much sleep. So ended my tenure with FBYPA, as fortunately Roy accepted our request for him to take over from me.

Appendix C
Resignation Letter
December 16, 1988

Dear Brothers and Sisters in Christ,

Although I find this letter difficult to write and read, I know it is God's time and will to do so. After seven months of wrestling with a new challenge and possible change in my ministry, I have accepted a call from our Fellowship executive in Toronto to become Home Missions Extension Secretary for Canada. This position will involve giving leadership in the area of church growth and renewal, church planting, ethnic ministries, chaplaincy ministry, church resources and internship ministry.

This decision has been the most difficult one I have ever made. It has not been made because of any pressure, problem or person, but rather after much time and prayer it became evident it was God's will. The Lord has since confirmed this decision in several ways. From a human viewpoint, it would have been easier to stay in the security and love of this great church family, but I've learned that God's will must come before mine. Knowing that this decision is God's will, we can have full assurance that He will provide and will bless Bramalea Baptist Church.

Sunday, March 12, will make the conclusion of my ministry as Senior Pastor of this fine church. However, as a family, we plan to go on living at our present residence and attend here for as long as it is possible and feasible.

On behalf of Bev and my family, let me express heartfelt appreciation and thanks for your love, support, encouragement and understanding over the years. You dear folk will always be an integral part of our lives. God bless you all.

Lovingly in the Lord,
Stuart Silvester

Appendix D
Noted Speakers Who Ministered at Bramalea Baptist Church

1. Chuck Swindoll from Fullerton California. He came in the mid 70's to speak at a Pastors' meeting for our Fellowship leaders. It was early in his ministry and he was to speak on leadership and asked me, as he met in my office, if he spoke on Joseph's life if it would be okay. I encouraged him to share as he felt led. He did a great job of challenging all of us. In the evening he spoke on the family to our congregation and other visitors. He is a humble and gracious servant of God.
2. Dr. Richard Dehaan from Michigan and Daily Bread publication. He spoke at our ninth anniversary services and was a great blessing. As I drove him to Toronto International Airport on Monday morning, he asked me if I knew any good illustrations for his Daily Bread booklets. I told him of a member in our church (Neilson Brooking) who had a small plane and used Toronto airport, but that he had the same rights and access as big jets. After a few months in September 20th, 1999, he wrote a devotional article entitled Equal Access and then it was reprinted on February 28th, 2006, and again 2017 as part of the one hundred and fiftieth anniversary issue for Canada.
3. Dr. Jack Scott – Toronto and Detroit, Michigan. He was an amazing speaker and delivered powerful messages.
4. Dr. Elmer Towns – Lynchburg, Virginia. He spoke on two occasions with great acceptance and blessing.

5. Sutera Twins from Stow Ohio. They ministered in 1976 and again in 1986 with wonderful results.
6. Chuck Colson from Prison Fellowship. He spoke to fourteen hundred people on a weeknight regarding morality and ethics. He was of Watergate notoriety and wonderfully converted, becoming a noted apologist and author of numerous books.
7. Dr. Erwin Lutzer – Pastor of Moody Memorial Church in Chicago. He was born in Canada but has a great preaching ministry as well as authoring several fine books.
8. Josh McDowell of California. He spoke to large crowds with great results in 1980. An interesting aside was that a couple who had just moved from California to Bramalea were looking for a new church. They said, if the speaker at Bramalea Baptist Church was from California, they would know it was God's will to join and they did.
9. Dr. John MacArthur from California. He was the guest speaker at our Fellowship Convention in 1986 and he also met with our pastoral staff for a time of encouragement and teaching.

One of the blessings of having a large and growing church was the ability to attract and afford gifted speakers and servants of God to challenge our people and others for Christ and His Kingdom.

Appendix E
Let us Clarify our
Perspective and Purpose[1]

Stuart N. Silvester

In the fall of 1976, I was approached by Dr. Roy Lawson and the Fellowship to see if I would be willing to become the Fellowship President for 1976 to 1977. I took this request to our Deacon's Board and they approved. It was an honour to be asked since I was young compared to Dr. Pickford from B.C., whom I was replacing. It was also a challenging responsibility of being chairman of the executive committee as well of our Fellowship, as well as travelling to numerous conventions and speaking at church openings and anniversaries etc.

I enjoyed the challenge and found it a time of stretching my vision and faith with the privilege of preaching God's Word from coast to coast. Unknown to me it was preparing me for a full-time ministry with our five hundred plus Fellowship churches in 1989 when I left Bramalea Baptist to give leadership in evangelism, church planting, and church growth.

I'm including a sermon of my address I gave at our Convention in Niagara Falls in November 1976, which was published in the Evangelical Baptist Magazine (E.B.).

I am grateful for the generosity of our Church Board and people for allowing me to serve the Lord in this way since our church was growing rapidly and required a lot of leadership, faith and work to keep up with our growing com-

[1] Stuart N. Silvester, "Let us Clarify our Perspective and Purpose," *Evangelical Baptist* (December 1976): 4–5.

munity and people's needs.

———————

God has been pleased to bless our Fellowship since its inception on October 21, 1953 with steady and sometimes spectacular growth. However, when something is growing rapidly; whether it be a child, a business, a local church or our Fellowship, it is a time of vulnerability.

Our doctrinal statement is definitely and unmistakably Baptistic and biblical. Leaders in non-Baptist churches often say about themselves, "We are Baptist in everything but name." They are thus recognizing and acknowledging that what we believe and practise is the divine pattern as revealed in scripture. Since we all, as local Fellowship Baptist churches, subscribe to the same doctrinal statement, it is imperative that we have similar basic objectives and goals which are based on the infallible Word of God. A company without clearly defined objectives and goals in today's competitive society is bound for bankruptcy.

Paul says in 1 Corinthians 14:8, "For if the trumpet give an uncertain sound, who shall prepare himself to the battle?" As individual blood-bought believers, and as a Fellowship, we must know both what we believe and why. We must produce a certain sound for uncertain and perilous days.

In a recent period of growth and transition in our own local church we endeavoured to clarify our perspective and purpose of existence so that both our message and methodology would be based on biblical principles. I believe the following three-fold objective is both biblical and basic for God's continued blessing upon our Fellowship of Evangelical Baptist Churches in Canada.

We Must Exalt Christ

Paul, in writing to the church in Colosse says, "And he is the head of the body, the church ... that in all things he might have the preeminence."[2] Exalt means to raise up, to prove, to extol and to place in high rank.

As evangelical Baptists, we have always prided ourselves on adhering to the Lordship and headship of Christ. Yet, too often I feel preeminence is given to buildings, budgets and buses, rather than to our blessed Lord. Granted these are important in the spread of the gospel but our thoughts and our talk must not be centred upon them but on him. Many people who have ceased to attend church have done so because the church rather than Christ was given the place of preeminence.

Since we acknowledge Christ as our heavenly Head and not some earthly vic-

———————

[2] Colossians 1:18 (KJV).

ar, we must not allow any person or program, or even our Fellowship of churches, to have preeminence over Christ and our fellowship with him. In our day, when there is a proliferation of false prophets and antichrists, let us remember the words of Jesus, "And I, if I be lifted up, will draw all men to Me."[3] Today, when many so-called preachers are denying Christ's virgin birth, his virtuous life, his vicarious death, his victorious resurrection, and his visible return, let us rededicate ourselves to the glorious privilege and great responsibility of exalting our Lord and Saviour Jesus Christ.

We Must Edify the Christian

To edify means to build up in the faith and to instruct. Romans 14:9 declares, "Let us therefore follow after the things which make for peace and the things where-with one may edify another."

Since conversion is the only commencement of the Christian life, it is important that we seek to build up our brothers and sisters in the faith. Without spiritual development, there will not be spiritual discernment, and this could lead to fighting amongst ourselves rather than against Satan and sin. Satan would love to fragment our Fellowship, and thereby weaken our witness. This need not happen if we follow Paul's admonition. In Ephesians 4:11–16 Paul speaks of the diversity of gifts given to church leaders so believers will be brought to maturity and they in turn may build each other up. The result is an increase of the body and a strength which enables us not to be "tossed about with every wind of doctrine."[4] As spiritual leaders it is important that we help our people discover and develop their gift(s) within the body.

As pastors, we must know that God has called us as undershepherds under the headship of the chief Shepherd and has entrusted to us the privilege of leading and feeding his sheep. Let us not be guilty of scattering the flock, either through lack of teaching, or lack of tending the sheep. When wolves in sheep's clothing come in to try and scatter the sheep, let us stay with them and not run from our responsibility.

As members of local churches, it is important that you allow your pastor to lead as the undershepherd. Some churches have been choked by people who have become overly possessive and provincial and have equated smallness with spirituality and largeness with Liberalism.

Our Fellowship will be only as strong as the pastors and people of its churches. Let us build each other up so that the life and love of Christ is growing and overflowing to others. Just as there is a ministry of edification within our local church, so we must assist in the edifying of our fellow Christians in our sister

3 John 12:32.
4 Ephesians 4:14.

churches across Canada.

We Must Evangelize the Community

A survey in the United States in 1975 revealed that out of twenty-four institutions the church was listed twenty-third with respect to its impact and influence upon society. This survey seems to point out a weakness in the witness of the church in society. As a Fellowship, let us pray that our ministry will he effective in our communities.

According to the dictionary, evangelism means "preaching the gospel and converting to Christianity." Evangelism should be the outgrowth of exalting Christ and edifying the Christian. We must evangelize for two reasons.

Firstly, because of the condition of the world. Our world has become a global village with four billion inhabitants and is seemingly balanced on the brink of oblivion. Our society seems to be sick with similar symptoms which led to Rome's fall: moral decadence, atheism, materialism and sensualism. Statisticians tell us one out of every five Canadians were Christians a hundred years ago and now it is one out of twenty. By 1984, it will be one out of fifty or two percent of the population. The many false cults are evangelizing at an alarming rate. People are seeking truth and hope. We have the answer for their needs! Are we willing to share it?

Secondly, because of the commission of Christ. We must remember that the Bible does not say "Come and hear," but "Go and tell." Our going is inseparably linked to our growing both numerically and spiritually as Christians and as a Fellowship. Beginning at our Jerusalem, we are to go in the power of the Spirit, not in the feebleness of the flesh (Acts 1:8). It is only as each church is carrying out this commission of evangelizing and discipling that we shall see our fellow-Canadians becoming brothers and sisters in the Lord.

However, we must not allow Satan to get us sidetracked from going with the gospel. He is pleased when he gets us riding hobby horses which may produce plenty of motion but get us nowhere. For example, the second coming of Christ must not become a "Doctrine for Debate, but a Motive for Missions." If we are to evangelize our communities in Canada, it must mean the establishing of many more churches and strengthening the existing ones. Just as evangelism is the overflow from building up the saints, so foreign missions is the outgrowth of home missions. It will be only as every member of every Fellowship Baptist Church takes his calling and commissioning seriously that the objective of exalting Christ, edifying the Christians and evangelizing the community will become a reality.

May the words of the hymn writer express our experience as we seek to carry out Christ's commission in Canada:

> Like a mighty army moves the church of God,
> Brothers we are treading, where the saints have trod;
> We are not divided; all one body we;
> One to hope and doctrine, one in charity!
> Onward Christian soldiers, marching as to war
> With the cross of Jesus, going on before.[5]

---

[5] Sabline Baring-Gould, "Onward, Christian soldiers," third stanza.

Appendix F
The New Age Movement in Canada
Article for Pastors Conference
June 1994
S. Silvester

The term "New Age" is a name and phenomenon often spoken of today. We hear about it on TV, radio, in books, school and literature.

What is the New Age Movement (NAM)? A religion, cult, world-view or fad? The NAM, according to the assistant editor of *Christian Research Journal*, 'aims to change our society by becoming the predominant and accepted philosophy.' It has been called "Spiritual Humanism". Douglas Groothuis in his book, *Unmasking the New Age* says, the old-fashioned secular humanist said, "There is no deity—long live humanity, while spiritual humanist (NA) says, "There is no deity but humanity".

I'm going to ask questions? What, When, Why, Where, How and endeavour to answer these questions relating to NAM.

I. When did the New Age Movement Begin?
Is the NAM new? Most NA teaching is just a revamping of old Eastern religious ideas. Some elements of NA teaching are an attempt to bridge the gap between a naturalistic science and a super-natural religion. Randall Baer writes, "The NAM is essentially Satan controlled modern day revival of occult-based philos-

ophies and practices in obvious and cleverly disguised forms. It is actually not anything new at all, for in many countries the occult has been active and more recently invaded North America. The magnitude and momentum is such it poses one of the greatest threats to Christianity."

Texe Mars in the book, *Dark Secrets of the New Age* lists nearly 30 rituals and beliefs found in ancient Babylon that NA practices today. "The NA is the revival of the Old Age and may well turn out to be the final age." Contrary to public opinion, NA isn't a religion. There are no NA Bibles, headquarters or statements of faith, but rather a loosely knit group of people who share a similar philosophy or world view. It has been in the 1980s that the NAM has gained momentum in the US and Canada. Some believe there is a NA conspiracy or overall game plan.

II. What does the New Age Movement Believe and Teach?

New Age Literature speaks of the need of Cleansing away the old superstitions and beliefs in order to usher in the New Age. Walter Martin in his book, *The New Age Cult* states that New Agers see themselves as advanced in consciousness; rejecting Judeo-Christian values and the Bible in favour of Oriental philosophies and religions. Other names for the NAM include Age of Aquarius, The New Age Consciousness, Cosmic Humanism, New World Order and New Globalism. John Stanhope says in *Faith Today*, "The NAM is best described as a growing social and religious movement that blends Eastern philosophy with Western culture, incorporating ancient beliefs such as astrology, reincarnation, occultism and pantheism with new phenomena such as trance-channeling. It has united people of all social, political and religious persuasion in the quest of a common goal, vison and way of life.

The teachings of the NAM can be put under four headings: Pantheism, Reincarnation, Relativism and Esotericism. In Genesis 3:4-5 look at Satan's message (lie) to our first parents, "You will not surely die, the serpent said to the woman. For God knows that when you eat of it your eyes will be opened, and you will be like God, knowing good and evil." In NAM today we have these same four lies being taught. Let me elaborate.

1. ***Pantheism "You will be like God"***

    Satan promised Adam blend Eve that they could set up a rival kingdom and they could be their own God. The teaching NAM is we are God, but in a sense are still becoming God too.

    A.W Tozer said, "No religion can rise higher than its conception of God." There are 3 views of God which are held:

    a. *Theism* is the belief that God is the Creator and Sustainer of the universe.

b. *Atheism* is the view that there is no God.

c. *Pantheism* is the belief that God is all and all is God. Word PAN means all. This belief permeates NAM. God is an impersonal force; God is energy and energy is God. Pantheism teaches that man is his own Saviour and that there never was a fall. Shirley MacLaine says we are both creator and creation and we can bring the two together. Pantheism says God fell and man redeems him.

<u>Pantheism destroys morality</u>. Charles Manson, mass murderer who embraced pantheism and NA said, "If God is all, what is evil?" At the heart of Pantheism is a denial of evil and since evil doesn't exist, the problem isn't sin but ignorance and all we need is to be enlightened.

Illus. In India rats eat 20% of food, non-productive cows 15% and monkeys 15%. They don't stop them because everything is God and everything should get equal treatment. (You could be eating a relative.)

In Canada, animal rights activists teach animals have equal rights with people. When we worship nature we end up in subjection to it.

2. *Reincarnation "You will not surely die"*

Satan's second fabrication (lie) to minimize the consequences of disobedience was the doctrine of reincarnation. Yes, you may die but you go on living in another body and you go around and around from one life to the next.

<u>Illus</u>. A couple of New Agers who kissed before jumping off the Golden Gate bridge, left a note in the car which said (man wrote it), "I love you all and wish I could stay, but I must hurry. The suspense is killing me." Shirley MacLaine says. "We can eliminate the fear of death because death doesn't exist." Reincarnation holds that plants, animals and humans are so interrelated that we can transmigrate from one form of life to another. She says it is just like show business. "You just keep doing it until you get it right."

3. *Relativism "You will know good and evil"*

In Genesis 3:1 Satan asked, Has God said?" He got Eve to doubt God's word. It led to relativism—nothing is intrinsically right or wrong; the situation determines the morality (what feels good). After all, if all is God and God is all, then evil must be God too! It removes distinctions between right and wrong. In 1976, 9000 university students were surveyed, 51% then believed in relativism. John Dewey, philosopher and educator, is credited with giving relativism respectability. (They say, "There are no absolutes!")

4. *Esotericism "Your eyes will be opened"*

The esoterics believe they are privy to special knowledge. They believe that reality can be reduced to a personal experience of enlightenment. The basic lie is; feel, don't think! This philosophy, known as esotericism, lies at the heart of NAM. We are told there is a "transformation of consciousness" that initiates us into true spirituality. The bottom line to these four teachings is the self-sufficiency of mankind. When we take a journey within we find that we are God, as we use channeling to contact Masters who have preceded us. We are told our problem isn't sin but ignorance, and we need to be enlightened.

Listen to the invocation used daily by New Agers who are interested in working together with God to bring peace to earth: "From the point of light within the Mind of God, let light stream forth into the minds of men. Let light descend on Earth. From the point of Love within the Heart of God, let love stream forth into the hearts of men. May Christ return to earth". The God referred to is the pantheistic God. The Christ of Maitreya; and the light is the enlightened mind. In a recent survey by Andrew Greely, 5% of North Americans claim they've already been "bathed in light." They have had an esoteric experience, a personal encounter that has given them special knowledge.

C.S. Lewis says that, "The highest form of deception would be for demons to duplicate spiritual experience". Potential NA Converts are told that they need not discard the past, just "transcend" it. Erwin Lutzer, Moody Church says, "The New Messiah will be the Antichrist of Rev. 13 and will usher in a counterfeit Christianity. Instead of prayers there will be mantras, instead of preachers, gurus, in place of prophet, psyches, in place of ten commandments will be a new set of commandments for a New Age and in place of the Holy Trinity an unholy trinity".

III. Why do People Join the New Age Movement?

Former New Ager – Dan Hardock writes, "NA is flourishing because of disillusionment with western values. As Christian Values are rejected, NA moves in to fill the void in every segment of our society including religion, politics, education, environment, etc. There is no area at personal, societal or global levels that NA doesn't attempt to replace biblical teaching with satanic counterfeit. The NA offers power! Power to get out of any situation, power to take over situations and to alter situations".

Thousands of people are paying hundreds of dollars to go to NA seminars. Why? Firstly, people are looking for spiritual fulfillment. Secondly, people are lonely and looking for meaningful personal relationships.

There are three social needs which are important and could be called 3 C's

of community:
1. *Comfortable* amongst their peers (Acceptance)
2. *Commitment*, a sense of loyalty to a cause and each other.
3. *Contribution*, a sense of satisfaction that comes from feeling needed. People get this from NA. (Our churches need small groups to experience the 3 C's of Community)

IV. Who is Involved in the New Age Movement?

There are dabblers and disciples—those who have been deluded and not aware of the involvement and those dedicated to promoting NA. In North America alone Shirley MacLaine has sold 11 million copies of her books. Nearly every Canadian book store carries NA books. In Montreal where a NA magazine has 85,000 circulation, it says 10,000 people in Montreal now make their living from NA related business. Bunyan Book Store in Vancouver offers 20,000 titles and tapes of NA. According to Chatelaine, Canada had only 4 or 5 such stores three years ago, and now 40 and in every major city.

Illus—US Corporations spend four billion annually on NA consultants to teach them conscious--raising techniques, and seven million (mainly professional people) have taken the Silva Method of mind control, all based on occult philosophy. Not only big Corporations such as Ford, Bell, Procter & Gamble, but well-known people ie. Alvin Toffler – author and futurist, Jonas Salk – biologist, Marguret Meade (late anthropologist)

In the film – "**Gods of the New Age** – "they estimated 60 million Americans have been involved in some form of the New Age! 52 Publishing Houses have formed the NA Publishing & Retail Alliance whose slogan is "A Consciousness Whose time has come".

Areas Where NA is Active include:
1. *Music* – There is even a Grammy Award for NA musicians. Many songs today contain NA teaching (illus. "Cosmic Energy")
2. *Educations* – Values clarification teaching used in Ontario is NA inspired. Students learn to use their feelings about right and wrong (no absolutes)

Illus. One of our college age gals from Bramalea Baptist quit a community college where she was studying Early Childhood Education because of NA teaching.

Illus. A lady from Norland Baptist Church quit a night school course because she had to begin class with NA meditations.

Illus. In Lindsay a kindergarten teacher had her children put their fingers into a mirror and then when they pulled them out they were covered in blood. The mirror wasn't broken but intact. One day her room burst into flames for no apparent reason. It was discovered that the woman, who had been a Sunday School teacher, was now a New Ager and witch and was getting her school children to join her coven. The principal tried to cover up for her.

Illus. On the cover of the Ontario Teachers Federation magazine from the fall of 1989 there was a picture of children lying on the floor and meditating and consulting the "wise one". The magazine was telling the teachers that this was a new method of teaching and learning.

In schools, notices are placed on bulletin boards for the teachers to attend "Zen" seminars which has Hindu teaching throughout it.

Illus. Another example of values clarification and NA teaching is where the teacher gets pupils to pretend they are in a life raft. However, there are too many to fit in, and the children are forced to make a decision as to who is least important and must be left out. This exercise not only teaches that life isn't important but also that some people are more important than others.

1. **New Age Games Dungeons & Dragons** is a game that has no board or moving pieces but requires an active imagination. Players take on identities of medieval warriors and battle monsters. Many young people have ended up committing suicide or killing others. Dr. Thomas Radechi say's "It causes desensitization to violence."

2. **Videos & Toys** NA is marketing many videos and children's toys which are aimed at the minds of those who are very impressionable.

3. **Health Food Stores** main motive is profit and then NA and holistic teaching. Leads to vegetarianism. It's not bad to eat vegetables but the problem is when meat is forbidden as Hindus do because you might be eating a relative who has become an animal.

4. **Counselling.** Many New Age counsellors are appearing and advertising their holistic approach. One such NA counsellor wrote a letter to me before I concluded my ministry at Bramalea Baptist. She calls it the "Positive Alternative Wellness Education Centre". She says, "My counselling has a strong, but subtle, spiritual component". According to her literature, her approach is holistic from a humanistic, transpersonal perspective, and from a feminist viewpoint. She invites clients to risk being themselves and to begin the journey into Self that does not reform but transforms. On her calling card she uses four concentric circles which are one of the NA symbols.

5. **Holistic Medicine.** NA offers course for everything including AIDS. They say with the proper alignment of mind, body and spirit we can tap

into latent resources to fight disease.

6. **Green Peace Movement** is staffed by New Agers who emphasize the saving of whales, seals dolphins and trees for all are seen as gods.
7. **Theology.** Secular psychology and NA Teaches that man has the resources to solve his problems and that he must accept himself as he is and will become and this has crept into modern teachings.

Wm. Kilpatrick, in his book, "Psychologicol Seduction" warns against NA philosophy, which elevates man and the idea of self-worth and human potential which minimizes or denies man's fall and sin. No biblical saint who met god ended up accepting himself unconditionally. <u>Illus.</u> Isaiah (Isaiah 6:5), Peter (Luke 5:8), Paul (rom 7:24). Martin Luther said, "God didn't love us because we are valuable; we are valuable because God loves us."

Robert Shuller's book, "Self Esteem – The New Reformations" replaces the Reformations doctrines of the depravity of man with a man-centered theology. He writes, "We need a theology of salvation that begins and ends with a recognition of every person's hunger for glory". He sees sin as against man and not against God primarily. When Schuller accepts a humanist view of man, he deminishes God. He now accepts Hindu meditation as compatible with Christianity. He writes, "The most effective mantras employ the "M" sound. You can get the feel of it by repeating the words I am, I am many times over. Transcendental meditation isn't a religion nor is it necessarily ant-Christianity".

V. Where Does New Age Teaching Lead?

Randall Baer in his book. "Inside the New Age Nightmare" who is a former NA teacher, holistic doctor and activist says. "Seeking truth I found only masterful counterfeits designed as truth, yearning for inner fulfillment and peace I experienced seduction and Satan's lies and bondage. Through drugs, yoga, T.M. and Eastern religions my mind had holes blown in it and allowed demons to enter and control. The ultimate seduction has over-take me. What I thought was heaven was hell and what I thought were ascended Masters and angels were demons". The By Product of NA Teaching Includes the Following:

1. Erosion of Biblical morals resulting in fornication, adultery etc.
2. Self-gratification and self-glorification and selfishness is common.
3. Family devalued and breaks down because of self-centeredness.
4. Men become feminine and women masculine. Unisex is widely held.
5. Feminist movement and emphasis on idea of goddess worship
6. Homosexuality is broadly accepted as normal and good.
7. Nudity is a sign of self-acceptance (nude saunas and swimming).
8. Abortion is practiced a lot.

9. Drug use is common for expanding consciousness.
10. Death is only an illusion and therefor no victims in killing or dying. NA leaders tell follower, "Just remember you are God and act accordingly".

    One guru says, "Kneel to your own self. Honour and worship your own being. God dwells within you as you". Self-empowerment is their quest in order to gain more power, attention and possessions. There is virtually no thought of helping others. (this is where we as Christians can be effective).

VI. How Can we Reach People in the New Age Movement?

Witnessing to NA people is difficult for two reason;

1. The great variety of NA terms and beliefs means you must get to know the person and what he believes.
2. Because NA doesn't deal with absolutes, but all is relative, New Agers create their own reality and therefore they believe that what is true for them isn't necessarily true for others. You can't impose your truth (the gospel) on them. They will say Jesus may be Lord for you and your reality, but it isn't theirs.

To New Agers, Christianity is Old Age and they won't listen very easily. The Bible is accepted, but only conditionally as one scripture among many sources of truth. The following four areas of teaching are interpreted by the NA as follows:

1. The Sinful Nature of Man – NA says that man is inherently perfect and a god.
2. Man's Need of Redemption through Christ – NA says there is no need of redemption.
3. Final Judgement – NA holds that each person is ultimately his own judge and the lake of fire is a myth.
4. The Personal Return of Christ – NA maintains another Christ (not Jesus Christ) or Christ-consciousness will lead the world to the New Age.

Some Don'ts re: Witnessing

1. Don't use shot gun blast approach. Treat them with respect and don't just spout off.
2. Don't just tell them they are wrong but ask questions.

The following three things are needed to rescue New Agers.
1. <u>Intercession</u>. It is a spiritual warfare (James 5:6 and I Cor. 10:24).
2. <u>Patience</u>. It takes endurance and time.
3. <u>Kindness</u>. It is love that can win them. If they come to Christ get them to remove all evil practices and paraphernalia.

VII. How Can We Identify New Agers?

The NAM has its own particular way of expressing itself with its own words, terms and vocabulary. Knowing some of these NA "buzz words" can be helpful in identifying and witnessing to them. Many of their terms seem harmless, but behind them usually lies a NA teaching or world view. However, it would be naive and unfair to assume that all groups or individuals who use a symbol or term (e.g. rainbow) are New Agers.

1. <u>Symbols</u>. The rainbow, pyramid, triangle, eye in a triangle, Pegasus (flying horse), concentric circles, ray of light, swastika, unicorn, goat's head, 666.
2. <u>Buzzwords</u>. Holistic, New Consciousness paradigm, transcendent, personal transformation, Karma, the aquarian-conspiracy, cosmic energy.
3. <u>Terms for God</u>. Infinite intelligence, Infinite principle, force, energy, the principle of cause, the light force, Essence, Principle Being, The spirit, The all in all.
4. <u>Terms for Inner Divinity</u>. Cosmic consciousness, God-realization, self-realization, At-one-ment. Higher-self, Attunement, Enlightenment, Illumination, Nirvana, Christ Consciousness.
5. <u>Tools and Methods Used</u>.
6. <u>Channeling</u> is a blending and touching between humans as evil spirits inhabit channeler or medium's body. His voice changes while in a trance, and spirits claiming to be "Ascended Masters" speak with predictions and sometimes accompanied by miracles.

<u>Mass Hypnotism</u> is used in seminars when channeling, so demons' messages are absorbed into the body, mind and soul.

<u>Familiar Spirits</u>, where person relaxes and contacts spirits on his own as a counsellor or guide and they intercommunicate. This is a dangerous and common practice in psychology and NAM.

<u>Crystals</u> have no power or light in themselves but are used to stimulate and activate psychic power centers located in the brain, so as to awaken superhuman higher mind power and abilities.

<u>Divination Practices</u> i.e. Tarot cards, palmistry, astrology, tea leaves, Ouija

Boards, all lead to depending on occult practices for every decision. New Agers use them 20 to 30 times a day.

Summary

We must never forget that the war which has raged since the Garden of Eden continues to be fought between the forces of God and Satan—Good and Evil. We must remember Satan comes as an angel of light to mislead and ultimately destroy. The teaching of Ephesians 6:10-16 must not only be read but practiced if we are to be victors and not victims. The Bible warns us in both the Old and New Testaments about practices which the NA espouses, i.e. Deut. 18:10-12; Acts 8:9-11; Acts 19:13-19; Gal. 5:20 and Rev. 22:15. We must also be careful not to allow our own reasoning to replace God's revelation in His Word. Too much emphasis on experiences can create an unhealthy hunger for supernatural demonstration of power. We must remember the words of Christ found in Matthew 24:24, "For fake Christs and false prophets will appear and perform great signs and miracles to deceive even the elect if it were possible". But, thank God, "Greater is He that is in you, than he that is in the world" (I John 4:4). Never forget as believers, "The weapons we fight with are not the weapons of the world. On the contrary, they have divine power to demolish strongholds" (II Cor. 10:4).

Appendix G
Happy 40th Birthday Lois

As the hours ticked down to the time of your arrival.
Your mother grew larger; her goal was survival.
Several people including the doctor said it would be a boy.
As an expectant father, my heart leapt for joy.
When your Mom went to the delivery room, I could not stay.
So, I went to the waiting room to wonder and pray.
There was another young father there awaiting some news –
As the hours passed by we both had a snooze.
Finally, a nurse appeared and said, "It is a girl."
I didn't even look up, this baby must be for Earl.
When the nurse re-appeared, she spoke much louder.
She said, "Mr. Silvester, aren't you coming to see your daughter?"
When I saw Lois' beautiful face, I was filled with joy –
And forgot the prediction that it was to be a boy.
She had lovely blond hair and a perfect round face,
We realized at once that we'd be blessed by God's grace.
Lois was a joy to raise and she used to be shy.
She was a very happy child and seldom she would cry.
When sisters Dale and Faye arrived on the scene,
Lois' mothering skills were quickly seen.
Her schoolwork was done with diligence and zest –
She was an excellent student and passed every test.

While vacationing in Florida at Thelma and Bruce Fitters place,
Lois noticed a family portrait and spotted Bruce Jr.'s face.
Back at Bramalea Baptist Church, Bruce noticed our daughter.
And wanted to date her before we felt she oughter.
Lois headed to Central Baptist Seminary and then Mothercraft –
To prepare for Day Care work and help lead the staff.
As Bruce and Lois' friendship grew to romance a wedding was planned.
Bruce designed their dream home to build on his land.
Lois and Bruce were married at Bramalea Baptist in September 1982.
It was the beginning of a busy life together and God's blessings too.
With a teacher for a mothers and preacher for a dad,
Lois, this is probably why you have the gift of the gab.
You've accomplished a lot for a girl of your size.
And with God's help you can face whatever may arise.
We sometimes wonder how you manage to do what you do.
Shopping, chauffeuring kids, making meals and keeping Bruce in line too.
You've been a loving mother and a faithful and caring wife.
And now at age 40, you've arrived at mid-life.
With your gift of hospitality and generosity too,
You have made many friends; some now are here with you.
You're always the take charge person and well organized.
But for once in your life we've pulled the wool over your eyes.
As your parents we thank you for the love you have shown,
And how these 40 years you have succeeded and grown.
Happy 40th Birthday Lois from all of us today.
May the Lord continue to bless you each step of the way.

Appendix H
Open Season on
Prime Minister Stephen Harper

Hunting season is a popular time for many hunters in this area whether it be deer, moose or small game. However, as our election day drew near, it seemed that Stephen Harper had become the target for many political critics. As I read the recent letters in the Forrester nearly everyone has been attacking Harper and the Conservatives. As I watched both the French and English debates on TV last week it was open season once again by the four opposing candidates against our Prime Minister. I was personally appalled by the accusation, rudeness and vilification of Stephen Harper. An old adage says, "The boat lost in the fog makes for most noise." There was a lot of NOISE and only Stephen Harper had POISE and conduct befitting a Prime Minster.

The old rhetoric of Harper being scary and extreme right wing is wearing pretty thin. In two and a half years as Prime Minister in a minority government he has proven very competent and trustworthy. It seems that some fear-mongers are afraid of a majority government but this what traditionally had been used to accomplish the will of the people in Canada.

Since when has having a strong military become extreme right wing? If it wasn't for the sacrifice of thousands of Canadians in the past, we would not be enjoying our freedoms today. When has law and order, moral values, traditional marriage and protections of life (unborn and living) become extreme right wing? These values are not extreme right wing; they are just right. When hugging trees becomes more important than hugging babies who can't protect themselves there is something systemically wrong with our value system. The Bible predicts a day when people will call good evil and evil good…has that day arrived? May we return to the value of our founding fathers who used their freedom and faith to build our political framework and our nation of Canada. On the arches of our Parliament building in Ottawa we read what our founding fathers uses as the basis of the name Dominion of Canada taken from Psalm 72:8. "And He (God) shall have dominion also from sea to sea and from the river unto the ends of the earth."

In the final days before the election with world economies struggling to survive an "economic earthquake," it was noteworthy to hear our Canadian banking system was ranked #1 by world economists. Why? Because Harper Conservatives had been "Pro-active" and not "Re-active," like the opposition parties and had taken steps to strengthen our banking regulations. This created stability for our banks and financial institutions, which encouraged the Canadian electorate to have greater confidence.

In conclusion, remember this truth, a leader is a person who influences people to accomplish a purpose. Stephen Harper is this kind of a leader and is deserving of our prayers and support as he continues on as our Prime Minister.

Stuart Silvester – Huntsville

Appendix I
Close the Back Door and Open Your Heart[1]

Stuart N. Silvester[2]

As we enter a new millennium churches face a myriad of challenges. The issues include questions about worship style, how to minister to "builders," "boomers," and "busters," the evaluation of evangelism methods, and the list goes on. However, the age-old problem of integrating new people into active membership remains a major concern in almost every church.

It is one thing to reach new people and quite another for them to become part of the church family. Current statistics indicate a decreasing percentage of attendees becoming participating members and a growing percentage becoming adherents or slip out the back door. This matter of retaining new people and involving them in active membership is largely resolved by establishing a viable assimilation process.

Next to preaching, the integration of new people was always my first priority in ministry. In my 20 years of pastoring at Bramalea Baptist Church in Southern

---

[1] Stuart N. Silvester, "Close the Back Door and Open Your Heart," *The Evangelical Baptist* (November/December 1999): 10–11.

[2] Stuart Silvester has 35 years of experience as a church planter and a pastor (including 20 years at Bramalea Baptist Church). He also served as a church growth consultant with the FEBCC. Now that he is "retired," he is Interim Pastor at Bethel Baptist Church in Orillia, Ontario and is actively involved in the FEBCC's Quick Build programs. He and his wife Bev live in the Muskoka area. They have three grown daughters and 9 grandchildren.

Ontario, 1640 people became church members and 80% of them participated in ministry.

Attracting people is why they *come* to church. Incorporating people is why they *stay*.

Studies show that visitors decide whether or not they will return to a church during the first 12 minutes of their first visit. There is not a second chance to make a good first impression. The following six steps are essential if outsiders are to become insiders and active participants.

Welcome people

Church buildings can be a turn off or a turn on to new people. Key factors are the nursery, women's washrooms, general cleanliness, pleasant lighting, and a good sound system in the main auditorium.

Most churches need to increase the number of greeters or hosts. A greeter shakes hands, but a host is responsible from the time visitors arrive until they leave. A host does not have to stay with the new person constantly but he/she must make sure the visitor feels welcome, meets others, and enjoys the experience.

At a large church, new people should be met in the parking lot to help them find their way to the church foyer. Hosts should be at a centrally located and well-marked "Welcome Centre," where visitors can gather a floor plan well as Sunday school and church ministries information. A host should be willing to sit with the guests in church and introduce them to other people.

In the church service, methods such as visitors' cards, a friendship booklet that everyone signs, or shaking hands with those around you can help in the integration process, but need to be done with sensitivity.

Some churches offer fellowship for newcomers after the morning service. At Bramalea we used to have two deacons and their wives as well as some staff members meet with new people to enjoy refreshments and fellowship. This was an informal occasion to get to know our visitors and inform them about the church and its ministries.

Accept people

Romans 15:7 says, "Accept one another then, just as Christ accepted you in order to bring praise to God." James 2:1–9 gives a strong warning concerning prejudices and the need for being accepting of everyone. People come in all shapes, sizes, colours, and manner of dress. We need to treat them all with the same care and courtesy. Remember, "People don't care how much we know until they know how much we care."

Befriend people

The word friend comes from the same root as freedom and good friends have the free run of our hearts. As Evangelicals, we tend to be friendly with our friends but not very friendly with strangers. My wife, Bev, often travelled with me when I ministered in various churches, and she would deliberately enter the foyer after I did. Almost without exception no one would speak to her, even though she stood in conspicuous places in the foyer. Only when they found out who she was, would some risk talking to her.

If we are to see people join our churches we need to be willing to say, "I don't believe I've met you before. My name is _____." Win Arn states the importance of the friendship ratio in this way: "Each new person should be able to identify seven friends in the first six months in a church. Friendships are the strongest factor to building people into Christ's body. If new Christians don't establish new friendships they will return to old ones. The faster friendships are made, the faster assimilation takes place."

While wintering in Florida we visited several churches, the main reason we attend the church we do is because several couples our age invited us to join them for lunch in restaurants and for fellowship in their homes. Some churches actually designate two or three couples to invite visitors to their home for lunch or out to a restaurant after church on Sunday.

Follow-up new people

In the first week after new people visit your church several steps need to be taken to favour integration.

a. Send a Follow-up letter within 24 hours. Visitors' names can be gathered from the guest book, visitors' cards, friendship booklets in the pew, or during fellowship after church.

b. Make a phone call within 12 to 24 hours to get information as to whether people are looking for a new church home. If they would like a visit, schedule when it will take place. Ideally the person (host) who spent the most time with the guest the previous Sunday conducts the follow-up contact. the host should offer to meet the person or family the next Sunday at the church and possibly invite them for a meal in their home.

c. A visit to the new person's home is important. Studies reveal that the visitor-return rate is greatly influenced by the length of time between when the newcomer visits the church and when the follow-up contact is made. My personal goal as a pastor was to visit every new person before the following Sunday. This continued for about 10 years at Branalea until, because of continued growth and a multiple of staffs, my visits became more selective. They were primarily to interview people for baptism, membership, and other needs. I would tell the family this might be the only time I would be in their home, unless there was a crisis.

During visits, I would share the history and vision of the church. I got to know the family, the children's names and their spiritual status, their church background, ministry experience, and special needs. The visit would last about an hour and I'd try to do three per evening. The fruit was incredibly encouraging.

The goal of the follow-up, whether done by the pastor or a properly trained church member, is to see the visitor return. According to recent statistics the average "affiliation rate" of first-time visitors in North American churches is 12 to 15% (That is 12 to 15% join the church in the following year). Growing churches average a 20 to 25% affiliation for first-time visitors but the average affiliation rate for second-time visitors jumps to 40 to 45% and third-time visitors average 60 to 75%.

d. A class for newcomers is an integral part of the whole process. It can be 8 to 10 weeks in duration and orient newcomers to the church, its beliefs and ministries. If you want further information regarding classes for newcomers see the article by John Mahaffey in the FV2000 Resource Manual under the theme Discipleship. One of the main benefits of the class is the friendships that develop between participants.

One of the problems of trying to get new people linked with existing members is that most members have little time for new friends. The children's toy called Lego illustrates this well. Like Lego blocks, some people have 2, 4, 6 or 8 connections. Most active church members have all their "connections" made. They have little or no time, energy or vulnerability for new people. Therefore, it is paramount that new people become connected with new people as quickly as possible and a newcomers' class is an ideal place for people to become acquainted.

Involve people

Commitment grows through involvement and people know they are welcome and wanted when they are needed. A Gallup survey showed that 10% of people are active in ministry, 50% had no interest in it, and 40% said they'd like to be involved but had never been asked or didn't know how to get involved. When we interviewed new people for membership it Bramalea, we sought to discover their spiritual gifts in order to develop them and deploy them within the body. Whenever possible, we limited each member to one ministry.

We didn't ask new people "if" they wanted to serve but "where" they were willing to serve. We had hardly any committees but chose to involve them in meaningful ministries within the church. My slogan was "Minimize the machinery and maximize the ministry." It is important to take new people from an "entry point" to an "entry path" and active involvement. The first reformation under Martin Luther gave the Bible back to the people in the pew. The new reformation is giving the ministry back to the people in the pew. Be willing to let people start new ministries as they see the need for them.

Most unchurched people join a church because of friends and relationships they've developed. Therefore, it is paramount to help visitors find a group where they can build such relationships, i.e. a small group, a sports team, a Sunday school class, etc.

Build up people
This is done through worship, teaching, involvement and small groups. Evaluate the effectiveness of existing groups (i.e. Sunday school classes, Bible studies, growth groups, etc.) and see if they are producing the desired results. Check to see if you have too few or too many groups for the same clientele. Integration isn't complete until newcomers are growing in their faith and actively serving the Lord in your church.

Pastor Rick Warren of Saddleback Valley Community Church says that in order for people to mature in Christ they must be given the opportunity to be involved in the church. He wrote, "People become what they are committed to and pastors have to ask them for commitment."

In conclusion, statistics reveal that of the first-time visitors who live in the church's ministry area, three of every ten should be actively involved within a year. If not, it indicates a lack of openness by members and a poor integration process.

We must work hard at closing the back door of our churches and opening our hearts to all who make the effort to visit. Hebrews 13:1–2 says, "Keep on loving each other as brothers. Do not forget to entertain strangers, for by so doing some people have entertained angels without knowing it."

Appendix J
Our 50th
Wedding Anniversary

Our three daughters and husbands planned a wonderful celebration for our 50th Wedding Anniversary at MBC on Mary Lake on August 13, 2010. We enjoyed delicious food, speeches, music and great fellowship with over fifty of our family and close friends. Bev shared some beautiful thoughts with me, and I gave her a ring with 3 diamonds, along with words of appreciation. Many pictures of us and our loving family were taken, that we cherished deeply. Our granddaughter Megan produced a great album entitled "50th Anniversary Memories" – All Because Two People Fell in Love. This celebration and the album have been a wonderful reminder of God's love and faithfulness to us and our family.

MY 80TH BIRTHDAY PARTY
Bev and my three daughters, Lois, Dale and Faye planned a great party for my 80th birthday on July 9, 2015. It was done in a "Nautical Theme" with my 1937 Ditchburn boat being a focal point. About eighty family members and friends attended this event. We all enjoyed fantastic food, great fellowship and a time of reminiscing at our lovely home on Bayshore Blvd in Huntsville. They gave me an Apple i-pad as a special gift and I continue to use it to this day. It was another reminder of God's goodness and faithfulness, both to me and all our family.

Our 50th Wedding Anniversary at MBC - 2010

FIFTIETH ANNIVERSARY SERVICE
AT BRAMALEA BAPTIST CHURCH

I was invited to speak at the fiftieth anniversary of the church I had pastored at from 1969–1989. The date was October 6, 2013, but Bev could not accompany me because of her cancer. I told her before leaving home that this might be my last time to speak at Bramalea Baptist and so I wanted to deliver my soul. I prepared and prayed more that I had ever done for any sermon. I drove to Brampton on Saturday and stayed at the Holiday Inn across from the church so I could be rested and ready for the two morning services. As I entered the church at 8:15am I was met by Weity and Kathy Siderius. He said his brother John (who had been our business administrator) was critically ill and asked if I would visit him (I'll return to this incident in a few minutes). As I entered the auditorium it was filling with between 1,200–1,500 people from around the world. Following an inspiring time of worship, I spoke on "Five Important Words to Remember"—Church, Memories, Anniversaries, Trinities and Victories. I spoke about the centrality of the church (Matthew 16:18) as well as the "Life Cycle of the Church." Then the four New Testament words describing the church—Body, Bride, Building and Brotherhood.

Secondly, I reviewed 20 years of ministries and memories at Bramalea that Bev and I had experienced together. Thirdly, I spoke of special anniversaries, 10th, 25th and now 50th. I dealt with the "Year of Jubilee" from Leviticus 25:8–17 and thanking God for His past blessings and trusting Him for the future. Fourthly I dealt with "A Trinity of Trinities 1) Heaven's Trinity—God the Father as Creator, God the Son and Saviour and God the Holy Spirit as Comforter and Teacher. 2) Hell's Trinity—The world, the Flesh and the Devil, our enemies. 3) Human Trinity—Body, Mind and Soul/Spirit. Last I concluded with Victories—the source of victories, the scope of them and the secret of our victories.

I challenged the congregation to come to Christ for forgiveness and victory, no matter their failures, brokenness and sins, as well as for obedience for Baptism, Membership and Serving the Lord. I then witnessed a response I had never experienced at any time in my ministry. Between two and three hundred responded to the invitation and filled the front and the aisles with many weeping. I, along with counsellors did our best to pray and counsel for the next 30 minutes. By then hundreds more were arriving for the second service. With little time to rest or pray, I preached again to about seven hundred people. Again, many responded to the invitation, with at least 100 being counselled. I felt humbled as well as tired and inspired as we concluded the 50th Anniversary Celebrations.

I return for a moment to the matter of John Siderius' critical condition. Following the second service Mike and Ruth Brandon took me out for dinner at Red Lobster. Then Mike offered to drive me to the hospital to visit John. Upon arrival we found John and his wife Francina and daughter Rose singing and reading God's word. John knew his death was imminent and asked me if I'd conduct his funeral and I said I'd be honoured to. John died in about a month's time. I conducted his funeral on November 14, 2013 which was attended by several hundred people. Following the internment and a luncheon, at which I met with many friends from the past, I picked Bev up at the Fitzell's home where she was staying because of the cancer. We then headed to London for six weeks so Bev could receive radiation treatment. While there we stayed with our daughter Faye and her family. Following the new year, we headed home to Huntsville.

Bev Awarded BA at Lauier University - 1987

Appendix K
Bev's Essay's While Studying for her B.A.

I found 20 Essays that Bev wrote from her BA while living in Cheltenham. She majored in Religion and I choose 3 essays. The professor had given A+ on them and written Excellent work on them.

1 - *The Vineyard Story and Love and Hatred*
November 7, 1984 By: Beverly Silvester

God the Father is portrayed as the gardener. Jesus us the vine, firmly planted and rooted. The followers of Jesus are the branches. The Father's desire, as a gardener, is for an abundance of fruit, produced by Christians whose lives must be rooted in the vine (Christ) in order to produce fruit which reveals itself in love, kindness, gentleness, etc. especially listed in Galatians 5:22. Branches which bear no fruit are cut off and discarded and those which produce are lovingly pruned so they'll continue to produce well. Without fruit there is no proof that a person is a Christian.

Jesus continues to explain that when one is rooted in Him (the vine), there is a common residence as both are abiding in the vine. Much fruit is produced in this relationship of working together but as a branch separate from a vine is barren, so is a person without the partnership in the vine or without Christ. Another factor in abiding in Christ is that our words will be His words and when we pray, we will have our desires fulfilled because our desires will be those of

Christ. This oneness of character with Jesus will glorify the Father and make a true disciple.

Jesus says He is all that a vine can be to its branch, that is, its nourishment. He thus teaches absolute dependence and perfect confidence in Him in the life of a believer. He explains that He has had this kind of relationship with His Father. All that Christ is and has, he has not of Himself but in the Father and that's how a Christian should relate to Christ. The purpose of a branch is to bear fruit. In this Christ illustrates that the reason for the Christian's life is to bear fruit pleasing to God and to accomplish this through partnership with Christ. The branch is like the vine in all aspects. It has the same life, the same place and the same work. The purposes of God become the purposes of the Christian. However, the vine is great, strong and the branch is little and feeble and needs strengthening. What a lot of lessons can be found in his simple illustration.

Jesus then changes his allegory from abiding in the vine to abiding in His love. He explains that He has been an example of abiding in the love of His Father by being willing to obey His commandments. He says further that this love leads one to even go so far as laying down one's life for friends – referring to what He was soon going to do. There is, He says, no greater love. There is a stipulation for being able to be part of the love of Christ and that is a willingness to be obedient to Him. When a person decides to be obedient, then Jesus says the relationship between them is no longer one of Master and servant but of friends. It is a love relationship like that of the branch and the vine. In verse 17 we see both a command to obey and a fruit to display in loving one another. One's ability to love another comes from Christ to the Christian as nourishment comes from the vine to the branch.

When a disciple abides in Christ there is not only the wonderful experience of love but Jesus warns that there will so be hate. Again, He uses Himself as the example. Although He abides in God's love, the world hated Him. In order to explain this hate, He shows how because of His presence, His teachings, His signs they have seen their sin and have no excuse for hiding it or continuing in it any longer. Instead of being willing to ask for forgiveness and forsaking it they hate the one who has revealed it to them. Believers, Jesus says we will have the same difficulty and He infers that same reasoning. The purity of the Christian should show up the sin of those who reject Christ. "Ye are the salt of the earth" or "lights shining in the darkness" describe the life of the one abiding in Christ—provoking antagonism in those around them who are still in darkness and don't like seeing themselves as God sees them.

There is a real contrast between these two kinds of people—those of the world and those who have been chosen out of the world (now part of the vine).

Those of the world will hate believers and it is made clear that this hatred is also towards Christ and God since all are one. Jesus explains that just as the vine/branch relationships is rooted in Him, so the hatred believers experience is because of Him. The behaviour or reactions of the people toward Him during His ministry is an example of what believers can expect as reactions to their godly lives. They will be hated or persecuted because they have come to know the Father of love.

Jesus predicts what will happen to His disciples in sharing that they'd be put out of the synagogues and their lives would be hunted by those who would think they were pleasing God by getting rid of them. Paul would be a fine example. There seems no escape. To abide in the love of Christ brings with it the hatred of the world. The reaction of Christ to the hatred He experienced was that of gentleness and pitying love. Only those abiding in Christ can react as He did. My observation is that the kind of Christianity that can endure the world and with which the world is pleased must have in some measure lost its power.

We realized in the beginning of this discussion that God was represented as the gardener. When Mary at the tomb did not recognize Jesus but thought He was the gardener we may have an illusion to the fact that He has taken on His glorified, heavenly body and therefore is now more a representative of God the Father.

2 - A Comparison of the Gospels Accounts of the Death and Resurrection of Jesus—February 1985 By: Beverly Silvester

Reading the separate accounts of any one of the Gospels without looking at them all gives an incomplete picture of the events surrounding the death and resurrection of Christ. We will compare the accounts to see the emphasis each has made and the events each has included or excluded for its own purpose.

Matthew emphasizes the joy of the miraculous to convince the Jews of the Messiahship of Jesus. He tells of the healing of the soldier's ear which Peter had cut off. He's the only one to explain the soldiers and the stone being put before the tomb because of the rumours that Jesus said He'd rise from the grave. He follows through this event by telling of the earthquake, which removed the stone and frightened the soldiers and then the scheme to pay others to spread the rumour that the disciples had stolen the body. He says the purpose of this "is not to impress the reader with miraculous detail, but to demonstrate that God was at work throughout the whole of the earthly life of Jesus, and that his action had culminated in the greatest of all miracles, the Resurrection."

Matthew also tried to convince the Jews by showing how the events are a fulfilment of prophecy. Several times he states, "that the scriptures might be fulfilled." One case of this is in the thirty pieces of silver Judas got for selling Jesus, prophesied by Jeremiah. Another is Pilate washing his hands to demonstrate his innocence, which was stated in Deuteronomy 21:6–9 and would be familiar to the Jews.

Mark is very similar to Matthew, but it says that Mark stressed that the "suffering and death of Jesus are essential stages on the path to glory." Some events included here but not in Matthew are the anointing of the body by the women and their concern about getting past the stone; His appearance to Mary Magdalene and the scolding Jesus gave the disciples for not remembering and believing in his resurrection teaching. This gospel ends abruptly according to Matthew's apocalyptic style. It emphasizes the fact that the disciples are not only to preach but to expect signs to prove they're believers. They'd be able to cast out demons, speak in new tongues and heal the sick.

Luke gives us three more saying of Jesus on the cross. In chapter 23:34, he tells of Jesus saying, "Forgive them for they know not what they do," to his crucifiers. He included the discussion of the thieves on the cross with Jesus in 23:39-43 and the finale statement of Jesus, "Father, into thy hands I commend my spirit." These statements give us a deeper understanding of the person of Christ in His forgiving nature and His complete dependence upon His Father. Luke also looks at the events with a more political and historical perspective. Jesus is declared as being the Christ as prophesied in Psalm 110:1 and Daniel 7:13 in Luke 22:69-70. Herod is glad to meet Him and wants to see a miracle. He mocks Jesus and allies himself with Pilate (23:6-12) Neither Herod nor Pilate see any fault in Him yet allow Him to be crucified. Luke is the only writer who predicts again the suffering to occur at the destruction of Jerusalem. He gives a good account of Jesus' words, explaining concisely His mission in fulfillment of scripture (Hosea 6:2) and His command to await the coming of the power the disciples would need before ministering.

John says in Ch. 20:30–31 that he is selective in the events he related but he adds interesting ones to those of the other gospels. He also states that his purpose is to get his readers to believe that Jesus is the Christ and in so doing he emphasizes the fact of the bodily resurrection, so we realize that it was not just a vision or an idea. Twice he has Jesus displaying His wounded hands and side. He is very clear in showing Jesus' claim to be the Christ. When Judas betrays Him, he says, "I am He." In 18:36 He says he is a King but that his kingdom is not of this world. During the trial John shows how innocent he is first when examined by Annas: "If I have spoken evil, bear witness of the evil; but if well, why accuse me?" Then with Pilate He is declared innocent twice in 18:38 and 19:14. This is the only gospel that quotes Pilate saying, "Behold your King." More detail is given about the superscription over the cross telling how the Jews wanted it changed, but Pilate said, "What I have written I have written." (19:22). John, as do the other gospels, refers to prophesies which have been fulfilled. Psalm 22:18 mentions the casting of lots for Jesus' clothing and is related in John 19:22-24. Psalm 34:20 says none of Jesus bones would be broken. John is the only one to show that fulfillment. A touching scene in John tells of the care Jesus showed, though in agony, for his mother. He asked John to care for her. Perhaps John, the writer, was John the beloved disciple and knew this scene especially.

Although the gospel writers have varied some in other presentations, I like to fit all of the parts together into a more complete narrative. Then, to me, it becomes a beautiful, almost complete rendering of the last days of Jesus' life and the appearance before the ascension.

3 - Irony in the Figure of Nicodemus: In the Gospel John —October 4, 1984 By: Beverly Silvester

Nicodemus is not only a Jew but a leader among the Jews. He is a teacher, one of a group called Pharisees who are students of the Jewish law who stress the keeping of the law above all else. He is also a member of the Sanhedrin which had considerable power in criminal jurisdiction. These people were the religious leaders of the day, teachers of the people. They knew the Old Testament Scriptures well and were looking for the coming of the Messiah, thought to be coming as an earthly king. With this background it is interesting to note the events which take place in the life of Nicodemus and the irony it entails.

Knowledge of Jesus and the signs he had performed had spread, evoking curiosity about Himself even amongst those in high places in Jewish religious circles. Nicodemus came to seek out Jesus. He does not come with a question but with the statement, "We know." It is ironic to see that he claims to know and what he comes with is "righteousness." He assumes that he will enjoy the privileges of God because of his race and his loyalty to Jewish traditions. However, very quickly Jesus knocks all these assumptions out from under him and he no longer knows but really becomes confused.

Nicodemus most likely did not want his peers to know of his interest in Jesus for fear of his reputation, so he came secretly at night. Now night is equated with evil or sin. Nicodemus has heard of or seen the signs Jesus has done and it has made him believe that He may be a teacher sent from God, but these signs do not bring him to faith in Jesus. Being a Pharisee, he has been looking for the Saviour but ironically, he does not recognize Him when he comes.

When Jesus says, "Ye must be born again," the double meaning causes confusion in the mind of Nicodemus. All he sees is the physical birth being repeated which is a rather comical idea. Even when Jesus explains that there is first the water of physical birth and then a spiritual birth, which is separate from it, he still wonders, "How can these things be?" Double meanings are ironic and so is the fact that this knowledgeable, spiritual leader is blind to see these truths and Jesus even says, "Don't be surprised at what I am telling you."

Jesus Himself is an ironic character to Nicodemus. He is a man in the flesh and yet He is God. He says He has come down from heaven, yet He is still in Heaven. How confusing to Nicodemus and yet we as readers can comprehend this because of our knowledge of the whole story which the victim, Nicodemus has not the advantage of.

Jesus proceeds to explain heavenly things, although he wonders how Nicodemus could believe when he doesn't understand even earthly things. This seems foolish unless it is intended primarily for the reader. To help make clear his mission, Jesus refers to Moses. Here again is an ironic message. Jesus is compared to the serpent that Moses lifted up in the wilderness. Perhaps Nicodemus could understand that looking at the serpent gave life, but it is unlikely that he could comprehend that Christ would be lifted up (on the cross) and bring life (eternal). Equating Christ with a serpent seems strange, especially coming from the lips of Jesus. The opposites here are ironic and of phenomenal contrast. Of course, as latter-day readers we can see that Christ is said to have become sin for us or to have become like a serpent when he bore the sin of the whole world.

Later, when Jesus is being rejected by the authorities, Nicodemus speaks up for Him by asking if it is fair for a man to be judged before he is heard. We now wonder if he has become a secret follower since he shows concern for Jesus and takes up His case. To be a member of the Sanhedrin and be partial to Jesus speaks of irony. They asked Nicodemus if he was from Galilee and inferred that he was believing this man to be a prophet. Then they tried to show Jesus couldn't be a prophet since He was from Galilee. We know that they were mistaken about the place His birth, but Nicodemus did not have that advantage.

The final note on Nicodemus in John 19 finds him busy helping in the burial and anointing of Jesus' body. This leads to giving us the idea that he is now truly a disciple but still a part of the Pharisees—a dichotomy of irony in that the Pharisees were the prime instigators in Jesus' death. He believed but he hid his faith, which is also ironic.

The whole of Nicodemus' mentioned encounters spells out ironic messages, which keep the victim and the reader fascinated and thinking.

Appendix L
Six of Stu's
Sermon Outlines

1. Three Responses to a Roadblock: Exodus 14:10–18

Introduction:

If by a miracle you could choose any period of history in which to live, which would you choose? Columbus and New World? Shakespeare and Drama? Greece and all it's glory with Aristotle and Plato as contemporaries? I'd choose now. We live in a day of conflict and contradictions. Knowledge without wisdom; speed without direction and it seems technology enables us to go backward more rapidly. In this chaotic world we are called as Christians to Live, Love and Labour. In the midst of despair, we can bring hope; in darkness, be light. Bring faith vs. fear and wholeness vs. despair. However, as we seek to serve God and man, we can expect resistance and roadblocks.

In Exodus 13 & 14 we see children of Israel after over 400 years of slavery in Egypt heading to the Promised Land. Ex 13:18 says "God led the Israelites to the Red Sea." Ex 14:1–4 Moses led people to Baal Zephon by the Red Sea. The Egyptian army was pursuing them and there was no escape. Let's look at 3 Responses to some Red Sea Roadblocks:

1.   Israelites Said—Go Back (v. 10–12)

Filled with fear, better off in Egypt. Blamed Moses and wanted to return to slavery. Satan tries to get them to return to world and miss God's blessings. 2 Timothy 1:7 God has not given us a spirit of fear but given wisdom and sound mind.

2.   Moses Said—Stand Still (v. 13–14)

I'm impressed with Moses reply for it reveals faith and obedience. God doesn't help those who help themselves, but He helps the helpless. Word Baal Zephon = Baal = God + Zephon = God's Hidden Treasures. God stopped the Israelites to teach them invaluable lessons. Eight times in the Bible it says "Be Still" v. 14. The Lord will fight for you, you need only to be still. We need to listen to the Lord's voice.

3.   God Said —Go Forward (v. 15–18)

Moses told to use his shepherd's rod as a weapon of war to open the Red Sea Roadblock v. 19–20. God moved a cloud from in front of the Israelites to behind them to create a "Buffer from the Egyptians and able to hear God's instructions and see God's miracle.

vs. 21–31 The Red Sea opened and the Israelites went through on dry ground. The enemy tried but God closed the Red Sea and all perished.

4 Timeless Lessons from a Roadblock:

1 — It takes Roadblocks to change us and our habits.

2 — When hemmed in the only place to look is up.

3 — If God is to get the glory, He must do the fighting.

4 — Red Sea Roadblocks open and close at God's command, not ours.

2. Freedom from Fear: Psalm 27 & 91, Luke 12:32

Introduction: "Don't be afraid little flock." Edmund Burke said, "we have nothing to fear but fear itself." I prepared and preached this sermon after 9–11 to my congregation in Florida. Many emotions produced by 9–11 including anger, sorrow, frustration, but primarily fear. Consider three aspects or dimensions on fear:

1 — The Characteristics of Fear

The dictionary defines fear as "Painful emotion caused by impending danger and evil, state of alarm, anxiety and death."

Fear is the first emotion recorded in the Bible. Genesis 3:10 "I heard you in the garden and I was afraid." Fear is a natural response when physical and psychological well-being are threatened. Rational fears are learned and basic for survival. Illustration: Parents warn not to touch a stove or use sharp knives to their kids.

Phobias are irrational fears that lead to irresponsible actions and phobias are characterized by their objects.

Acrophobia = fear of high places

Claustrophobia = enclosed places

Monophobia = fear of being alone

Pathophobia = fear of disease

Toxophobia = fear of being poisoned

In order for fear to be legitimate it must have two attributes. Must be imminent (present) and potent or powerful. Illustration: Fears and phobias like coils of a snake that squeeze life out. Philippians 4:6–7 "Do not be anxious or fearful of anything."

2 — The Cause of Fear

It can be traced to three things — Death, Man & Satan.

The main cause of fear is ¬¬¬lack of faith in God.

I want to focus primarily on the fear of death.

1 Corinthians 15:25–57 & John 11:25–26 "I am the resurrection." What people fear most (poll of 1000 US adults) reveals it was related to death and finances just before 9–11.

    a.   Car Crash

    b.   Cancer

    c.   Inadequate Social Security

    d.   Food Poisoning

    e.   Getting Alzheimer's

    f.   Victim of Violence

    g.   Plane Crash

    h.   Natural Disaster

    i.   Stock Market Crash

    j.   Victim of Mass Violence

3 — The Cure for Fear

There are two Biblical cures for fear:

a.   Fear of God

The fear that expels all other fears. From Genesis 20:11 to Revelation 19:5 speaks of fearing God. 1 John 4:18, How can we love God and fear God at the same time? It says, "Perfect love casts our fear."

God is superior to all fear objects, but He is kind and good

Psalm 22:23, Psalm 119:10, Psalm 34:9, Psalm 22:8–12, Psalm 103:13, Psalm 76:7–10, Isaiah 8:13.

b.   Faith in Jesus Christ

Matthew 10:28, Jesus said "Don't be afraid of those who kill the body but cannot kill the soul but fear Him who can destroy both body and soul (in hell)." In Matthew 10:29-33 Jesus used two little things to illustrate and prove His love for us.

1 — Sparrows

2 — Hairs

V. 30–31 "Don't be afraid for you are worth more than many sparrows."

John 14:27 Jesus said to His faithful followers "Peace I leave you, my peace I give to you, not as the world gives you. Don't let your heart be troubled or be afraid."

Hebrews 2:6–15 and John 14:1–3 & 6

3. Bodily Sickness and Divine Healing - 2 Timothy 4:9–22

v. 20 "Trophimus left sick at Miletus." Why wasn't he healed, for, twice Paul exercised a healing ministry? He was a child of God and a pastor yet remained sick. I'll ask pertinent questions regarding sickness and divine healing and try to answer them.

1 — Do the Lord's People Suffer with Illness and Bodily Sickness?

Are Christians subject to sickness of body and mind? Yes. Sometimes subject to all the church. Illustration: Gord Barwell, a strong Christian and athlete and dead at age 44 with brain cancer, in spite of much prayer. My Mother died at age 52 from cancer. Recently Bev in spite of much interceding prayer and faith exercise and doctors' treatments.

2 — Does the Lord Ever Heal His People?

Yes, He does. In Philippians 2:25–30 Epaphroditus, Paul's friend, almost died but God raised him up. Acts 9:36–45 Dorcas a fine Christian lady in Joppa died and Peter raised her from the dead. Illustration from Bethel Baptist Church in Orillia, Artist Arnold Nogy's wife was expecting but large tumours were found and doctors said either she would die or else the baby would. He asked me to pray for her. A deacon and I, after fasting, praying and using oil to anoint her, a week later the tumour was gone and she gave birth to a son and they invited Bev and I for a meal and gave a painting to us.

3 —Does the Lord Always Heal His Children?

No. He doesn't. Even though much prayer is made and a sick person is a Christian, and some teach, it is always Gods will to heal. Text Trophimus left sick. 2 Corinthians 12:7–10 Paul wasn't healed in spite of much prayer. Otherwise Christians would never die of sickness.

4 — Why Do God's People Experience Bodily Sickness?

Consider the following three reasons:

A — Often Because of Breaking Laws of Healthy Living.

Exodus 15:26 contains a promise "I am the Lord who heals you." But note it was a promise to the Jews related to diet, cleanliness, work and relaxation (conditional promise).

If we neglect our diet, sleep, exercise and overworking we'll pay the price. We can't burn the candles at both ends and remain healthy.

B — Sometimes Sickness Comes Upon Christians as The Direct Result of Wilful Sin.

Not always the case 1 Corinthians 11:29–32 God's judgement come to some Christians in Corinth. 1 Corinthians 5:1–5 see sin resulting in sickness.

C —When God Permits Sickness & Suffering & Withholds Healing, He Always Has a Loving Purpose in View.

Nothing happens by chance in a Christians life. Romans 8:28

5 — What is God's Purpose in Permitting Bodily Sickness and Suffering?

A — That He May Draw Us Nearer to Himself

Illustration: Shepherd breaking straying lamb's leg and carry's it. Psalms 23:2 As we walk through valleys He comforts and leads us.

B — He Permits Sickness and Suffering in Order to Sanctify Us.

Hebrews 12:5–11 Purity produces power. John 13:7 "You don't realize what I'm doing now, but later you will."

C — He Permits Sickness and Suffering in Order that Our Testimony May Bless Others.

Philippians 1:12 "What has happened is for the gospels advancement."

Romans 14:8 "Whether we live or die we are the Lords."

Philippians 1:20–23, 2 Timothy 4:6–8

Illustration: My Mother illness, death and prayers motivated me into ministry.

4. A Model Church — 1 Thessalonians 1:1-10

v. 7 "You became a model to all the believers."

People become models and model homes but what does a model church look like? Consider 3 dimensions of a model church according to the Bible.

1 — Motivation for Ministry — v. 3 we see a trilogy of faith, hope and love that motivated churches in Thessalonica.

A.   — Work Produced by Faith — Book of James treaties on faith. Ten times it speaks of both faith and works. Need balance work produced by fear or force won't work. Faith needed then and now. Faith is the Root and works is the Fruit (cause and effect). Man says, "Seeing is believing." God says, "Believing is seeing."

B. — Labour Prompted by Love — 1 Corinthians 13 says love is the greatest. Love motivated early Christians and our Love for God and people is needed now.

Saying "People don't care how much we know until they know how much we care." Needs to be a labour of love.

C. — Endurance Inspired by Hope — Saying "The character of a person is revealed by what is takes to stop him." Running marathons and bad weather. No pain, no gain. Distraction by people gets our eyes off the goal.

Proverbs 13:12 "Hope deferred makes the heart sick."

Romans 15:13 "May the God of all hope fill you with joy and peace."

Hebrews 11:27 Moses endured because he saw God who was invisible. It is my prayer that your life & Ministry will be modeled by faith, hope and love.

2 — Matured for Ministry — v. 4–6

A. — An Elect People (v. 4)

Knowing your election of God. Greek word for election or chosen was used seven times in the New Testament.

John 15:16 You did not choose me but I chose you to bear fruit. Ephesians 1:4 "He chose you in him before the creation of the world to be holy and blameless. In love he predestined us to be adopted as His sons through Jesus Christ, according to His pleasure and will. We are chosen as Christ's bride and He is the Bridegroom. Ephesians 5: 25–27 "Christ died for us and we're to be his radiant bride or church."

B.   —An Enlightened People (v. 5–6) "Gospel came with power, the Holy Spirit and deep conviction. Conversion is instantaneous but growth and maturity is in process. Thomas Carlyle said, "No person ever becomes a saint in his sleep."

What produces maturity? (4 ingredients needed).

i- Feed On God's Word.

ii- Faith in Prayer, we have not because we ask not.

iii- Fellowship with Christians

iv- Filled with the Spirit (Galatians 5:20-23)

3 Magnitude of Ministry v. 7–10 (Breadth and Influence of Ministry)

Saying: "If we look after depth of our lives God will look after the breadth of our ministry. Note three concluding characteristics:

A. — An Exemplary Church (v. 7–9) Are we content with mediocrity or do we want to be a model church? v. 9 They turned from idols to serve the living "God." Are there idols in our lives? Things, plans, sins?

B. — An Evangelistic Church (v. 8) "The Lords message goes out from you…

everywhere." v.7 Speaks of examples models and v.8 of evangelists and missions. Remember if we fail to evangelize, we will fossilize. A fossil is a relic of a former condition.

C. — An Expectant Church (v. 10) says Each last verse in each chapter speaks of Christ's return. Illustration: expecting Lois in the waiting room. V. 10 says we'll be saved from the wrath. Matthew 24 lists signs of Christ's coming. Deception, Divisions, Disease, Dangers, Death. Matthew 24:14 "And the gospel of the kingdom will be preached in the whole world as a testimony to all nations, and then the end will come." Are you ready?

5. Evangelize or Fossilize

Luke 19:10 "For the Son of Man is come to seek and save that which is lost." Illustration: We have lost and found departments for dogs and cats and clothes and Bibles, but what about people? Soul winning has become a sideline rather than a lifeline in many churches today.

Consider Four Essential Ingredients for Evangelization:

1-The World That Needs Evangelization — A global village and getting bigger yet smaller with jets and email.

A. It's Size — 1 AD = 170 million

1000 AD = 265 million

1900 = 1.590 million

1950 = 2.525 million

Now = 7 billion

Dr. A.B Simpson wrote, "A 100,000 souls a day are passing one by one away in Christless guilt and gloom, without a ray of hope or light, they're passing to their doom."

Each week a city the size of Toronto is born at 500,000 daily.

B. It's Sin — Gibbon's book says Rome fell because of moral decadence, atheism, materialism and sensualism. Our country is suffering from similar symptoms as well as murder, rape, strikes, drugs and even terrorism. The Bible describes unsaved as Lost, Perishing, Condemned and Spiritually Blind. If we believe we are only sick and not dead with sins and that God is Impotent and not Omnipotent we'll do less to reach out to lost and dying humanity.

2-   The Word Needed for Evangelizing —Two key passages regarding Evangelism in the New Testament.

a.   Matthew 28:18-20 — The Great Commission or Omission?

i.   Unlimited Power (v. 18) "All authority in heaven and earth."

ii.   Unlimited People (v. 19) "All Nations," not just Jews or white people.

iii.   Unlimited Precepts (v. 20) "All things" I have commanded you.

iv.   Unlimited Presence (v. 20) "Always" GO & LO I am with you. It doesn't say, "come and here" but "Go and tell —show and tell."

b.   Romans 1:14–16 — Paul makes three tremendous statements regarding Evangelism.

i.   I am Debtor (v. 14) The obligation of the gospel. He owed his prayers, presence and preaching. Paul's creditors were last in Rome and in debt to reach and win them to Christ.

ii.   I am Ready v. 15 The Preparation for the Gospel. Dedicated in body, soul and spirit. Prepared to go to hell for the lost.

iii.   I am Not Ashamed v. 16 The Satisfaction of the Gospel. It's the Supremacy, it's Sufficiency and it's Simplicity. Even a child can understand.

Hebrews 4:12 "Too often we defend the Bible rather than use it.

3-   The Work Needed for Evangelization —God's work takes work.

a.   1 Corinthians 3:5–8 One sows and waters, but God gives the increase. Remember, God cannot bless what we do not do.

b.   Psalm 126:5–6 "They that saw in tears shall reap in joy."

Only 1 out of 24 is reached for Christ by Media and the rest by one-to-one relation.

Story: Karl Marx

At age 17 he wrote an essay based on John 15:1–14 as he saw a need for union with Christ and spoke of people seeking for a higher being who could satisfy man's search for truth and light.

Quote "Our hearts reason and history" and the Word of God call out to us that union with Christ is absolutely necessary and without Him we would be rejected by God. Marx was exposed to five years of Christian education, yet there was no conversion of his life to Christ and he entered the University of Berlin and became a militant atheist and founder of World communist. Someone failed in the task of personal evangelism.

Paul said there are three kinds of work in Acts 20:20:

i.   By Example — "I showed you" = Lifestyle

ii.   By Exhortation — "And taught you" = Lips

iii.   By Experience — "From house to house." = Legs

4-   The Workers Needed for Evangelizing

Joseph Aldrich says in his book "Lifestyle Evangelism, excessive relational demands have crippled our relation capacities and because of so many people our attitude of isolation becomes a way of life." We allow crowds to crowd out the individual and we say I won't bother you if you don't bother me. If your lives are carnal and not committed, we have little desire to witness. Illustration: Like the Dead Sea fed from the Sea of Galilee. No outlet.

2 Chronicles 7:14 "If my people shall humble themselves and pray and seek my face and turn from their wicked ways then I'll hear from heaven and will forgive their sin and heal their land."

Story: Col. James Irwin who walked on the moon was asked how he dealt with being a celebrity. He said, "When I returned to this planet, I realized I had not become a celebrity but a servant, I'm here to serve God for the rest of my life and share the purpose, the love and glory of God." This is why God leaves us on earth as well as Christians.

1 Corinthians 3:9 says "We are to be labourers together with God."

Poem: A Voice From Eternity
"You lived next door to me for years
We shared our dreams, our joys, our tears,
A friend to me you were indeed –
A friend who helped me when in need.
My faith in you was strong and sure
We had such trust as should endure,
No spats between us ever rose
Our friends were alike, also our foes.
What sadness, then, my friend, to find
That after all, you weren't so kind.
The day my life on earth did end
I found you weren't a faithful friend…
For all those years we spent on earth,
You never talked of Second Birth,
You never spoke of my lost soul
And of the Christ Who'd make me whole.
I plead today from hell's cruel fire
And tell you now my last desire,
You cannot do a thing for me,
No words today my bonds will free.
But do not err, my friend, again,
Do all you can for souls of men,
Plead with them now quite earnestly
Lest they be cast in hell with me."

Story: Alexander the Great was a courageous leader who had conquered world and wept when no more to conquer. He sat on his golden throne and accused some of his men of cowardice. A 17-year-old caught hiding from an enemy stood before Alexander the Great. Was asked, "what is your name?" "Alexander, sir," believing because, he had the same name would benefit him. Asked two more times his name. Alexander the Great said, "Either change your conduct or change your name." Lord asked our name. We say Christians could He says the same to us because of hypocrisy and fruitlessness.

6. Revival and the Church —Psalm 85

Introduction: "When man wants to do something, he starts with a method but God starts with a man." God is more concerned with the worker than the work. The Bible speaks of revival in several places. It doesn't mean a charismatic movement. D.L Moody said, "The symbol of the Holy Spirit is a Dove not a Hoot Owl.

Let me ask and answer four questions regarding Revival.

1-   What is Revival? In the USA they speak of Revival meeting, but they are referring to Evangelism meetings. Church renewal is more about program than purity. A definition of terms: It refers to the Body of Christ.

Revival in the church is like springtime in nature (Warmth vs. Cold). It involves the sovereignty of God and the freewill of man. It is God's response to man's obedience.

3 Dimensions:

a.   Revive Me — (Psalm 137:8) Intensely Personal

b.   Revive Us — (Psalm 85:6) In Family or Church

c.   Revive Your Work — (Habakkuk 3:2) "Revive they work in the midst of the years."

The Dictionary defines revival as reawakening fervour and the restoration to life and consciousness.

Definition of revival itself — Many definitions from man and God. Our spiritual experience catching up to our biblical theology. Judgement day is coming early and calling sin SIN. Revival is God's finger pointing at me and asking two questions

i.   What about sin in my life?

ii.   Who is going to control my life?

Revival is the Spirit of God controlling the surrendered life.

Revival is a Two Directional Experience.

i.   Vertical with God

ii.   Horizontal with Man

The roof is off and walls are down and open and honest with God and man. Acts 3:19 is best "Times of refreshing from the presence of the Lord."

2- Why is Revival Needed? Because often our lives don't honour God. Psalm 85:6–9 Reveals three reason why revival is needed:

a. That we may Rejoice in God v. 6 — Not ourselves accomplishments or churches.

b. That we may Hear the Voice of God v. 8 — We listen too often to man.

c. That we may See the Glory of God v. 9 — Not our glory.

In Isaiah 6:1–4 Isaiah saw the glory of God and saw he was a man of unclean lips.

— Albert Einstein said, "If we could cleanse the Christianity, we see today to what Christ taught we would have a religion that would save the world."

— Martin Luther said, "I don't fear the Pope and all his cardinals as much as I fear the king who lives in my heart."

— Revival won't break out in the masses, but in the few who have gone to the cross and died to sin.

—Dr. Raymond Edmund says, "God sends revival for 1 or 2 reasons. 1-That judgement might be averted. 2-That Gods people might prepare for persecution and service."

-Revival is needed in our Hearts, Homes, our Churches and our Country.

3- What Must Proceed Revival?

True revival is never worked up, it comes from above. Revival is the result of Agonizing Prayer not Organizing People.

2 Chronicles 7:14 Notes four conditions for revival:

a. Humble Themselves

b. Pray

c. Seek God's Face

d. Turn From Sins

Note Three Promises:

e. Will Hear from Heaven

f. Forgive their Sins

g. Will Heal Their Land

Finney said "Revival may be expected when Christians have a spirit of prayer for revival.

Illustration: The Welsh Revival of 1904 was proceeded by 13 people praying for six years and resulted in 100,000 conversions.

— A.T. Pierson says, "From the day of Pentecost there hasn't been one spiritual awakening in any land which hasn't began an answer to prayer."

Three things must take place if personal revival is to take place:

1. Deal with SIN for Forgiveness and Cleansing

a. Psalm 66:18 "If I regard sin in my life the Lord won't hear me."

b.   Proverbs 28:13 "He that covers his sins will not prosper but whoever confesses and forsakes sins shall have mercy."

c.   Psalm 139:23–24 "Search me Oh God and see if there is any wicked way in me and lead me in your way."

We need to keep current accounts with God regarding our sins.

d.   1 John 1:9 "If we confess our sins God will forgive them."

2.   Deal with SELF for Deliverance

Take sides with God against ourselves to deliver ourselves from ourselves.

Romans 6:6 "Knowing this, that our old man (self) is crucified with Christ."

John gives us 3 steps to Death:

a.   John 3:30 "He must increase."

b.   John 5:30 "I can of myself do nothing."

c.   John 6:63 "The flesh profits nothing."

Galatians 2:20 "I am crucified with Christ."

Hebrews 12:1 "The absence of death (to self) is killing the average church."

3.   Deal with the Holy SPIRIT for Victory

We must be emptied of self and sin before the Holy Spirit can fill us.

Ephesians 5:18 "Don't be drunk with wine but filled with the Holy Spirit."

It's not getting more of the Holy Spirit but allowing the Holy Spirit to have all of us.

4-   The Results of Revival: I saw six results in our church following revival meetings.

a.   Liberation — From shyness and defeat to openness. Shyness is inverted pride in what people think of us.

b.   Liberty — Witnessing and Prayer. Some couldn't lead in silent prayer before revival. When revival becomes the experience of the church, evangelism becomes the expression of the church.

c.   Liberality — In giving of finances, time and abilities to the cause of Christ.

d.   Love — Not human, but divine love. John 13:34-35 reads

e.   Loyalty — To the Lord and His people. Love is the greatest.

f.   Lordship — of Christ needs a servant heart like Jesus Christ had.

The Problem is we've been strong and right too long and we need to be weak and wrong. May we not resist God the Holy Spirit but respond and experience Revival of the Heart.

Epilogue

When my wife Beverly first suggested that I write a book I had little idea of the time and work it would require. She had encouraged and assisted my dad in writing an autobiography of his life, and this was my intent when I started writing. However, it has grown into more of my memoirs as well as some of Bev's memories of our life and ministries together. I have been amazed at the magnitude of God's blessings, mercies and guidance in our lives over approximately eighty years and fifty-eight as husband and wife. As the old hymns say, "Count your many blessings, name them one by one; And it will surprise you what the Lord has done."

At a Fellowship Convention in Toronto on April 4, 2016 Bev and I were surprised and blessed to be given the "Eagles Award" for a lifetime of ministry for the Lord. The award is based on Isaiah 40:31, "they will soar on wings like eagles".

My life has been full of blessings and surprises and it is easy for one to forget them, until we take time to remember and record them. The Bible says, "The blessing of the Lord, that makes rich and adds no sorrow to it." Thanks to the Lord for a strong constitution and good health, it has enabled me to be involved in numerous sports, hobbies as well as many ministry challenges at home and abroad.

Following Bev's death, I asked myself what I needed to do to keep going straight and strong and to finish well. Using alliteration as I did in my sermon outlines, I came up with Faith in God, Family, Friends, Fitness of body and mind and Finances to live on. They are in the order of importance and it gives me a checklist in my latter years, until Christ calls me home.

I am indebted to several people who assisted me in the writing of this book. First my late wife Bev, who encouraged me to start writing and was instrumental in writing and recording some of the events of almost 58 years together. Secondly, my youngest daughter Faye who laboured for hours typing the majority of the book and deciphering and interpreting my writing (no small task). Thirdly, my granddaughter Katelyn who finished most of the typing and stored it on a USB stick for review. Fourthly, my friend Peter Gibson an English major who spent countless hours working through the manuscript, making needed grammatical changes. Next I want to thank Keith Jerry, a long-time friend from Bramalea Baptist. His expertise on the computer has been a "God-send" as he assisted me in electronic editing and placing pictures in their proper place. Then, Janice Van Eck of Guelph was enlisted to enhance the 65 pictures for my book, and did a wonderful work, and Michaela Jerry assisted on three special ones. Lastly for, Dr. Michael Haykin who generously offered to help me when he heard I was working on a book. As a result of several meetings and numerous phone calls and emails, Michael gave invaluable assistance. Michael enlisted Dr. Dustin Benge, a colleague from The Andrew Fuller Center for Baptist Studies to do final editing of the manuscript and placement of pictures and captions. Dustin moved from Louisville, Kentucky to a Christian Seminary in Wales, United Kingdom in the middle of assisting me. However, thanks to emails we were able to communicate, and he finished the manuscript, designed the cover, and prepared the manuscript for publication. God bless you all for your gracious contribution to *Blessed Beyond Belief*.

I have been the beneficiary of many people's prayers, love and encouragement. It is my prayer that this book will encourage you to trust and serve the Lord with all your heart, soul and strength. Remember, we only have one life and it will soon be past. Only what's done for Christ will last.

* 9 7 8 1 9 8 9 1 7 4 6 6 1 *